www.fast-print.net/store.php

CALL THEM THE HAPPY YEARS
Copyright © Martin Everard 2011

ISBN 978-184426-987-7

First published 2011 by
FASTPRINT PUBLISHING
Peterborough, England.

Contents

Acknowledgments

I am most grateful for the help received in various contributions to the preparation and publication of these memoirs.

My brother, Anthony, was the guardian of the original type and hand-written pages and numerous family photographs for many years and, but for his safe-keeping, this story would never have been able to be told nor the publication undertaken.

Our friend, Kim Nixon, has been hugely patient in reading and correcting grammar and syntax and, being American, has shown up the differences in the English on both sides of the Atlantic. This editor has reserved the right to accept or refuse ultimately but it is amazing just how many typo's can slip through. But more importantly, I have valued her comments that highlighted inconsistencies and understanding.

Tessa and Stuart Wheeler opened their home at Chilham Castle to allow me, with the guidance and resources of Michael Peters, their curator and superlative guide, to add so many historical photographs of that part of the time that Barbara spent there in the 1930's as companion to Lady Davis. The wealth of archive material, which they offered, has added so much in illustrating what a magnificent heritage they have in their home. I entreat you to have a look at the website and arrange a visit.

David Morris was looking forward to showing me around Telscombe Manor but sadly died very suddenly before my visit. I am indebted to his widow, Felicity, and his family graciously showed me around and allowed me to go and photograph inside and out. I enjoyed their confirmation of Barbara's descriptions and what changes had taken place since she was last there.

My thanks here to Sophie Cheshum and her team at the National Trust for their assistance.

I am also indebted to Suzan Thompson of Elegant Address Ltd for unearthing the Villa Fiorentina pictures for me; to Jonathan Moffat of the Malayan Volunteers Group for his research into the facts in Ray's story and to Dr Henry Oakeley and his committee at the Orchid Society of Great Britain, for their permission to use the painting that has become the logo for the centenary.

For the majority of these memoirs, I was able to transcribe Barbara's typed pages but later ones, from Chapter Fifteen onwards, the narrative remains in her own handwriting, some in green biro, some black and some blue. All of these were written in a flowing hand that sometimes I found hard to decipher. This was particularly relevant with the plant names, most of which occur in Chapter Sixteen. I am most grateful to the internet, many a search throwing up the correct name and spelling of words even from the minimum of interpreted letters.

It will not go unnoticed that these later chapters, transcribed from their raw state, never received the polish and were never finished by Barbara. They are shorter and there remain many corrections and revisions to sentences and paragraphs and if I have misinterpreted any of these, then I would have to apologize. Barbara was in her seventies when she took up writing her story again more or less at the same time that she set up her Trust for Orchid Conservation and the thirty eight paintings and designs for the Orchid Society of Great Britain.

Finally, many people, friends, family, artists, botanists and others, may have memories of Barbara and meeting her during her life. This celebration is not a 'closed' book and I do invite you to add any reminiscences that you might have on her website. There is a special section for you to do this.

I do hope you enjoy the book.

Martin Everard,
London, 2011

Book One: Chapter One – A Sussex family

I belong to an old Sussex family, the Beards, which will be extinct in the 20th century. The first records start in 1200AD with just the name Berd. Gradually the family acquired land and wealth.

Beard Family Crest

Sections from the Beard Family tree as prepared by the Chester Herald of Arms

In 1627, one Thomas Berde changed the name to Beard. They lived around Rottingdean since the time of Edward IV and it all came to my great grandfather, Steyning Beard, J.P., Master of the Brookside Harriers.

Steyning Beard (possibly painted after his death)

He was born at Rottingdean in 1849, was married twice and had four sons by his first wife, all born at Rottingdean. He died in 1909, at the age of 64. He is buried in the family vault in Rottingdean churchyard, his wives, his sons and their wives. There are precious few more to be put there and then the vault can be closed for ever.

St Margaret's Church, Rottingdean

One of the Beard family memorials

One of the stones marking the last resting place of one of the Beard family

He inherited this great slice of Sussex at about 21 years and by the time he died, he had mortgaged it nearly all away and it was found there was very little left for Charles, Ernest, Bertram and Ralph.

Telscombe, Sussex

They salvaged Telscombe Manor and the farm of 500 arable acres of Down land and my father, Charles, and Ernest settled there as 'gentleman farmers'. Shortly after, Charles married Rosalie Anne Digby Russell, second daughter of Philip Cecil Crampton Russell of Co. Wicklow. Her family was a branch of the Duke of Bedford Russell's and, going back to Norman times, probably came to this country with the Conqueror.

Rosalie Russell

She was very pretty and, by today's standards, with make-up and perms, she would have been quite a beauty. I often wondered why my father married her. True, she had a small income but, except for her looks, they were totally unsuited. He was a most attractive man to women. He had golden red hair and fair skin and blue eyes. He was well used to women running after him and there is a scandalous tale that he seduced the Rottingdean cook at the age of 16!

Possibly my mother was shy of him and held him off and to his temperament this could well have made him determined to marry her. her. During the first few years, my Uncle Ernest continued to live with them, which couldn't have been very nice for a young wife.

Children do not know about their parents. One can only go by hearsay and surmise and one was only told what was suitable 'for the children to hear'. I don't think my mother was too happy and I cannot for the life of me see my father as a devoted young husband! She was of a nervous, highly strung disposition, artistic and painted water colour landscapes rather delicately. The gross sex of married life was rather a shock to her as apparently my maternal grandmother had to be called in 'to talk to her' about wifely duties. For a man such as my father, used to easy sex, mother's reluctance must have been quite a shock to his ego.

And worrying! Ernest, also by this time, had left Telscombe and married an Irishwoman called Elizabeth Tweedy (incidentally a kinswoman of my mother's and cruelly described as a 'half-blind, old parrot' by one nameless member of the family) and it was imperative to Charles, head of the Beard family, that he should have a son before Ernest to carry on this impoverished line on.** Elizabeth Beard had a daughter, my cousin Alice, and my mother, a few months later, presented my father, not with an all-important son but a girl, on July 27th 1910.

Thank you card announcing Barbara's birth

I was a bitter blow. It is possible the whole course of my father's life would have been altered had he had a son to be handed down the lovely, old Beard furniture. But it was not to be because seventeen months after Barbara Mary Steyning, there arrived Evelyn Ursula Steyning. And, four years later on, all hope was abandoned by Ruth Patricia Steyning.

Ursula was his favourite perhaps because she mirrored his fairness. I had his beautiful red hair but was darker like my mother.

Anyway, I had let him down and I do not think that he ever got over his disappointment of my unfortunate lapse in being a girl.

** Ernest did have a son, Steyning, who later had twin daughters. Hence the line became extinct.

Telscombe Manor, 2010

The aged and beautiful Manor House of Telscombe is the first building on the road from Lewes, surrounded by its farm land. The two brothers laid out a very fine garden on the South side of the Down with two deep terraces.

They made a lot of improvements but were clever enough to retain the house's character and mellowness, leaving the great open fireplaces or putting a simple brick one inside the original. The fireplace in the dining room had a somewhat naïve legend:

"Better a dinner of herbs than a stalled ox and hatred within."

Over the mantelpiece, written in large, whit letters on the great, dark oak beam. I can only remember this in the early days – perhaps it was removed as it didn't ring true later on.

Modern interior of The Manor

This room was festooned with guns, aged pewter plates, hunting horns and a murderous man-trap hung on one side of the fireplace. Paintings and prints of departed Beards on horses surrounded by hounds covered other walls and masses of blue Spode platters and soup tureens and fierce gaping masks of dead foxes made up the décor. When my father felt in a jokish mood – and he loved a practical joke – he would, much to our shrieks of delight and terror, place these foxes in our bed! I can't think why we are not nervous wrecks. For sheltered children such as us, the effect of these dead animals, with their dreadful canine teeth barred, leering between the white sheets and pillows, was truly horrific.

The house had its original oak staircase, which was dark polished with a patina of age and was uncarpeted. Off the staircase on the right was the hall and over the mantel in this room was the old Beard motto: "Pax in Bello." More literary decoration! Both the dining room and this room had fine oak panelling and beams and supports. The hall was also something of a museum as it housed my father's magnificent collection of flints, found on the Downs and turned up by the plough. Also there was a Bronze Age burial urn, which his shepherd had come on while pitching hurdles for a sheepfold.

On the other side of the stairs was a brick passage to a large kitchen. Under the stairs were winding steps to the big vaulted cellars. Off the kitchen, to the North, were the back door and my mother's dairy. Here were great, flat bowls full of milk, waiting for the cream to rise, then skimmed off and put into the churn. We greatly loved being allowed to turn the handle and listen for the cream's change of note into a gentle schlop, schlop and to know that the butter had arrived. To see the buttermilk poured off (which was given to the villagers and the pigs) and the big lump of dripping butter lifted out and formed into neat squares with wooden butter-pats – we were very good at it. Under the dairy, so my father told me, was a deep well but it ceased to be used as it became tidal.

In the early days, the lighting was probably oil and candles but next to the dairy was an outhouse, which housed a new innovation, a petrol gas-lighting plant. I did not have much to do with this thing as it was kept locked but it hissed in a most unpleasant way and always broke down at inconvenient moments.

On the South of the house, next to the hall, they added a corrugated roofed billiard room. Five or six steps led down to this room, it being built on the same terraced land as the garden. The room was decorated in green and crimson baize, with settees all round the room and three dilapidated old armchairs by a small fireplace. The whole centre of the room was taken up with a vast billiard table. This was my parents' sitting room. It was quite in keeping that no alteration had been made to make my mother a drawing room in a bachelor household. Perhaps she had a 'boudoir' upstairs, I wonder? This I can't recall nor can I remember her bedroom and my recollections of the day and night nurseries are vague but the nursery walls were salmon-pink, glossy paint.

Georgian Pavilion, being restored   *View across the tennis court to house*

To the east of the billiard room opened off into the peach, nectarine and grape houses and more doors to the south led on to a terraced walk, a herbaceous border and a narrow strip of grass. Here the garden ended rather abruptly in a steep cliff overlooking an aged barn and cow and pig-sties and the roof of a cottage, in which Gregory, the cowman, lived. Eastwards, the terraced path led to the kitchen gardens and a fruit orchard and below these was another terrace and a tennis lawn surrounded by a pergola-ed walk. Daddy had built several little pillared summer houses along the terraced walks and, overlooking the tennis court, was a curious little building on pillars, which was intended to be used to watch tennis.

The 'hay-loft', 2010, somewhat altered

Recently, in the last published 'blurb to the glory of the reigning Telscombe benefactor' (the only person not to have published such a book seems to have been my parent – he was too poor!), I have seen this building described as an 'old hay-loft'. It was never this but it used to store the tennis nets and posts. This, my father built before I was born. We liked as children to climb its rickety steps and throw open the cobwebby windows. But I was frightened of the walk round the pergola. I thought tigers lurked there!

This was the end of the garden, right at the bottom of the dip in the Down, and over the garden wall was the village pond, a muddy piece for ducks and where the carthorses were watered.

The Rectory

The next big house on the other side of the road was the Rectory. A not-unpleasant looking house with double eaves and a nice old garden, a place we also loved to play in. Between 1910 and 1914, two Rectors came and went and I can remember nothing of them. The first Rector I remember was the Rev George Street. My mother had an elder sister, Lucilla, hereafter called Auntie Lilla. She was a tall, thin, gaunt girl and somewhat put in the shade by her sister and, so, was always jealous of her. Later, in 1918, she astounded everyone, except my mother, that is, who had been busily matchmaking, by marrying the Rector.

Blacksmith's Cottage, Telscombe

Below the Rectory, level with Gregory's cottage on the other side, was the blacksmith's cottage. Windlass, his name was. He had a large brood of children of all ages, the older ones mostly working for my father..

The Old School

A bit further on was the school, where some eighteen or so children were taught by Miss Shenton. When we happened to visit the school, all the children had to stand up!

Nearby, on the Manor side of the road, was the village well, rather jutting out into the road. I can just remember this, I think, but it was done away with when the water was laid on from Brighton. (The well is just where the entrance to the 'club' is now.)

The Club, 2010

Church of St.Laurence, Telscombe

Up the road was the Church of St Laurence, where I was christened in the old family christening robe, an heirloom. Here we were taken to

Morning Service regularly. Memories of old Hymns and age-old Psalms sung and responses in good, strong Sussex accent come back to me – the harvest Festival Service and Christmas and Easter. The fresco rather upset me right above my head of a mournful looking Christ with enormous spiky rays, reminiscent of railings. It is beyond me to describe a church, but I came on this from S.B Mais's booklet on 'Around Telscombe" of Telscombe Church:

"Kipling probably had Telscombe in mind when he wrote of 'Little Lost Down Churches', for here is a tiny Norman flint church with a shingle, witches-cap squat spire, all hidden away in a fold in the Downs with a road leading to it but not through it'

And

"It is a model village, with a picturesque Manor house in the centre, a few cottages but no inn' (and I would add, no shop!)

Above the church and higher up the hill on the North side was a row of terraced cottages. I only knew of one family living in them, old John Reid, the carter, his wife and eighteen children. These were tied cottages and Grays and Read were mostly employed either on the farm or in the house. Servants did become very difficult later on. Or they were working for the other 'big' house in Telscombe, The Stables.

The Stables

Until the breaking up of my grandfather's estate, this had been a Hunting Box, and then a wealthy bookmaker, called Ambrose Gorham bought it. I think that, from the very beginning, there had been some rivalry between the Squire and Gorham. Gorham, rich and powerful did not like my father being Lord of the Manor and Squire, though he was Patron of the Living. In fact I think he did not like the Beards and the old traditions and what they stood for, more or less penniless to him and yet standing in his way of being the 'Power' in Telscombe. My father, for his part, disliked Gorham's money. It rankled that Gorham could pay out for this or that improvement and hardly notice that he had. Any venture that the two men started ended in a row. To this day can be seen the start of one and that is the road on the Tye, which was never finished and ended in a quarrel.

Ambrose Gorham was my sister Ursula's Godfather. We found him a rather gruff, alarming person but we loved the magnificent toys he sent us for Christmas. And the Meets of the Southdown Hunt at The Stables were a great excitement. He kept a string of racing horses and actually won The Grand National with one called Shannon Lass. So much has been written of Telscombe and its benefactor, Ambrose Gorham, that I do not intend adding to it. He was one of the new gentry of England with money made from grocering, tailoring and what not and my father and his brothers belonged to another England, which was rapidly disappearing.

So, that is Telscombe, during my baby years, with its Squire, Manor farm and cottages, wealthy rival power in The Stables and the Rector, who probably had the job of keeping the peace between the two. There was no Mrs Gorham, which was perhaps just as well. Telscombe – surrounded by farmlands and, beyond the arable land, were the Downs and the Gallops, where the racehorses were trained.

But the place I loved more than anywhere else was a part of the Downs called Croxdean. This was an ancient place, a curious bit of land with obvious earthworks, having terraces or steps running along the Down and honey-combed with rabbit warrens. I later learned that these terraces were probably Saxon gardens. Here grew cowslips and great pats of wild violet and thyme-covered anthills. Orchids - Fragrant, Bee, Early Purple and Butterfly - grew there. (*Butterfly is extinct now – BE*) Just over the top of Croxdean was the road to Lewes and along the old bridle path, known as The Links, lay the road to Piddinghoe. To the south of this path was the virgin grassland, which, later, was to become that horror, Peacehaven.

According to my father, who fought a hard battle on Newhaven Council against Peacehaven, this forerunner of all 'subtopias', "would ruin some of the finest partridge shooting in Sussex and only damned fools would build a town right in front of the Brighton sewer".

How right he was!

Telscombe Tye

Going down the Tye to the coast road, there was only rolling Down to Rottingdean and a farmstead here and there and the patchwork of fields. Not much than thirty years before, most had belonged to Beards for generations. From Kemp Town to Falmer, to Piddinghoe, to Newhaven, most of Ovingdean and Rottingdean…all gone. What would the land be worth today? To own all this and vast tracts of what were new suburbs of Brighton. Had my grandfather hung on, as his sons implored him to do, we children could have been very wealthy heiresses, some of the richest in England. Ah well, such is life.

I have a pretty thought – sheer imagination – but could an ancestor of that solitary Berd, did he, could he well have lived at Croxdean and farmed and gardened there? And a few yards away, there is even a telltale patch of slow and other stunted trees, which could well have been a building. I wonder.

But undoubtedly he lived on the Downs, somewhere around Telscombe, Rottingdean or Ovingdean. His ancestors saw Harold beaten and further back were the Beaker people, an ancient tribe, who used to bury the dead in urns like the one found. We know little of our forefathers, really, and of an England that can never return.

Memories of childhood must be jumbled, of course. We lived a nursery life, surrounded by nurses and later governesses. Panting nurses pushed our prams up the road. Dreadful grey powders in spoonfuls of jam and being taken to our parents after tea for play. A memory of crawling around and being told off.

"Mind my foot!"

Daddy undoubtedly suffering from an attack of gout. Always baby lamb orphans, which we bottle-fed; a beloved Jersey cow, called Daisy. My sister, Ursula, used to call the cows in. To see this tiny child stand by the gate calling:

"Come along Daisy! Come along! Cuwp, cuwp, cuwp! Come along!"

And bring in some twenty cows with her arms lovingly round Daisy!

There was a pig, too, we were rather fond of, and this animal was called Ursula! It had her fair complexion. And there were the great carthorses. We rode high on them. Boxer or Steamer, Blossom and Flower....yes, and flowers. I noticed them around me even at that young age. I must have met Adonis annua in my father's cornfields as I've never to my knowledge seen it growing and yet I saw it at Telscombe. And Corn-cockle too. The banks by the roads were full of flowers....the chalk lovers, Scabious, Knapweed, Sainfoin, clovers and Lucerne..oh! many such.

And such was my young life, with the seasons coming and going. Hot summer days of play and garden and farm life; winter, when the damp chill set in; Telscombe, when the drifts of snow came, could be well cut off.

Daddy was very anxious that I should learn to ride as befitted a granddaughter of Steyning Beard, and I can remember very clearly, even now, being put in a chair saddle on Queenie, the nervy, little pony-cart horse. I fell from the bank to the flint road and was rushed, screaming, indoors by my frantic mother, who hated and feared horses but who had to ride, being the Squire's lady. I had a nasty cut on my upper lip. I was three when this happened. Daddy took that poor little horse to the stable and thrashed her! Most unfair as she had only reared up a little because her girths were too tight and she did not like the extraordinary arrangement that had been placed on her back.

Queenie did further disgrace herself by bolting in harness and trap from the Lewes side just above Telscombe. Daddy and I had got out to look for my hair ribbon. The pony and trap ended up in the yard and my mother, frantic once more, tore up the road expecting the worst only to meet us walking solemnly down the hill, Daddy saying to me:

"Naughty Queenie! Did she run away then!"

Telscombe was not at its best in winter. One of the great disadvantages was that the Tye became impassable from the first onset of winter. It was annoying because the way over the Tye to the coast joins the Newhaven-Brighton road at what was then known as Portobello but is now known as Telscombe Cliffs. So in winter there was only Newhaven by way of Southease or Piddinghoe or Lewes for supplies.

Shortly after the runaway and the debacle of my riding lesson, Daddy decided to give up horses for transport because he bought a car – a Humberette. Memories of this vehicle are somewhat vague…slithering down the Tye and the return journey, invariably getting stuck, halfway, where the land steepens, stuck, stuck so firmly that no entreaties or pushing from front or rear could move her. In the end, Daddy would leave car and passengers, either to freeze in a howling, off-channel gale or be soaked with rain from the dripping hood while he went off, swearing like mad, to fetch the carthorse to pull us out.
Other recollections of this car are of my father perpetually spread-eagled underneath it, of fascinating dirty innards of car and sparking plugs, which he seemed always to be 'changing'!

We played around happily in the old coach house, which had housed Queenie's trap and many others for years and now had to give way to this dirty, oily, noisy machine. Incidentally, we picked up a fine vocabulary. While he wrestled with the bowels of his car, we played with our dolls, lovingly saying to them:

"Damn your eyes! God, damn your eyes! Blast you!" etc in fond imitation of our parent.

My father tried hard to teach my mother to drive this car. Hopeless, as with the horse, she was nervous. Once, instead of turning at the junction of the Newhaven-Lewes road, she went straight up the steep bank on the opposite side and, also, on another time, ran clean over the old roadman, who was harmlessly minding his own business while making up a pothole. She went right over him, Daddy looked back and saw him jumping about, swearing like mad. I hoped they stopped and were not the first 'hit and run'!

Chapter Two – The First World War Years

Then the First World War was upon them, though people on farms did not feel the food shortage. There were always the rabbits and game in season, plenty of butter and milk, fruit and vegetables. Sugar was difficult but what really hit Daddy was the shortage of petrol. And men!

And it was no joke groping in the pitch dark night with no lights on, Daddy roaring at the top of his voice, the Hymn:

"The night is dark and we are far from home, Lead, Thou, me on."

He got rid of the Humberette (and a good job, too, I would think) and bought a Studebaker. He completely gave up journeys to Brighton and used Newhaven, for which we had to have passes. This new car did signal war service, besides being used for transport and provisions for all our workers. And also for our own use. And it was extremely difficult to get help with getting the harvest in and during one unforgettable year, he got it in, load by load, with that car.

We children didn't see much of the war although, standing on the cliff edge at the end of the Tie, I saw three ships, minesweepers, circling and firing into the sea at a German submarine trapped below. There was an aerodrome then on what is now 'bungaloid' Peacehaven and there was once a sudden explosion and an enormous column of smoke thrown up by a mine below the cliffs. And Canadian soldiers were based in the village. All our barns were taken over as billets. The barn at the bottom of the garden was the cookhouse and men's mess and I can still hear their "Come to the cookhouse door, boys" and see them swinging down the road.

I adored the bugler boy and held his hand and gave him apples. My mother, who always had difficulty keeping servants, said this was the only time at Telscombe when she did not have trouble.

We also had a series of governesses. Things between my parents were not well. Daddy was a perfect nuisance with every young woman he met and the governesses were no exception. Sooner or later, each one would have to go as and when my mother discovered what was going on; not only governesses but young servant girls as well. In fact my mother was very unhappy and how lonely she must have been. With an unfaithful husband, stuck on a farm at the back of beyond, in wartime, with young children and not equipped in any way to do the housework.

Of course, I was too young to know the truth of the trouble and will never know but, judging from his behaviour later on, I would say that my father was to blame.

Barbara Beard, aged 5 years, 7 months

In 1915, my sister Ruth was born. Whether this was a last hope to have a son or to patch up a breaking marriage, one will never know. Ruth was a strange infant, quite unlike Ursula and me.

In 1918, the rector, the Reverend George Street returned from the war and the marriage engineered by my mother took place. Daddy had a fine bonfire on the Tie – four hundredweight of coal, six wagon loads of furze were used and it burned for a week. We went to Brighton for the 'Celebrations' and stayed at the Queen's Hotel, sat on the balcony and were thrilled at the Royal Sussex Regiment going by, the band playing:

> "Oh, Sussex, Sussex by the sea
> Good old Sussex by the Sea
> You may tell them all that we stand or fall
> For Sussex by the sea."

Daddy was 40 at the outbreak of the war. He never actually served, nor did Uncle Ernest. Both were needed for work on the farms. He did, however, have a uniform, complete except for one puttee, he would recount with glee.

Then he decided to sell Telscombe. I can only think he must have been losing money or that he was tired and sickened by the struggle to run it during the war. But sell it he did and it was a great mistake. It was bought by a retired Indian Army General. I do not know very much about him. The auction sale was painful, the agonized farewells to treasured animals, all soon forgotten in the exciting move – to Hove! Of course, we went back there quite a lot, to see Uncle George and Aunt Lilla at the Rectory but it was not the same.

It must have been quite a business, the move to Hove, and quite a wrench, particularly for Daddy. His whole life until this move had been a country one and of country things and for him to be cooped up in a town must have been very strange. As for my mother, she had been born in Hove so, no doubt, she welcomed the move after the loneliness of Telscombe.

Wilbury Gardens, Brighton, 2010

They rented a house in Wilbury Gardens, at the top, north corner, overlooking St Anne's Well Gardens. The only remarkable thing about this house was the bath – an enormous affair, panelled all round in mahogany and with white enamel right up to the ceiling at the waste end. It had fifteen or so taps, all of which turned on different types of water jets. A sitz-bath was one and in the middle, the sitz-jet emitted a most powerful jet of water. Much pleasure was had by getting one's sister on it and turning it on, forcefully. There was a shower, of course, and a gadget called the Wash. This was ferocious, sending out a solid sheet of water out of the wall from a thin slit. The wall, too, was punctured by many tiny holes and when this was turned on, it was excruciatingly tickly. Many happy times were spent in that bath.

My parents were very gay. The tension of the war relaxed, there were lots of dinner parties and the first night club opened in Brighton. We went to tea dances in the afternoons.

Daddy was setting himself up as an antiques dealer and at first he didn't do so badly. But they must have been living above their income as, after a couple of terms at the expensive Hoove Lea, we left as he could not afford the fees. I was not sorry to leave as, always with this sort of school, there was a mixture of children from 'good' families and the rich, new war-jumped-up, tradesmen's children, so inclined to bully and snobbish in that dreadful way about what one had an wore. That which is known as 'keeping up with the Jones's' today'!

One suffered agonies of hell if clothes deviated in the slightest. "Oh look! Barbara's got a straw hat" (when it should have been a Panama). The hat would then be torn off and thrown up onto the top of a cupboard. There followed tears and misery until some kindly girl got it down.

Things between my parents were rapidly getting worse; both were engaged feverishly in enjoying themselves. Daddy was involved in affairs with young girls all over Brighton. My mother also had admirers. I think that she tried to go back to her old way of life in Brighton before she was married, as she used to take us each Sunday to church at Hove Parish church and after that we would walk on Church Parade, a quarter mile strip of lawns in front of the sea. This was the 'done thing' and one met or was seen by friends and so on - dressed very smartly with Mummy looking most attractive. But it was not 'done', however, to take a step further than where the grass ended and the tarmac front started, not vulgar Brighton! My mother and her sister took all these now seemingly ridiculous nicenesses very seriously...one did not rub shoulders!

But bit by bit our lovely furniture was being sold. The financial state of affairs became steadily worse and Daddy had 'bloody tradesmen', as he termed them, sending him unpleasant letters. It all came to a head in the Brighton Bankruptcy Court. Daddy salvaged what was left of the furniture by making it all over to my mother, moving hurriedly from Wilbury Gardens to a dreary house in Clarendon Villas. In the crash, my mother's small, private income disappeared, swallowed up by some debt, I suppose.

All of this happened, but happened over our heads, and we rather liked the move but we missed the bath!

This new house had four stories. By now, my parents must have been quite estranged because they had separate rooms. We and Mummy all slept in one room on the ground floor. The second and third floors we had let to some people and Daddy had a room on the top floor. The first floor front room was Mummy's drawing room. This was mainly full of enormous, unsellable furniture (Daddy's furniture dealing mistakes!) together with some two hundred pieces of Spode from Telscombe, stacked on the most colossal side table I have ever seen. It had about twenty-four different types of leg and how the floor didn't collapse remains a mystery.

There was a basement; the front room was the dining room and was where we had all our toys. Our enormous dolls' house, beautifully made by Daddy, took up one wall. And in the windows, Ursula and I had tables each, on which we used to draw (me) and make scrapbooks and the like. Ruth didn't have a table – too young!

The garden was a dilapidated cat-run. Daddy did try to garden it but what with the cats and us, mad children, it was too much. One of our jobs was to collect stones and put them on an upper landing window sill as ammunition for him to shy at the cats. As we were all devoted cat lovers, except him, and always had at least one adored animal each, we thought this most cruel.

We found a Mills bomb in the garden. We couldn't think what it was but Mummy didn't like the look of it so we put it on a plate and, later, Daddy took it in his pocket to the police station, where it was exploded in a bucket of water.

All the best people in Brighton by now had dropped us but the scandal about Charlie Beard was far from over. We were sent to a non-descript school, somewhere nearby, where, to my mother's disgust, we caught measles. She promptly took us away but I cannot remember where we went for a time.

Daddy gave up antiques dealing. There weren't any more family things to sell and all that remained was that unsellable furniture. However, that and the Spode went as a Bailiff came and sat for days in the drawing room. We rather liked him and took him frequent cups of tea.

Daddy got a job in London, selling carbon papers. Mummy had the most frightful financial troubles and, if it hadn't been for the Uncles' and Aunt Lilla's help, I cannot think what would have happened. Daddy, then, ceased to live at Clarendon Villas and Mummy's spiralling struggle became even worse because she now had the greatest difficulty in getting any money out of him. She felt this 'poverty' deeply and made great efforts to keep up 'appearances'.

It all came to a head in 1923 with my beloved mother's death, at the age of 44, from double pneumonia, brought on through nursing us three children with raging flu. A good woman; a brave, proud woman, unequipped for the life she was lately thrust into. We were not at Clarendon Villas when she died. We had been taken away, I suppose, while she fought for her life. Ursula remembers leaving the house, the bell by her bed furiously jangling. She probably thought we were being taken away from her. Ruth and Ursula did not feel her death as I did. I was just thirteen and she had been starting to tell me some of her troubles and, to me, it was a terrible loss.

From now on, I loathed and hated my father.

For a few weeks we were separated, living with Mummy's cousins and then, after all was sorted out and Aunt Lilla, much to Daddy's rage, had sold all the contents of Clarendon Villas to a dealer for fifteen pounds, we were all collected together by Daddy. To the horror and disgust of everyone, within a week of Mummy's death, he had married, the woman, Ella. To make matters worse, he announced that it was to give us a home! Ursula and Ruth took it quietly enough but, as for me, it was a pitched battle between Ella and me from the first half-hour. I hated her from the very first moment. I hated everything about her, her blond, wavy hair, blue eyes and drooping mouth. I saw her as the archdevil and the cause of my mother's death, which was not so as she was just incidental.

Ella must have had a pretty tough time with me, being difficult and grieving for Mummy. She got on best of all with Ruth, naturally, as she was only six or so. We lived in their flat in Sussex Terrace. She had a little bit of money, which was fortunate for daddy as all he had was his carbon paper selling.

In March 1923, Daddy had a taste of what all his old friends thought of the whole affair. It was Ruth's birthday on the 17th and he thought to have a birthday party for her and some other people he had invited, who were old friends and had lived in Rottingdean when Daddy was a boy. One was Dr Whittington's daughter, Kitty, one of our oldest friends. Her mother was Lucy Ridsdale and one of the Ridsdale sisters married Stanley Baldwin. Well, old friends like these loved my mother and us and Daddy had a nasty shock when he got the invitation back with 'A disgrace to public decency!' written across it. And so it was! I don't think there was a party after that.

Memorial to Lucy Ridsdale, St Margaret's Church, Rottingdean

We were sent to school in Sussex Square and we forgot our sorrow as children will. We played in the private garden there, which, for children, was rather exciting. There were Euonymous and Tamarisk shrubberies, a long tunnel under the road to the lower garden, games with other children in the garden, Julian Ridsdale and his sister, Raymond and Dorothy Cox, who were to become lifelong friends of mine, walks along the beach, bathing and swimming.

This part of Brighton is nice. The Downs rise from here, and here the beach changes from pebble to chalk seaweed covered rocks. The sea is rough and, with strong, violent currents along there. Since my father was a boy, the sea took back a couple of roads and some cottages, which I can remember. This is called Black Rock. At very low tide to this day can be seen the big blocks, which are the remains of the first marine railway. This went at the time the old Chain Pier disappeared.

There is still a little railway but it runs safely above the shingle. Many a ride have I had on it. Fares then were tuppence, I think.

Then Daddy and Ella moved to a house on Davigdor Road and I went to Brighton and Hove High School as a day girl. I liked this school and was happy there. Drawing was the only thing I was good at and at that I shone. Arithmetic was quite, quite hopeless. And still is!

Ella had an Alsatian dog called Romus. He was a magnificent animal and promised to be a good show dog. At about a year, Ella did show him and he got a first. Unfortunately, a little after that, he went down with distemper. For three weeks we all fought for that dog's life and it was only the fact that he was such a glutton that he pulled through. He was nourished completely on expensive chicken essence. When he was better, he was semi-paralysed in his hind-quarters and for a long time had to be carried everywhere. He was weeks recovering and had to be helped to walk by holding him up by his tail. In the end, he recovered his strength but was left with a twitch in his front paws, which was maddening when he used to rest them on the fire fender. Ella worshipped this dog. I admired his handsomeness but I thought him an awful fool. His brains, which did not equal his looks, had not been helped by his illness, but he was a good natured animal.

Then Daddy and Ella decided to move out of Brighton and took a house at Five Ashes, near Heathfield. This was a nice, old-ish house with quite a bit of land.

The battle between me and Ella just continued. I was difficult and intractable about everything. I hated everything. My bedroom upset me very much as it had egg-yellow curtains. Ella loved Alsatians and, to this day, I dislike them.

It was arranged that I should still go to the High School but as a boarder. This was wonderful and in my year there, I was very happy. But then came the holidays and life at Woodcote, Five Ashes; quite a nice house in its way with a lot of ground dropping away to a huge and deep hammer pond. Daddy, good gardener that he was, was busy making the garden. He wasn't content with just one pond, no! He dug out nine in all, connecting them up with little streams and bridges with the banks planted very naturally with primroses and bluebells.

Ella had decided to breed Alsatians and had fourteen and, at times, a lot of puppies. Experience with these dogs has left me with a hearty dislike of all Alsatians. I have never liked dogs, having had so many beloved cats killed by them all through my childhood. These were murderous animals, bullying and fighting each other. Romus was the stud dog but, poor thing, the duties expected of him were rather a trial, with his weak legs giving way. When a bitch was in heat, Ursula or I used to have to help him by holding up his legs. So we had the facts of life well demonstrated, though I do remember Ella telling me but I was not much interested at the time.

We had to do quite a lot of chores for these dogs. Fourteen Alsatians take a bit of feeding and the daily job of cutting up and cooking the meat was revolting. In winter, it would be quite a procession to the outhouses where the dogs were kennelled, preceded by Daddy or Ella with a hurricane lamp, followed by us three with each dog's bowl of meat, with the dogs creating the most appalling din, snapping and snarling and the puppies yapping.

Exercising the dogs was pretty awful because we had to have at least three each and they were very nearly a match for us. Dreadful things happened – puppies died and there was even a murder among the larger dogs. Furthermore, they were always escaping and there were complaints about sheep worrying. Relations between Ella and myself were no better except it must have been a relief for her when I was away at school.

In the holidays, I was very much thrown on my own, Ella having given up punishing me for things, such as stopping me having butter and pocket money, as it had no effect. Long ago, Daddy, at Wilbury Gardens, had given up whipping me because on the last occasion it had happened – I had been rude to Kitty Whittington – I had, without turning a hair, held out my hands, saying,

'You had better do these as well!'

Daddy turned away and I had beaten him. So Ella resorted to putting me in Coventry until I apologised. This was no good either because nothing would have induced me to do such a thing. This meant that Ursula and Ruth were forbidden to talk to me, even being expected to ignore me. In a way, they had to so I was very much on my own.

One of Ella's dogs, a fox-like bitch called Dorris, I did like and we would for hours hunt voles around the pond. I, in the boat, would creep up silently on the vole on the bank and it would either drop with a plop into the water with Dorris after it or into the boat with Dorris after it! Why that boat didn't capsize I can't think but it was great sport!

And I went for long walks, collecting flowers and pressing them.

Daddy was going to London on his carbon job, selling a bit but not nearly enough. It was Ella's money that was sending us to school and financing the dog breeding adventure. Daddy used to give me things to do in the garden while he was in London. Some of these were money-making jobs, such as in spring collecting the hundreds of pairs of mating frogs into large barrels for him to dispose of. Sixpence a hundred! Dorris was also very good at this sport and learned to listen for the tell-tale croak of a couple and would stand over them, quivering with excitement as I caught them.

In the summer, we and the dogs had good fun swimming in this pond. It was not too muddy, being so very deep. Red-orange scum would form on the surface of the water, which had to be skimmed off before the melee of children and dogs could swim in it. Daddy thought that, being an old hammer pond, that this would be something coming up from the bottom from the old workings. There was one place we could never find the depth. A spring rose at the northern end, which ran out to the copse at the other end, with steep, deep banks, which daddy planted with primroses and a path cut half way up and round the bank. There was a kingfisher and large carp, which I like to watch on the surface on hot, summer days. And very difficult to catch!

The pond gave me great pleasure and, during the times when I was in Coventry, I spent hours and hours by it, watching its life. Should Ursula or Ruth happen to be in the pond neighbourhood while I was and Ella was out, then we all played together and were happy.

It was always Ella, who gave in first. After three or four weeks, she would say: 'Look here, Barbara, haven't we had enough of this?' and then we would be on speaking terms for a while, which meant we three could talk openly once more until the inevitable time when I would once more defy her and I would be in Coventry again. But it did not worry me after a while. I was perfectly happy in the garden or taking myself off for long walks with Dorris. And then there would be the relief of returning to school.

Ruth, at this time, was too young for school and I think Ursula was taught by Ella, as nothing would induce Daddy to send his daughters to the Council School at Five Ashes. Possibly they could only afford the one schooling and, naturally, Ella wanted me out of the way. The other two were quite good with her but I was perpetual trouble.

During the long, hot summer of my fifteenth year, Ella filled the house with people coming to stay. Mostly new friends would come and see us and people we met at Sussex Square. The Cox's, father and son, were the only people who came with whom I had anything in common. Raymond Cox and I had a mutual interest in pressing wild flowers and all the things that I liked. Ella thought him very dull.

It was during these holidays that I found out what Ella was really like. Daddy, obviously, couldn't satisfy her and there was no sign of pregnancy so she assumed she could not have children. I can see her now, proclaiming with drooping mouth and plaintive, pleading eyes, 'Of course, I'm barren!'

There was a young boy, Dennis, and his sister, who came to stay. Just on seventeen, he was. I disliked him intensely probably because he liked Ella. He became quite in love with her and she encouraged him. It became quite an affair, which all knew about, except Daddy, who doted on her and thought her quite perfect. We came on a most interesting letter from Dennis, stating everlasting love, among other things, and longing to meet. Well, she probably got bored and the boy went back to school; but there were a few others.

I disapproved of all this but I was neither interested nor jealous of her admirers as, yet, boys meant nothing to me and I was very gauche and virgin. Maybe because I was so unattractive with my high aquiline nose and straight, fine, brown hair and was always somewhat plump. One of the men friends staying one week was Gordon Birch. He was a man of about forty, very good-looking and rather alarming. I didn't like him but he was a different cup of tea to the other admirers, cultured and polished, very musical. One time, when he was week-ending with us, Ella was ill and had ot go to bed. She was always racked with indigestion. Daddy, Ursula and Ruth had to nurse her with hot water bottles during these bouts and she would drink boiling water to ease her pain. Of course, I never went near, so Graham Birch and I were left to amuse ourselves.

What he thought of the prospect of this Saturday evening, left with an unattractive lump of a girl of fifteen, I can't think, when he could have been dancing with Ella while Daddy looked on, smoking his pipe. We played games of Beggar-my-Neighbour once or twice and then Gordon said, 'Next game, we'll play if I win, I'll kiss you. If you win, you can kick me'.

I agreed. We played and I lost and he kissed me, flat on the mouth. I found this rather upsetting and somewhat bristly. I was startled and angry but a little pleased with myself that this attractive and most adult man had bothered to kiss me. Also, pleased to steal a march on Ella. We played another game. I won and I did kick him and I then decided to go to bed, leaving Gordon to amuse himself. I always had to go and say goodnight to Ella. Daddy wasn't in the room a\t that moment and I went and blurted out, 'Ella, Gordon kissed me!'

My God, hell was let loose! Why I had to tell, I don't know, but it was, I suppose, two females, and I was female enough not to be able to resist telling her and, with my hatred, it was a glorious revenge. Ella raged. She burst into tears. Daddy was told and all about herself and Gordon! Daddy bore down on him and there was a shocking row and he took Gordon to Mayfield station the next morning. Ella smoothed Daddy over but things were never the same. I was rather pleased about it all. I had scored over Ella at last, jarred her pride, badly, and shaken Daddy's faith in her.

I couldn't feel any sympathy for him. His treatment of my mother, I had not forgotten and I remembered and missed her terribly, still. But I felt very much better after this little episode and I remembered Gordon's kiss, very clearly indeed. And, I think, after this, I began to take an interest in boys. But there was not much hope with Ella around, she being so very attractive to men, and so it went on. I realised that if I worked on Daddy right, I could help this marriage break up.

Diabolically, devilishly cunning, I did everything I could for him, helping him in the garden, clearing up endless little heaps of weeds, mowing lawns, weeding, weeding, weeding and he thought what a "dear little thing" I was becoming!

The "dear little thing" actually had realised he was just a man and that it was easy to get him to think her way! Every row, and there were many now, I sided with him. I told no tales, of course, but there were other men. Whether Daddy knew about them, I do not know. Ella used to take herself off to Brighton, taking Ruth with her. My schooling came to an end. Her money was beginning to get a bit low but she packed me off to stay with some friends of hers at Brighton and I spent two terms at Brighton School of Art at the age of sixteen, taking Fashion and Antiques. I loved it but what useless subjects!

This friend I stayed with was a rather spinsterish girl called Muriel and, during this time, she came to stay with us for a weekend and foolishly brought a man friend with her. This man was just on the brink of asking her to marry him and then he met Ella…and that was that! Even him, she had to have and she didn't even want him. There was no more Muriel and I came back to Woodcote, grown up a little more because I had fallen rather in love with Muriel's young brother. We had gone out together in Brighton and this had been fun but then I forgot him and never saw him again.

Then Ella's money ran out completely and we had to exist on Daddy's carbon sales earnings.

Things came to a head and Ella left Daddy but took Ruth with her. Ruth, about eleven, was a strange looking child, unlike me or Ursula. She had a squat, snub nose, big, hazel eyes and large freckles. Decidedly quaint, she was described as. Ruth's experiences with Ella while in London with her were pretty grim. She had no memory of Mummy and she was a good little slave to Ella, having to do all sorts of errands for her, messages to men and so on. She says she had to ask a black man for money once.

Later, when I asked her to elaborate, she told me that a rich, young Indian was staying at the same hotel with his mother. He fell for Ella and said that he would do anything to help her at any time. Ella then sent Ruth to his room with a note requesting a loan. He read it, said, 'Well, of course!' and picked up a few fivers from the mantelpiece. She thanked him and returned to Ella, who said Ruth had done very well. Ruth also told me that she pawned the family spoons for her in Brighton. The pawnbroker looked very doubtful when he saw her. She also asked Ella's solicitor to lend her money but he was not at all cooperative!

Ella then met a man called Fisher, who wanted to marry her. She asked Daddy to divorce her, which he did, and Fisher paid for it. He paid but he never married her. The last I heard of her, she had had two children. Barren, indeed! Ruth returned to us at Woodcote and we settled down to housekeep for Daddy. And we enjoyed ourselves very much. Daddy went to London each day, returning in the evening, leaving the running of the house divided between the three of us.

Woodcote was right on the main road between Heathfield and Mayfield, right in the heart of old Sussex iron country. Huggett's Furnace – 'old man' Huggett and his man John – cast the first cannon! There were other fascinating names around. It's a nice part of Sussex and I love it all but my Susses heart is in the Downland.

Life was very pleasant with Ella gone. The house running was shared out. I had the housework to do. I have never been madly keen on house-cleaning ever, then or now. I think it is a boring chore. My unalterable routine was to sweep out Daddy's lonely room, out into the top landing passage, then Ruth's room and mine, and with all these rooms' refuse on the landing, brush the whole lot down the stairs! I would not clean Ursula's room on the grounds that it was impossible until she mended her eiderdown. It was a mass of chicken feathers and dog-hairs from the two of Ella's Alsatians that were left behind with us. One of the first things I did was to swap curtains with Ursula and it was a fact – I felt much better with those dreadful curtains gone!

Having brushed all the dirt, dust and dog-hairs down the stairs to the hall, I did the same to the drawing room and collected the whole lot up. A rapid dusting of all surfaces that showed and that was my work done for the day other than any gardening job I had been detailed to do by Daddy.

Ursula was the cook and was supposed to cook an evening meal. Daddy was no cook and Ursula only knew the rudiments of cooking and this had to be done on an oil stove. Ruth's job was washing up. This was really quite a hardship as there was never any hot water because no one would go and pump up water from the well into the tank.

My idea of a day well spent, having raced through the housework, was to cook up an enormous plate of fried potatoes, well garnished with pickled onions, take it and one of Ella's novels, which she had never hitherto allowed me to read, my drawing paper and pencils, get out the boat and moor it right in the middle of the pond and there remain all day until the very last moment when I hurriedly did my gardening before Daddy's return.

Ursula amused herself with the cottagers living near the house. Ruth collected her washing up until Daddy came home in the evening and pumped water. But she was busy all day in her bedroom, writing her Heathfield Magazine. This journal, to which we were all expected to contribute, came out each month and copies were sold to unfortunate Uncles and Aunts for a shilling each, so Ruth, at least, was well employed! She also wrote The Cockpit Chronicle in the pig-sty, which was the Editorial Office as she called it!

Conditions in that house must have been grim, but we were very happy doing just what we wanted to do. Ruth's days were rather overshadowed by the Educational Authorities, who wanted to know why she wasn't at school. She spent a couple of years hiding from them so she really had no schooling at all. But she was to become such a brilliant, vivacious and lovely woman that it never mattered in the end. Daddy would rather his children had no education than mix with village children and, up to this time, we never had.

Ruth and I did have some inclination towards personal cleanliness because we did bother weekly to take the trouble to pump up water, taking well over an hour, and light the boiler and wash our clothes and ourselves.

But, as for Ursula, something had to be done! To me, "Barbara, Ursula is filthy. She must have a bath." To Ursula, "You must have a bath."

"I don't want a bath. I'm all right!"

"Unless you have a bath, we will make you. It's weeks since you had one and you *stink*!"

Ruth and I went off, pumped water and got it nice and hot. A lovely bath was ready.

"Come on. Your bath's ready."

"I do not want a bath!"

"You're going to have one. Come on Ruth, let's undress her."

This done, we carried her, protesting and in tears, heaved her into the bath and made her wash and, although she wouldn't admit it, she probably found she liked it as there was no more trouble after that.

After a while, I must have got bored with the boat because Ursula and I took to hanging over the gate, watching cars and bicycles go by. We were on waving terms with everything male that regularly went past the house. Ruth was most disapproving and thought us stupid. In fact, had she wanted to join our junketings, she didn't dare to for fear the Educational Authorities would see her and haul her off to school.

Gradually, these yokels and hobbledehoys stopped at the gate during their lunch hours and after work. Woodcote was so conveniently placed that we could see Daddy's bus approaching in good time to allow our admirers to disappear. Ursula wasn't bad looking with corn-coloured, straight, fair hair and good features. She had far more followers than I did. I was most unattractive with my hateful nose and hopeless hair. All the same, I had a somewhat bucolic affair with one of those boys. He worked on the farm on the brow of the hill and I encouraged him on. One day, when we were alone at the gate, he came into the house on some excuse and I found myself fighting like mad. I don't know what would have happened but, luckily, Ruth walked in and probably saved me from a 'fate worse than death!'

I was a bit more cautious after this and had another admirer, called Reggie, who was a gardener's boy, but I kept him at a safe distance.

Well, things went on very happily and Daddy never had an inkling of what his daughters were up to. Then he met a Mr Worrall on the train. He lived in Heathfield and he had a daughter, Maud, and he introduced her to Daddy. She was about thirty, liked horses, and was short-sighted with wiry brown hair. Daddy and she fell in love. Much to her father's disapproval, she decided to marry Daddy. I liked her rather and I had no objections to her as a stepmother. I was getting rather tired of my housework, too! Maud and I went out in the boat and anchored it in the middle of the pond, where we had a long talk.

"No, I don't mind you marrying Daddy. I think you are making a big mistake. When you are fifty, he will be eighty." I said.

"But Barbara, I love him! I love him! I must marry him."

"Well all right then but I have told you what I think. I like you, Tommy." This was her nickname – Maud was an impossible name for her!

"And I think that we shall get on very well. It will be better for Daddy, anyway."

Before they married, we moved to London to a house called Sunnyside in Ealing. It was rather a wrench leaving all our farm cronies. I can't think what happened to the Alsatians. All the cats would certainly have come with us as Tommy was as devoted to cats as we were and that was a great point in her favour.

Chapter Three – The Slump

The wedding was very quiet, only the uncles and aunts and Tommy's parents were there. I suppose they went for a honeymoon and we probably went to stay at Bosham Vicarage with Aunt Lilla and Uncle George Street. They had left Telscombe a few years after we did. But we all settled down in Ealing very well. I was just eighteen.

It was somewhat of a change to Sussex, this suburb, but it was a novelty. I loved going to Kew, which was reasonably close, and we enjoyed seeing the uncles more, Bertie at his Kensington flat. He still treated us to gorgeous lunches at expensive places. He lived by playing poker at the Cocoa Tree Club and, later, at Crockford's. And Uncle Ralph, my godfather, had an antique shop in Beauchamp Place. One would drop in and 'Well, young Barbara' he would say. His wife, Auntie Elaine, was one of the most beautiful women I have ever seen.

We got on rather well with Tommy, and life at Sunnyhill was rather uneventful except for the occasion when the kitchen ceiling fell down and narrowly missed me! Then, Daddy thought it was time I had a job. He went to some old friends of his, Ernest and Walter Thornton-Smith, who had a faked-antique business in Soho Square and I got a job in the Studio.

Ursula wanted to be a children's nurse, so she got into a children's hospital. Ruth, who was still young, stayed at home, and still had no schooling, of course! She was still issuing her Journal and she also loved the place. Once, she played a rather nice little tune, which she had composed, to Daddy and Tommy and some friends. Fond parent and all making admiring noises at clever little daughter, who, turning round on the music stool, pronounced gravely and with great aplomb: "That, ladies and gentlemen, was the _fin ale_ from 'Refrain from Spitting'."

I used to go off every morning on the workman's train to Oxford Street, and it was a very new life. The hours were from eight to five. The Studio was in Dean Yard, off Dean Street, on the top floor of the workshops, where really wonderful antique furniture was made. The whole place was filthy dirty. Some thirty girls and a few men worked in the Studio and it was managed by a little bird-like, lumpy woman, called Miss Ward. She had two artist cronies, who worked with her in draped-off seclusion on the north side. One was Miss Kathy, Botticellian, rather like Edith Sitwell in looks. They were all brilliant artists of their kind; working for weeks on an accurate copy of a Canaletto or minute work on a Chinese painting or mirror glass. These had to be painted back-to-front, so to speak, starting with the highlights or the pupil of an eye and working backwards. They also did a lot of retouching of old Masters, all very intricate work.

Fanny, as Miss Ward was called, was a nice little woman but as she worked, she kept control on the rest of us. There was chatter always and, if it got too much, she would say 'too much chatter, girls,' but, if there was too much quiet, she would leave her own painting and slip round and see how our work was going.

The main work we did was fake Chinese wallpaper. I think that it was in the Prince Regent's time that this paper was very popular, so what we were doing were fakes of those 17th century, English painted, Chinese wallpapers. There are very good examples to be seen in the Victoria and Albert Museum. The Studio variety started as ordinary wallpaper, painted eggshell blue, cream or some other pale colour, about eighteen sheets to a set. Two senior girls would 'block out' in white paint designs of the flowering trees, well sprinkled with butterflies and gorgeous birds. The design would sprawl on and on from a peony tree to lemons, chrysanthemums, carnations. These two girls were paid one shilling and tuppence an hour, which was a very high wage.

When they had finished the blocking, Miss Ward would have it hung up to see what it looked like, and she would criticize or praise it. After this, it would be passed to us lowly ones with our own parts to do. Beginners just had to do leaves and make tea, do the shopping errands for all and sweep the studio, and whether one was a success and could stay on rested on whether one could master these leaves. They were tricky until the fact was grasped that the light in China always came from the left. Many times I saw papers hung up for criticism, and whole sheets of leaves would present themselves with the light apparently springing from the ground. Withering sarcasm from Fanny ensued!

It didn't take me long to get the hang of the leaves and I used to take great pleasure in painting them, very smooth and graduated from extreme dark to extreme light with perfect veining, which was done with a special brush called a 'duck'. When I started, I was paid eight pence an hour and I worked from eight in the morning, Saturdays included, doing a forty-nine hour week and earned about thirty shillings a week. But after about three months, I had a raise of a penny an hour. I was now taking on whole parts of the paper, taking on a whole peony tree and not letting any other girl share it with me, so that I could plan the whole colouring of that section, birds, butterflies and all.

When the whole set was finished at last and all the tears in it mended (it didn't matter how much it got torn, it just had to be patched on the back),

the most dreadful thing had to be done to it. We all had to help and it was called 'dirtying the paper'. We got dried, powdered paint and, with filthy rags, rubbed it all over the brilliant colours so that they looked hundreds of years old!

I was given my first designing job to do, a Dutch wallpaper. I was delighted, but most upset as Miss Ward had put a girl called Bob on to work with me. We had terrible arguments as she set herself up to rival me and I knew she couldn't draw. In the end, she gave up and I finished the Dutch paper myself.

We had rests from the paper occasionally. Thornton-Smith had an interest in Fortnum and Mason, and now and then we had to go there and work. I don't suppose it's still there today, but I did an awful frieze for the Grocery Department with camels and all, loaded with provisions. And there was a set of tea tables to have designs of people ballooning on them. Miss Ward put me on these, working with and on the same level as Miss Kathy, doing them at her standard, which was no effort for me, but there was much speculation in the Studio over this. Then, on one of Thornton-Smith's visits to the Studio, he looked at this work of mine, and Miss Ward whispered to him and, when he had gone, she told me I was to have a penny an hour raise.

This was indeed a triumph. Ten pence an hour meant that, in about eight months, I was one of the best artists and well on my way to designing. I was earning about two pounds a week, which was good pay for an artist then. Round about this time, Ruth at last was not too young to start and was taken on at five pence an hour, and she did her stint as tea maker and errand girl.

Unfortunately, soon after she arrived, the terrible slump of the thirties started and she had to leave. As for the rest of us, we were all put on short time, those that stayed, but gradually most left. I stayed on until we were down to three girls and seven hours a day. It was a dreadful situation with no work in the Studio. We would hang on to our precious sheet of paper and spin out the painting of each leaf so as to make it last. I think that Miss Ward and Miss Kathy also did the same on their side of the Studio.

The buildings the Studio was in were wooden and a terrible fire risk. I reckon they must have been a death trap. I do wonder there was not a serious fire as, when we were all painting, quite a bit of terebine and turpentine were used and this would accumulate in paint rags. If these were screwed up tight, they would get hotter and hotter. Suddenly someone would sniff 'the rags are burning' and the waste paper basket would be turned out and the rags, smoking, would be spread out to cool off.

And one day, a girl set the whole place alight. We were painting the curtain for the new Dominion Theatre in Tottenham Court Road. And she threw, by mistake, a lighted match into a pot of shellac varnish. This burst into flames and set alight the enormous fringe, which was hung up all over the place right up to the ceiling. It was all so old and mostly wood. It was a near thing and damn dangerous. I was in the upper studio at the time and I saw smoke belching out of the windows. We got down those little rickety stairs a quickly as we could into the yard and the carpenters came and put it out. The girl, who did it, was the daughter of a friend of Walter Thornton-Smith. He came and looked at the damage, shook his head and looked at her reproachfully. I think it would have been dismissal for anyone else.

All kinds worked there. There were gorgeous society girls, who played at work, intriguing us with their lunch dates and so on. And there was Winnie, a heavy-featured blonde, always around wherever a dreadful youth, called Bert, was working, and, as they painted, sniggering over dirty stories. No one could say a single sentence in his presence without him making something horrible out of it.

Mr. Pluckrose, the designer and draughtsman, a little, tiny man, didn't say much and did not think much of Miss Ward. There was Emily, who blocked out and whom I disliked; Sybil, who was having a terrible affair with some man, whom I believe she married; dreamy Elizabeth Worthington, blonde, good-looking, sister of the Mrs Fox, mother of James and Edward, but like a fish out of water, not very good at painting, but, then, so many were the same. These types of girl came and went.

There were serious artists, but so many were like Winnie and Elizabeth, to whom it was just a job. Some were content to paint leaves, month in and month out. It wasn't dull. Sometimes one would be detailed off for a special job in some big house, touching up furniture or re-gilding carvings on walls. And to Fortnum and Mason a lot – murals for the Mezzanine floor of tropical trees with trailing lianas and magenta orchids and monkeys.

Of the two Thornton-Smith brothers, Walter was our favourite. Ernest managed the business side. They were very wealthy. Walter had a magnificent house filled with very fine and opulent antique furniture. Those of us in the backrooms didn't have much to do with the Salerooms, which were in Soho Square, in a big, black, Georgian house; room after room full of sepulchral gloom and filled with, seemingly, aged furniture.

The years at Thornton-Smith's were a good time, very formative as regards painting. Here was my training. Here I learned that I WORK - in heat, in cold, with a cold, under any conditions, with no artistic whimsies of 'not feeling like painting. One painted! This basic training has stood me in good stead and, to this day, the detail of the Chinese wallpaper still lurks in my paintings.

I didn't have much money left over from my wages. The workman's train ticket and paying Tommy for my keep took a lot, but my great joy was the opera at the Old Vic. I used to queue for three hours for a Gallery seat. And there were the Promenade concerts too. And life at home was peaceful, although Ruth and I were not there much other than at weekends. We went out of the house so early in the mornings and, when I got back in the evening, I went to night classes at Ealing School of Art. I took Life class twice a week, and Lettering, the latter because I was a bit taken by the Lettering master, who was rather good-looking. This infatuation has proved of great use in later life as it did seem that I learned a little and as, from time to time, I've had notices to write out.

Ursula was still away at her baby hospital, not making a success of it because she hadn't the foggiest idea of routine. Then I had a row with Daddy. I suppose he must have been short of money for some reason.

One of his 'bloody tradesmen' wanting payment! I found out that he had sold my Georgian silver christening spoon and fork.

"Why did you sell them? They were mine!"

"I didn't sell them."

"Then where are they, where, may I ask?"

"I don't know where the bloody things are!" A long pause. "Oh, all right, I did sell them."

"You DID!" I was furious. "How dare you sell them without asking!"

"Well, I've sold them. And you've no business to speak to me like this."

It churned on and on, and then Tommy took my part and said he shouldn't have sold them if they were mine. This was the last straw.

"Look here, Barbara, I've had enough of this. I think you'd better go."

"All right, I will."

And so I did, within a week. I took all my things and went to Bosham, leaving Thornton-Smith's, which, anyway was nearly finished. The depression and slump of the Thirties was right on us and there was no work for artists.

And I never returned to live at home again.

When one looks back, Auntie Lilla and Uncle George at Bosham were our port for all storms. We seemed to make for the Vicarage from now on when jobless, because it wasn't very long before Ursula and Ruth followed me, having been turned out of the Ealing house. Tommy later denied this but both sisters confirmed that this was only too true!

I looked at advertisements in the *Morning Post* and, after a week or so, I got a job as a mother's help to a Mrs Morgan, who had a naval sea captain husband. And three children! To my dying day, I shall always have great sympathy towards mother's helps. Of all the most unpleasant and unrewarding jobs, I think that this just about takes the biscuit. I fully understand why servants have died out. Women are so bloody to work for!

I must have been just nineteen when this disastrous existence and constant battle for work started. Aunt Lilla was very much keeping an eye on me and was glad the job was at Bognor Regis. She was very anxious that I should only work for 'nice' people. This 'nice' person was a colossal woman of about forty. She had three horrible children, who quickly found out that I could not manage them and, when their mother was out, made life hell for me.

I had to get up at six, light a boiler and two fires, and clean two rooms before the lady of the house came down to cook breakfast. Then I had to wash up and do all the housework while she shopped and took the children to school. Then I had to get the tea ready and amuse the children, which usually meant that they played me up. Then they went off to bed and I think I did too, dead tired.

I was paid eighteen shillings a week and my food. Wednesday was my half-day and I was off every other Sunday. Wednesday was the cruellest thing of all. I was desperately unhappy and longed to get over to Bosham to see Aunt Lilla, to be with someone of my own kind. But this wretched woman had to have boiled cod for lunch on that day, which she cooked in a four tier steamer. Boiled cod, boiled potatoes, cabbage and so on - not to forget steamed pudding. It never dawned on her to hurry up the lunch so that I could catch the bus to Bosham, which only ran once an hour. So what with the time it took to scrape these damned pots clean and wash up, I would miss the 2 o'clock bus and only get to the Vicarage before four, so didn't have much of a half-day!

And, when I got back, I would find that the children had been rummaging through all my things. This was all too much so I took to locking my door, giving the woman my key. She didn't like this. Aunt Lilla did not think that she was a very 'nice' woman after all and that she overworked me and thought that I had better leave and find somewhere else. So back I came to the Vicarage to look around again.

The Vicarage was enormous, flint walled, with seven bedrooms with attics above. There were a dining room, a drawing room, a big study and an enormous area of kitchen and pantries. The house stood on the main Chichester to Portsmouth road, not far from Bosham railway station, and a mile or so from Old Bosham.

In these gaps between jobs, I would do whatever Aunt Lilla was doing. There was a lot of parish visiting and, like a lot of clergymen's wives, she did much of the Vicar's work while he practised his excruciating notes on his violin in an attic or pottered in the garden or snoozed in his study – typical country parson. Aunt Lilla, always a social girl, longed to be gay and doing things. She had been smothered and buried at Telscombe, and the move to Bosham had meant lots of tea parties, prayer meetings, and so on. Uncle George preferred Telscombe. Bosham was too much under the eye of the Bishop for him.

Whenever Ursula, Ruth or I was staying with her, she would do her best to arrange parties of 'young people' for us. Only impeccable members of the best families around Bosham were invited. People in trade, or farmers, were not considered thus. On the whole, during this Depression, the time spent at the Vicarage was the only bright spot.

Ursula had now left her hospital. It had rather knocked her and she wasn't very well. She took a job as a nurse in Emsworth, so I did see a bit of her as we were able to meet at the Vicarage on half-days. This job decided her life for her. The servant at her workplace, Florence, had a brother, a thin, dark-haired youth called Cecil, who was then a grocer's boy. Ursula fell in love with him and in spite of six years of pleading from the family, she eventually married him.

Ruth, now fifteen, having left Ealing, was having an equally grim time, with a series of frightful jobs. She tells a tale with much gusto and embroidery of a job with an old lady with bedsores!
The next job I had was with a woman, with no children, living in Selsey. She did no work at all in the house but expected me to keep it spotless. This job only lasted three weeks. Aunt Lilla discovered she was definitely not 'nice' because she was being divorced by her husband and it would never do for me to be connected with scandal as it might affect Uncle George.

So I was looking for yet another job, and I got one through Elisabeth Worthington, with whom I had kept in touch. A friend of her mother, a Mrs Douglas-Hamilton, wanted someone to take with her back to Dinard. Her husband was first cousin to the Duke of Hamilton and Brandon. Aunt Lilla was delighted with this. It was very much her cup of tea and she even found that the Hamilton family crest was the same as her stepfather's. So she saw me go off with Mrs Douglas-Hamilton, feeling I was going off with relatives! Dear Aunt Lilla, she did so try to take Mummy's place and help us but her social views were so out of date in a changing England.

I was very thrilled at going, getting a passport and all the preparations. I loved the short sea journey and my first experience of seeing England left behind. Mrs Douglas-Hamilton was very 'nice'! She was a 'gentlewoman' and knew how to treat me, and I was very happy. Also, I did not have to do the menial jobs such as I had done at the other two horrors. She had a lovely, old, wrinkled Frenchwoman for the rough work. She was a gorgeous cook, and I loved to shop for food with her in the market - veal and butter, cream and great langoustines...oh yes! I lived very well.

Also, I had a bit of free time, which I used to explore. There was a fine walk out of Dinard by the slopes of the Rance, with overhanging pines and masses of wild daffodils and the sounds of the St Malo church bells, sounding, from across the water, as they never sound in England. Being early spring when I was there, I loved the camellia bushes, thick with red and white mottled flowers, mimosa, too, and lots of magpies. I investigated St Malo on my days off while on another day Mrs Douglas-Hamilton took me to Mont St Michel, when the tide was out, and I saw the terrifying sands which have trapped so many.

Mr Douglas-Hamilton was a horrid old man. I saw very little of him, thank God. Even his wife was disgusted with him. I came across her one day, scrubbing the drawing room fireplace.

Then she saw me and exclaimed furiously, "Disgusting old man! Spits in the grate!"

"Oh, look, couldn't I help?" I asked.

"No, this isn't your job. This is a wife's job!"

This job came to an end because she decided to leave Dinard. So, regretfully, I left her and came back to England with a few pounds and four yards of black and green checked silk, which she insisted on giving me and had wrapped round my waist under my dress. I passed through Customs without a qualm. Actually, I think that I did not know what the

Customs really were! But, for all the useless bits of material to run all that risk for, that length of stuff was it, and it was years before I could put it to any use. I learned no French, of course, only what sounded like 'san fairy ann' from Marie, and a taste for good food!

Next, I took a situation in Brighton with a couple in a flat. On the whole, this was uneventful but I was expected to know how to make a soufflé, having been in France. She also made me mad because I was back to doing all the housework and I was determined not to be found fault with. She had a ghastly bath, which stained badly. I put my heart and soul into trying to get this bath clean and each time, on my day out, she herself would clean the bath and every time, there it was, pure as driven snow. So I nearly wore my arms out trying to get it like she did. At last, I mentioned it to her.

"Ah!" she crowed delightedly. "I've been waiting for you to ask me! Look, this is what I use." And she produced a bottle of peroxide or bleach. I was not amused and went straightaway to an agency and put myself down on their books as a cook.

I was hired to go to London with a Lady Hall. This was a real below stairs affair, as it was a ground floor flat with an old fashioned basement kitchen. She had one other housemaid to do all the housework, but I had to do the cooking and kitchen cleaning. I cannot think what her Ladyship thought of her new cook, who was certainly not in the usual run of cooks. And I took care that she should know it. My dressing table brushes and combs were every bit as beautiful as hers, being Mummy's beautiful wrought silver set with cut-glass bottles and all very elegant. (These were all lost to the Japanese in 1942.)

This job came to an abrupt end when Lady Hall wanted me to cook jugged hare. There I was confronted, confronted with a skinned corpse of hare, and I had not the slightest idea how to cook it. The maid and I read and read the cookery books but we couldn't make sense of it at all, so I stewed it all up and served it to her in a jug! This wasn't quite her idea of jugged hare so she called me in to her room and gave me a lecture, asking me what I was going to make of my life. She pointed out that we couldn't all just get married. Maybe she thought that I was so unattractive that any hopes of getting a husband were out of the question, especially with my cooking!

And so, it was back to Auntie Lilla to sort myself out once more. No sign of the slump retreating, and a great many unemployed. No one wanted artists, the only work available being domestic, and how I hated it!

Chapter Four - Return of the Native

I think that I must have got my next employment through Aunt Lilla, because it was as a help to Mrs. Winlaw at Telscombe. Mr. Windlaw was the Rector after Uncle George left. She was dumpy, white-haired, and twittered, being very nervous of her husband. I don't blame her. He was a dour, grim, hatchet-faced man. They had two boys and two girls – Roger, the eldest, an enormous and lofty person at Cambridge and idolised by his father; Jean and Dorothy (Dessie) and Peter. It was indeed strange to be in Telscombe again, in such different circumstances, not as Miss Beard of The Manor but the Rector's wife's help!

Strange to be living at Telscombe and at The Rectory and not sleeping in the bedroom I had always had, but in an attic, high up with the rooks caw-cawing outside in the trees. I overlooked Hindlass's cottage. I just had to help Mrs. Winlaw doing any old job but mainly the cooking. I did not have any meals with them, which I didn't mind at all. The less I saw of Mr. Windlaw, the better, and, on the whole, I don't think that they were very friendly to me.

My position in the village was rather queer and I learned an entirely new aspect of Telscombe life. I had my Wednesday afternoon off and every other Sunday and each evening I was free to amuse myself in the village. Except in the kitchen, there was nowhere for me to sit in the evening at The Rectory, so, having nothing to do, I went to all the village social dances, dancing with Mr. Gorham's stable lads and farm boys.

What the people in our old house must have thought of me, heaven knows. Dear Miss Kirkby, Gorham's housekeeper, I think, was deeply worried about 'little Miss Barbara' and said that I could come into her kitchen at the Stables whenever I liked. So, on many, many evenings, after my work at The Rectory was finished and if there was no dance or the weather was so bad that going to the cinema in Brighton wasn't an option, I used to watch Miss Kirkby cooking Mr. Gorham's dinner.

Of course, he could have done a lot for me but what did he care! I was Charles Beard's daughter and, possibly, he liked to see me in the position I was. So, I made friends among the village people and I was the talk and admiration of the farm workers, stable lads and the rest. I was also beginning to make something of my looks and get over my sense of inferiority, caused by my nose! Perms, too, had just arrived, which meant my straight, brown rats-tails had gone forever.

I think that I could have made friends with Jean Windlaw. She did try to confide in me. She was very much in love with someone in India and had saved up enough to go out to him and was arranging everything, unknown to her father. And she did go while I was there but I was too taken up with being the 'Belle of Telscombe' to bother much about the Windlaws. 'Dessie' Windlaw was a great favourite of Mr. Gorham's. He completely took to her and gave her a wonderful time. She was bold, good-looking, blonde, fearless on a horse and a good rider to hounds. She stood up to and was cheeky to old Gorham and he took it!

It is possible that, if I hadn't been who I was, hadn't been so nervous of him and could stay on a horse while riding it…but, no!..as I write now, I can see that I was not his type! I longed for Mr. Gorham to give me horses to ride and I felt, because Ursula was his god-daughter and I being who I was not, that he should have patronised me, Miss Beard, whose grandfather had owned his house. But what a fool I was! I couldn't hold a candle to Dessie Windlaw. She had an answer for him every time and shouted at him to make him hear. I was terrified of him and his deafness made me nervous so that I could never make him hear a word I said.

He did let me ride, twice, but, so much for my wonderful ancestry, I could not control his horses and, on the last occasion, I ended up over the horse's head in a haystack! So that was that!

Publicly, he was a great philanthropist. It was he, who gave Telscombe the mains water supply from Brighton in 1909. This was, indeed, a great blessing even more so than the electricity he had had brought in many years later. Prior to this, Telscombe only had brackish wells and rainwater for drinking but as my father said,

"Ask Gorham to give two and six to some old woman and he'd refuse but for something impressive, he'll spend thousands."

This was quite likely because he was that type, but, for all that, these were of great benefit to Telscombe. What it must have been like to live there before 1909, I can't think. What about a dry summer? I suppose they had to cart water from elsewhere.

Ambrose Gorham's Grave, Telscombe

When he died in June 1933 and his will was read, it was found that he had left Telscombe, with much ensuing publicity, to Brighton Corporation.

During the first month or so, on my Sundays off, after the Windlaw lunch was washed up, I would make my way to The Stables, where Mr Gorham would be finishing his lunch, at the coffee, port and liqueurs stage. As children, it had been usual to be taken to see Mr. Gorham in this way and it never occurred to dear, simple Miss Kirkby, who remembered that, that I was no longer 'comme il faut' with Mr. Gorham. She would usher me in to him, saying, "Little Miss Beard to see you, sir!"

This went on for a few weeks and, although very nervous of him, I hadn't realised the awkward pause in the conversation on my introduction. Then, one Sunday, Miss Kirkby aid, heavily:

"Miss Barbara, Mr. Gorham doesn't want you to go in after lunch." And then added, "But you can come and see me whenever you like."

I was utterly mortified and humiliated and, from that moment on, I don't think I ever spoke to him again. I was certainly shaken out of my ideas of being treated like Dessie! I realised that I was Mrs. Windlaw's servant and that is all I was as far as Telscombe was concerned. Miss Kirkby was very upset and worried for me. Seeing that she had known Mummy when she was first married, had seen me first when I was three days old, was devoted to Auntie Lilla and loved all three of us children, she was, of course, appalled.

So, I went to all the village do's and I had a wonderful time with all the young men. At this time, I suppose I had acquired a kind of glamour and found I could hold these lads. I was different to the other village girls. I was handsome, I think, never pretty, but for whatever reason, I caused much unrest in the village. I cannot think what Auntie Lilla would have done and while Miss Kirkby was worried for me, with Mr Gorham's attitude, she could do no more. I had my 21st birthday at Telscombe and Mr. Gorham gave me two pounds with this note:

'Dear Barbara,

Many happy returns of the day. I enclose you a trifle to buy a little present with."

Yours sincerely,

A. Gorham.'

One remembers the gorgeous gifts he used to send us three children from Hills of East Street, Brighton. Presents to the hated Squire, of course, were important and a far cry from Miss Beard in her home-help job at The Rectory.

Daddy, who had moved from Ealing to Kings Langley, sent me a watch and my great aunt, Annie Lowcock, my mother's aunt, wrote to me and sent me a superb sapphire and diamond brooch. I had not remembered seeing this before but, in her letter, she said it had been Mummy's and had been her brother's wedding present to her. Mummy, during one of those Clarendon Villas' financial crises, had asked Aunt Annie to buy it, which she did, saying that she would give it to me when I was twenty one. I was overpowered by its beauty. It had two biggish diamonds at each end of a bar with two oblong, navy-blue sapphires. In the centre was an open round of two rows of brilliants and inside this a large, matching sapphire. Later I had this made into a ring, using the circle, a handsome thing it was, which I have worn for forty years or more now.

(The other stones on the bar were made into a brooch and subsequently given to Barbara's grand-daughter, Louise. It is still in the family.)

I made good use of Miss Kirkby's invitation to The Stables' kitchen. From there, I could laugh and flirt with Mr. Gorham's employees. I got friendly with Dolly, his Irish housemaid, and we used to go out together on our half-days. She had a young man, Charlie, a farm hand, rather a nice person. She also had a cousin, Michael, working as a carter for Mr. Gorham. It was not long before I fell in love with him, really and truly in love for the first time.

He was an attractive devil, tall with twinkling grey eyes and curling, light brown hair, and, what with his brogue, if I was the 'belle', he was certainly the 'beau'! He had several girls all over the place and no doubt had a whale of a time with them all running after him.

Now, I couldn't get Mrs. Windlaw's meals washed up quick enough and, having dressed myself up as prettily as I could, I would go up to The Stables. At first, this affair proceeded with meetings at the social dances in Telscombe or over at Piddinghoe or Ovingdean and there were a few at Peacehaven. And all this during the winter months! It seems appalling to me now, to think of walking, perhaps in teeming rain, over Telscombe Tie in an evening dress and gumboots, carrying my dancing shoes. And then dancing waltzes, one-steps, Paul Jones's and gentlemen's excuse me dances in some village hall, reeking of perspiration!

The girls all sat together, some of whom had 'steadies' with them, but the majority of men, youths and boys, clumped together in a solid mass at the bar. Filthy coffee and tea and evil-tasting lemonade were drunk, accompanied by stale sausage rolls, buns and paste sandwiches. Then the piano and a violin would start to play and it would be a few minutes before a couple, brave enough to risk the stares, would get up to dance to be followed slowly by others. The huddle round the bar would begin to thin a bit and some would come and collect a girl. Some never left the bar the whole evening but stayed just staring, sniggering at the dancers. Some could not dance, anyway, and some were too timid and so self-conscious that once they got to the bar, there they were stuck. Not drinking alcohol, there was very little drunkenness as such. No one could afford it as money was scarce.

Then after the dance, there followed the walk back over the Tie and this is what made it so attractive, with the youth with whom one had by some tacit agreement or engineering, returned to the village. Sometimes, Michael would walk me back but, if he didn't I would walk back with Dolly and her young man, feeling very miserable.

There would be other meetings, daytime ones, sitting on the bank by the field where he was ploughing, watching the earth turned into neat furrows and the seagulls swooping, settling after him, hearing him chirrup to the horses and sing in rhythm to their plodding gait:

> "Oh I wonder! Oh I wonder,
> If the angels way up yonder,
> Have kept a place for me…"

This, on the misty air, the cold mist coming down and then to walk back to the village, leading the horses, and to then arrange to meet him that evening.

I didn't go to Miss Kirkby's kitchen for quite a while. Michael and I would walk up to the Tie, freezing, to find the nearest haystack to shelter from the wind and there we would make love. Harmless enough, I thought! But, he did play me like a cat with a mouse. He would say that he would meet me, perhaps at seven by the church, where I would go and wait, in the bitter cold, until I had to at last admit that he wasn't' coming. Like as not, I would hear the next day that he was seen in Lewes with some girl!

I can remember clearly, even now, one of these waits on the Tie with streaming rain and a gale off the sea. I asked someone, who was going into Brighton, if they had seen Michael.

"Oh, yes, he's following in. He's coming over!"

And he did but he went down into Ovingdean, avoiding me. I then went on into Brighton and went to the pictures. I came back on the bus and getting out at Telscombe Cliffs, left me with precisely eight minutes to get up the Tie and back to the Rectory before Mr. Windlaw bolted the door.

And to this day, my dear memories of Telscombe are overshadowed by the misery I suffered. With the sound of rooks cawing endlessly in the winter twilight while I waited and waited before eventually realizing he was not coming only to crawl miserable back to the Rectory with a broken heart. If I would then see him the next day, all would be well for that brief moment. He would be there, full of Irish charm, and we would find somewhere. He would spread his overcoat and we would snuggle up under a gorse bush. This would be around the month of

February. It didn't matter if the skies were clear, with the stars out, frosty and the wind blowing. Then, it would suddenly be five to ten, I would have to rush back to The Rectory, only to find Mr. Windlaw had bolted the door and he would be unpleasant to me and have to come down and let me in.

I think they must have had some inking of this affair going on; something of it must have seeped through as it rocked the village. I thought Jean and Peter used to try to catch up with me because, when they began to help me with the drying up, they began to go through the catalogue of young men and girls in the village. Dessie Winlaw never spoke to me nor helped with any of the housework. Indeed she was seldom at home. Her life was hunting and race meetings with Mr. Gorham. He married her off to Sir Dermot Cusack-Smith into just the sort of life she wanted. I cannot remember the name of the people at The Manor then, nor can I recall ever going there. Perhaps I didn't, perhaps I wasn't asked!

Spring and warmer weather gradually arrived and my alternating happiness and misery went on. May came and Croxdean was alive with grass snakes, warming in the sun. The great mounds of violets and cowslips were just as before and the baby rabbits! Once more, the orchis – Bee and Marsh, fragrant and green-winged, and Frog and I found one last Butterfly orchis. Long gone now,

I used to have a recurrent dream about Croxdean. I would be walking along the Links, that ancient track to Piddinghoe, and come to a place where the fields end, where the slope steepens, leading down and down into the dip, with all the anthills and along to the great terraces. In this dream, I would always be taking big, flying strides. It was a wonderful sensation, alighting on an anthill and taking off again, on to the very bottom. Then I would wake!

This was also where I can remember an open air service being held during the First World War and in the middle of it, the cowman saying to Daddy in a stentorian whisper, "Daisy, she be in the clover, zur!" Everybody hurriedly left to get the stupid animal out before she blew herself up.

This was also the place where I lost my virginity. To Michael of course!

One glorious afternoon in early summer, we were lying drugged by gorse blossom, bees humming and larks singing, on the steep bank of my dream, love-making as usual, when something changed. He was on me and had me in a vice. He hurt me excruciatingly/ I wrenched at him and got free. I was very shaken and, as we were returning to the village, hand in hand, Michael said:

"Let me know if you don't come on."

My God! And it dawned on me what had happened and I was terrified with fright and went up to my attic, literally shaking with terror and shock. There were other meetings like this but every time, I was so scared that I just would not let him again. This sheer terror of the consequences got the better of my feelings for him. I think I may have been getting fed up with being played with as well and at last, realised how bad he was, braggart and boastful about his girls and so on. And so the day came when he failed to meet me and I decided I was finished.

I told Dolly this and soothe whole village knew I had ended it. Typically, Michael tried all he could to get me to meet him again but I never did. What fools girls are! How easily I could have got myself pregnant! What on earth would have happened? I grow cold at the thought of Auntie Lilla's horror and Daddy's rage! What a mercy that I was so frightened. Also, I cannot see myself as the wife of an Irish farm labourer and I cannot think what on earth I was doing as at no time did I ever entertain the thought of marrying him!

After this, I was very sought out but I didn't go out with anyone else. I was through with men! However, Dolly went to Ireland on holiday and left Charlie in my care, feeling he would be safe with me. We went to the pictures and the like. He was a nice man and I believe she did marry him and still lives at Telscombe.

And, soon, I left Telscombe and the Windlaws and returned to Bosham and the haven of the Vicarage. Anyway, I had had a good fright and had had my first love affair. If blame is to be laid anywhere, other than on myself, I think it would be on old Gorham. He caused me to be flung in among the village Telscombe people and the shock of not being wanted by him as I had lost my 'class' so to speak, went very deep.

But then, how could it be otherwise? No, the whole thing was impossible and I should never have taken on the job in the first place.

Perhaps, it would be easiest of all to blame Auntie Lilla. I imagine that all she saw was me at The Rectory, safe and protected by the Rector and his wife. She did not realise the teeming and pulsating life outside its walls.

Chapter 5 - London

It was nice to see Ursula again, who was deep in a love affair with her Cecil. This was a nice, respectable walking-out affair, unlike my disreputable and unhappy experience.

Once again, it was Auntie Lilla, who got me another job, in London. An old friend of hers and Mummy's wanted a companion help and she took me on. She had a brilliant daughter, who was studying something though I cannot remember what.

I liked life in Addison Gardens very much. I had a nice bedroom, which was a change from the attic, and she had servants so my life was 'upstairs', giving me a rest from the eternal cooking and washing up of my previous employments. Shortly after I started, the daughter had a nervous breakdown, from overwork, I think.

One day, Mrs. H and I were sitting in the drawing room and suddenly we both realised that her daughter wasn't around. Then we heard a sort of moaning sound, which seemed to be coming from the garage yard. We rushed out and there she was, lying dead in a pool of blood pouring from her mouth.

We stared, horrified, for one second and then the chauffeur and other servants came and took Mrs. H away. The doctor came next and took the daughter inside. I helped quite mechanically and, with the chauffeur, washed her blood down the drain.

There was an inquest but no one found out why she was in the yard. I heard that she had wandered out there and, having a fainting fit, had fallen and fractured her skull. That evening, a reaction of horror set in and, later, I was glad to get a letter from Auntie Lilla, saying it would be better if I left. I agreed but I didn't want to go back to Auntie Lilla's this time. Having got back to London, the last thing that I wanted to do was to go back to more slave jobs!

So I went to King's Langley and stayed with Daddy and Tommy for a bit and saw Ruth, who was living just across the road with Tommy's mother. Then it seemed my luck turned at last. Uncle Bertie had a friend at one of his clubs, who was running a decorating business, and had heard that she wanted an artist. The dreadful slump was on its way out at last and things were beginning to look a little more hopeful. I was jolly glad to get away from ghastly housework jobs. Yes, to the end of my days, I will always have sympathy for mother's helps and home-helps, poor souls!

It was wonderful to be back at painting. Mildred, Mrs Spong, paid me thirty- five shillings a week, with a room at the back of the shop. This was close to South Kensington tube station and the room was pretty shocking, right at the bottom of a well and, if I craned my head out of the window, I could just about see daylight, way, way, up above. Nearly every minute or so, the floor would shake and I could hear the thunder of the trains below. Mildred had partly furnished it and gradually I acquired odds and ends of furniture. Dark and miserable a hole as it was, I was very happy. I was free! After my day's work, I could do what I liked – cinemas, dancing or meeting Ruth, who was by now staying at Uncle Bertie's flat.

I liked working for Mildred. Among other things, she supplied waste paper baskets to a shop in South Audley Street. Waste paper baskets of all shapes and sizes, screens, tables, trays, fancy goods really. They were all covered in parchment, which had been crackled by some secret process. After the parchment was dried on the cardboard, it was varnished and then a white, gluey substance was brushed on and then put in front of a fire to dry. The brown paint was rubbed into the cracks, after which they were ready for me to decorate. I did this in oils, painting bunches of flowers, a cross between Dutch flower paintings and the flowers on old china. I turned them out quite rapidly and they sold very well.

After a few months, I got tired of the perpetual dark of my basement room and heard of a room going free in Queen's Gate Gardens. It was an attic up a hundred and twenty stairs and the rent was thirteen and sixpence a week. I decided to take it and moved in with just some bare essentials to furnish it.

I was still working for Mildred and life became fun. I had got over Michael. Although I longed to be taken out by young men, I wasn't and I led a rather solitary life. I loved it as I was able to do the things I wanted to do, mainly frequently going to the cinema.

I went out with Ruth quite a lot. She was then about eighteen. She was pretty and very amusing with lots of young men wanting to take her out. She had big, wicked, hazel eyes, which she well knew how to use;

a pert, snub nose, covered with freckles, a nice mouth set in an oval face and a lovely thin body. I, however, had the same eyes as Ruth and a magnificent complexion and not a bad mouth, but my face was too square and my dreadful nose just ruined everything. While I went down to nine stone during the era of Michael, it wasn't long before I began to put on weight, which, as I am shorter then Ruth, made me appear dumpy and fat beside her.

Ruth Beard, Fashion Photograph, 1935 approx

She knew how to wear clothes and, to be truthful, I just looked frumpy. I was rather jealous of Ruth. I found her unsettling. I did get taken out, of course, but I just cannot remember them all except for one frightful person on a motor bike. That came to an end when I got an abscess in my two front teeth and they had to be pulled out. My front teeth had never been right owing to that fall on Queenie, the pony. They were very deformed with the two incisors slanting right back and the eye teeth protruding forward. I had had much senseless pain during Ella's reign and she had spent quite a bit of her money trying to straighten these teeth.. It really had been agony as I had to go to the dentist twice a week to have a brace screwed up. And it was not much better after it was finished and, as I had appalling teeth and much pain from them, when I lost them, good riddance! I was fitted with a plate and this did improve my looks a bit.

Life in London was good. The slump now forgotten and my new room, now up in the clouds, was so gay and airy.

45 Queen's Gate Gardens was an enormous terrace house, run by a husband and wife, both kind people. Most of the rooms they let furnished and I could never understand why mine was let unfurnished, as the attic room opposite mine was furnished too. These two rooms were in the eaves, facing each other at the top of very steep and perilous stairs. It was amusing when people first came to visit me, having puffed their way up to the top landing, to find that they had another flight to tackle. Maybe that was the reason they never let the one opposite to a woman as, while I was there, it was always rented by a man.

It was difficult not to get to know one's neighbour. Either doors would be opened simultaneously, with the usual expressions of politeness on an imminent collision or the inevitable crossing on the stairs as one descended as the other came up. My first neighbour was a rather superior sort of young man, a very literary, red-brick university product.

Ruth was making progress in London. Around this time, she had a job in John Lewis in Oxford Street. John Lewis had two shops and Ruth had to go between them and to get things.

One day an assistant asked her, "Staff, are you? Which J. L. are you from?"

"Dunno," says Ruth. "It all seems a bloody gaol to me!"

Oh yes, she could be quite a wag. Things would always be happening to her, which she would enlarge and recount with much gusto. Once, a photo of her climbing up the mast of a barge got into the local paper and, much to her delight, she received a letter from some gentleman, who wanted her to pose for him! Everything she did was amusing, even her minute studio in Chelsea had a large tree growing through it!

Ruth Beard, Publicity photo, 1937

Ursula was still living in Emsworth and engaged or walking out with Cecil. Nothing would deter her. It upset Daddy quite a lot. He felt it keenly, he, who had refused to let his children have any schooling if it meant going to a council school. And Ursula was his favourite.

Ursula and Cecil Ayling, Wedding day, 1936

Daddy and Tommy moved back to London and had a rather nice flat in Norland Square. In a very short time, Daddy had taken the sooty, cat-run of a garden in hand and had made a little gem of it, covering the walls with Polygonum, paved it and planted Iris germanica, London Pride and other resilient plants.

I used to see them at weekends or go down to Bosham or to see Uncle Bertie, who was not doing so well now. He had stopped playing at the Cocoa Tree Club, where the stakes were not very high, and was now playing at Crockford's, but he didn't have the same luck. He also dabbled in shares, disastrously, and was slowly getting more and more into debt and bankruptcy, from which he never recovered. His only means of living was thus taken from him. He had not done anything worthwhile except put in some pretty good service for King and Country in the First World War, on the front line in Delville Wood. He was the most generous, gentle, kind man I have ever known.

His love for dogs, in particular dreadful mongrels, was a passion and they absolutely revolted me. I had had a bellyful of Ella's Alsatians enough to last me all my life and so could never greet the current bag of hair, jumping up all over me, slathering with its tongue, as was expected of me.

"Barbara, say something to poor, old Bill! Look, you haven't said anything to him. Oh, there, there, old boy! Poor, old Bill!"

I could hardly bear to bring myself to touch it. His cat, however, would writhe itself around my legs and I would pick it up and stroke it with loving noises, and darling Uncle Bertie would be quite hurt, seeing my preference to a cat and not a dog. In his young days, he had a cottage, Dale Cottage, in Rottingdean and, one day, my grandfather went to see him and found him in bed surrounded by nineteen dogs!

"Dog," he said, "is spelled D-O-G. not G-O-D!"

Mildred's business wasn't doing so well after all and she couldn't afford an artist. She found me another job in an advertising studio, a subsidiary firm of Storey Brothers, her sister's husband's firm. I continued doing the wastepaper baskets for her as a freelance, but this new job was a dismal failure. I had no idea how to do a layout and the only lettering I knew was what I had learned at Ealing School of Art. It dragged and they were decent about it even though thoroughly embarrassed by my hopeless lack of understanding of commercial art. Obviously something had to be done.

Then Storey's started a publicity campaign to demonstrate their oil cloth in shops all over England, and asked if I would like the job. I did, and this work took me all over England. I kept my room on as sometimes I would be around London, say in Bentall's or Harrods so I would use my room. But frequently I would be, say, in Norwich for two weeks and then across to Swansea on the Sunday. I liked it and I liked the first class travel everywhere. Rooms had usually been booked for me by the buyer and I returned to many stores again and again. These were usually the biggest in the town and usually in the soft furnishing department.

I would have bolts of cloth, all bright and gay and shiny, stacked around me: Curtain Cloth for curtains, a wool backed table covering, and a new use wall covering, which was the primary material that I demonstrated. I had a large board and a bowl of paste and a brush. People would look on as I seized the brightest bit of Curtain Cloth, unrolled it and gathered it into folds.

"Isn't it lovely?" said I. "Rose Brand Lancaster Cloth. This is a curtain material for your bathroom or kitchen." Fetching a different length, a daring black, "What about this? ..So modern! And you can sponge it clean and it doesn't fade. And here is the Wallcovering. This has a special backing and you can cover your kitchen and bathroom walls. It will last about twenty years."

Seizing the brush, I would feverishly slap on more paste, and to the people who were about to move on,

"Stick it on! So! Smooth it down and it will stay on for years."

"How much is it?"

"The Wallcovering is one and eleven a yard, fifteen inches wide."

"Bit expensive to do a kitchen, isn't it, Miss?" asks a man.

I had an answer. "About twelve to twenty pounds, which is not expensive, if you think of the time it will last. It won't wear out."

"I wouldn't mind a bit round the sink, dear." Or, "How much would we need for the bath?" it would go.

And they would buy some, a yard or two here, sometimes enough for a room, which was good for me. I was not expected to make sales but it was all for the best if I did. The Buyer liked it if I sold it well but the main idea was to demonstrate what could be done with this cloth. Everyone knew it could be used for tables, but few knew it could be used for walls, where it made a very good, washable wallpaper, with fifteen years wear. The Curtain Cloth was beautiful and good quality. I wish I had some now, much better than the plastic stuff we have today.

I went to the Channel Islands and as far north to Stockton-on-Tees, where the women stood and gaped as they listened to my accent. It was tiring work, standing all day, demonstrating again and again how to stick it and heaving the great rolls of wallpaper about. The middle weekend in each town was the best as it gave me a chance to explore the surrounding countryside. I was paid two pounds ten a week and all expenses, which was very good then. The job lasted two and a half years and I made a lot of friends. But it didn't last as the demonstrations petered out and I found myself without a job once more. Having been out of London so much, I was very much out of touch.

I took on another demonstrating job. For this I had to be trained. Oh dear! What a difference!. The product, the Luckstone Beauty Secret, was owned by a vampire-like woman, called Miss Gordon-Stables. (*An internet search has revealed that its opaline pot this can still be bought on eBay and others though whether the contents are usable cannot be confirmed*) It was a commodity in the form of a face powder in a scented cake, which was to be patted onto the face with water. From the outset, I hated it and I would like to put it on record, here and now, that as soon as I had finished my 'training', I never demeaned my face with it, but stayed faithful to my Coty!

So, after two weeks propaganda on how to put the stuff on and how to extol its virtues, I washed my face and was sent to Great Yarmouth, which, I recall, was freezing cold. My companion demonstrator, a very

old hand at this and an ex-actress, used to scream about the Luckstone Beauty Secret right across the store. The only notable thing that I can remember about this visit to Gt. Yarmouth was that I caught fifteen flatfish off the pier and my landlady cooked them for my tea and they were superb!

Next, I was sent to Lewis of Leeds in Yorkshire. The Luckstone girls wore blue silk dress overalls and a pink carnation. The demonstration stand was on the ground floor near Perfumery. I quickly found out that the idea of 'demonstrating' had been killed by forcing sales on people and these girls were expected to sell, sell and sell more. They would get a woman to stop, put the stuff on her face and not let her go until she realised that the only way out of the trap was to buy a box. The result was that nine out of ten women, on coming into the shop and seeing the Luckstone stand, would say. "No, not that way" and beetle off in the opposite direction.

None the less, I sold quite a bit in the first week – perhaps it looked so well on me, Coty, remember! Anyway, I sold more than the old hand, who was working with me. Then Miss Gordon-Stables and a side-kick appeared and, instead of the approbation I had expected, they were not at all appreciative only expecting more and more sales.

So, that night, I sat down and wrote what I thought of them and sent in my notice. It was just as well I did, as I heard later on that I was going to be sent next to Carlisle, which would have made it very expensive for me to travel home. As it turned out, I took the bus back from Leeds and arrived in Queen's Gate Gardens with fifteen shillings. But I was very glad to be rid of that lot.

I knew quite well what I wanted to do next, and that was to get back to painting. Not so easy, and I had a rather thin time for the next few months. Ruth was also out of a job and she came and shared my room for a month or so. We got on reasonably all right but it was a bit difficult. The trouble was that she was so attractive. Night after night, she was asked out to do this or that and she usually had two or three young men to choose from. So she would go out and leave me behind. Try as I could to grin and bear it, it was a bit hard, on her as well, because she did try to include me.

One never-to-be-forgotten evening, she had two or three invitations to things and a young man turned up with ice skating tickets for Olympia. She said she couldn't or wouldn't go, and why not take me? He did, but with a very bad grace, sulked, and I felt awful. And this was my first and last attempt at ice skating as it was horrible and I couldn't get the hang of it.

Then Ruth, who was getting desperate, answered an advertisement for a typist at an art agency. How the interview went, I cannot think, as she couldn't type and couldn't spell, but she returned with a job. Apparently her future employer was so taken aback by her audacity and aplomb, walking into his office, selling herself and as a typist as well! I suppose he thought he would see how she got on in Fleet Street. In fact, Ruth had this job for years and years and became a well known and very good art agent.

Ruth Beard's Entry Photograph for the
£1000 Daily Sketch 'Smiles' Contest

She moved out and lived elsewhere, which was really better even though I was in a financial mess, struggling along, doing any old jobs. Then, somehow, I met Mr Pluckrose of the Thornton-Smith days. He was managing the decorative studio at Peter Jones. I went there to see it, as quite a few of the Thornton-Smiths' artists were working there. It was funny seeing them all again. I told 'Plucky' I would very much like a job, but there wasn't a vacancy and I would have to wait. He said he would remember me.

And so, a really appalling time for me started. I was drawing the dole, which just about paid my rent, leaving enough for Lyons' loaves at a penny three farthings each, tomatoes, butter, milk, tea, sugar and cheese. Just these were my staple diet for some time. So I was nice and thin. There was another love affair during this time but I will say it was uneventful and quite respectable. There was someone living next door, whom I used to hear moving about. I never saw him as he was never there, when I was, nor did we meet on the stairs.

Then, at last, I got a job. Painting!

It was with a little man in the King's Road, Chelsea. He made fancy goods: mat holders, table mats, trays, egg cups, gaily painted wooden things. I proved most satisfactory and I designed some nice things for him. One was a catchy design of the *Queen Mary*, which delighted him because she had just been launched. The third week I was there, I developed a dreadful boil in my nose, which became enormous, infecting my two eye teeth and my usually short upper lip. I looked exactly like the drawing in Leon Furtwangler's 'Ugly Duchess', with an enormous, swollen upper lip.

I became really ill with this boil and the landlady nursed me with a high temperature. Eventually, when I was able to, I went to the dentist and he took out my two deformed eye teeth. And, as with all those years in the past, it was to Auntie Lilla that I went to recuperate and wait for my new false teeth. Dear Auntie Lilla, I remember with her with love and gratitude. Dry, snobbish, withered and childless she might have been, but I reckon that when she met her sister 'up there', she could rightly say; "Rosalie, I did try to take your place."

I never knew her once refuse us staying there. So, there as always the Vicarage. One doesn't forget.

These new teeth were very expensive and were a severe blow to my finances. There was no National Health, and my bite right to the roof of my mouth was very strange. There was then no plastic in use, only gold, so it had to be gold. The little man in the King's Road had been awfully decent and even paid my wages while I was ill. Seeing that I had only been there for three weeks, it was very good of him.

My new teeth arrived and, back in London, the young man next door couldn't believe his eyes when he, at last, met his ravishing neighbour! Then Plucky rang up and asked, did I want a job in Peter Jones? Did I?

I felt awful speaking to the little man. "I've been offered a job at Peter Jones and I'll have to take it," I said.

"I knew you were too good for us," he replied, pathetically.

So I started to work in a studio once more and I liked it there. It wasn't at all like Thornton-Smith's, with only a few of the people, who had been there that Plucky had taken on. At that time, in 1935, the fashionable vogue was for white furniture. Wealthy people decorated their rooms completely white. The most beautiful, bow-fronted chests of drawers, antique tables, chairs and chaise-longues would be sent to be plunged into enormous tanks of stripper or caustic soda, there to lose their superb patina and ancient polish.

Next, they were painted white and sent along to the studio, to us, the artists, who decorated them with subdued designs and picked them out in silver and lacquer work. They then had dirty paint brushed all over, rather reminiscent of the Chinese wallpaper trick, and, when this was nearly dry, with a large brush, we would 'pull' it over the surface of the white paint so that it stayed in the ridges. It was effective, but an appalling act of vandalism done to much fine furniture.

I was twenty-five, the slump was over, and it was the year of the Silver Jubilee. During the week before, I had a good survey of the procession route and decided that the best vantage point and an excellent pitch was to be had just below Hyde Park Corner where Piccadilly starts. There was a large storage bin for gravel and road salt and I reckoned to take up my position there. So, at around six the evening before, I and three girlfriends took possession of this bit of pavement. Other people were doing likewise. We had plenty of food and drink, rugs and woollies against the cold night. This is quite an experience, all night waiting for a great event, and I wouldn't have missed it. It was difficult even to doze with so much going on around as people constantly arrived to take up a position. There was singing and much laughter and one got to know ones neighbours quite well.

Towards daylight, people still arrived steadily, and the crowd was in a very good temper, cheering at the slightest thing, even the arrival of the milkman and the postman. The police were helpful and happy too. There were the late-comers, who tried to stand in front of us, we who had waited all night. At this there would be an outcry and the police would move them on. The arrival of the soldiers to take up their places was greeted by terrific applause.

Eventually they came, King George and Queen Mary, a wonderful old woman, stiff as a ramrod, waving her hand graciously in acknowledgement. We certainly had an uninterrupted view of the carriages that followed with the Prince of Wales, the royal Dukes and Duchesses. Princess (?) Marina was too lovely and there was a 'coooo' from the crowd. I think I remember her hat with a fringe of feathers.

All in all, it was a happy time but, in the meantime, there were horrid things happening in Germany, which even I could not help noticing. Politics and the happenings of the nation rather went over my head so unless they impinged on my life, I did not take much interest. But I had to notice that Hitler's horrid screaming, which had been going on for some time, was steadily getting worse; the plight of the Jews and the papers with photographs of great rallies of German youth; Nazi salutes, Heil Hitler! I voted for the first time and put Stanley Baldwin, Kitty Whittington's uncle, into power.

I gradually got to know the young man next door. His name was Raymond Everard.

Raymond Wallace Everard, 1937

He was tall and rather thin, rather like Clark gable, having the same features, moustache, grey eyes, thick, dark wavy hair but a rather weak chin. He worked at Harrods in the Mail Order department. He was always broke and spent every evening dog racing, which perhaps was the reason. He took me dog racing once and I was never so bored in my life. It seemed hours went by with nothing happening and then about half a minute with everybody screaming themselves hoarse and a lot of dogs would rush by – over and over again!

Then, soon, he did not go out in the evening and the aroma of my lovely, gas-ring cookery, steak or sausages and onions, would waft across the yard of the landing. And so, it had to happen, so naturally that I should ask him to have some.

And he gave up dog racing!

He told me something of his family. His father had been a wealthy man, having a shoe factory in Norwich, called Sexton, Son and Everard, but he had died at the age of 44, when Ray was very young, of double pneumonia brought on by his refusal to stop working. Leaving his wife well provided for but with ten children, four of whom self supporting at the time their father died.

'Baba' Everard, Raymond's Mother

The children were: Ivy Mary, who renamed herself Althea, Alfred Clement George, known as Sonny, Algernon Charles – Algy, Olive, Vera Constance Maud, Kenneth Malcom – Ken, Barbara Mary, Lillian Margery Blanche, Bertha Mildred Joyce – Betty, Raymond Wallace – Ray and Herbert Edward Hilary – Hubie. I have never seen such a collection of names in all my life – any more children and they would have run out.

There was another child, stillborn. Hubie very nearly died at birth and had to be dashed into alternate hot and cold water. So Mrs. Everard – Baba – had at least five children, some at school age, Ray a toddler and Hubie, the weakly baby.

Herbert, 'Hubie',Everard, 1935

Each child had been left £2000 by their father and the older ones all got theirs but when it came to Ray and Hubie, there was none left! Baba had gone through it all in extravagant living and bringing up the children. Poor young men, what a bitter blow it must have been as, undoubtedly, they had been brought up to expect this inheritance. At this stage, I did not meet any of his family, with the exception of Vera, possibly.

'Baba', Betty, Raymond and Hubie

At the beginning of 1936, in early January, dear, old King George the Fifth died. The sadness of the BBC announcements warned us "The King's life is slowly drawing to its close". He was much loved particularly for his innovative Christmas Message to the nation, given in his fatherly, fruity voice.

I queued to see his Lying in State, joining the line after my day's work at Peter Jones at about 56 in the evening. It was about three and a half miles long and the steady crawl forward took me four hours to get to Westminster Hall. It was an unforgettable sight with the solemnity of those four, bowed mourners at each corner. And my companion on one side all the way was Prince Monolulu.

So now, we had a new King on the throne and this seemed very hopeful but Hitler, the Fuehrer, was in complete control of Germany and had taken the Rhineland. Even I had to notice all this!

Chapter Six - Chilham

A friendship developed even though I was still in mourning over my last young man. It was all rather fun. We didn't have much money, so we just walked about London and took bus rides to places like Kew Gardens and, of course, went to the cinema.

Sometimes, in the summer, we used to climb out of my window on to the dirty roof and sit there in the cool with a lovely view and talk. We went on like this for some weeks, just friends and it was such a happy time. Then, one day, we were sitting on my divan and he kissed me, very firmly, and I had a most frightful feeling of finality. "This is it...." that's what I felt. We were both jolly cross about it, neither of us wanted it and there we were. He was in love with me and it wasn't long before I was with him.

Thing were really quite domestic. We pooled expenses, with me, cooking lovely meals. No one seemed to notice the two turtledoves on the top floor. Then, rather late one night, we were lying on my divan when Ray stretched out his foot and, crash, over went the lamp, making a terrific noise in the silence of the night. We looked at each other in horror and I said;

"You'll have to stay now,"

So he did, and after that we slept together each night. Slept together! Just that! I had not forgotten my fright with Michael.

Then, an awful problem arose. Mildred had an aunt and uncle, Sir Edmund and Lady Davis, who lived at Chilham Castle in Kent. Mildred's decorating business had folded and she had been living with them as an aunt's companion. She wanted to go to America but she loathed leaving her aunt.

Mildred asked me if I would like to take it on. It was a temptation. I was so poor and they were so rich. I didn't know what to do. There I was now, at last, having a happy love affair with Ray and quite happy at Peter Jones. And now this most enticing offer of a job.

How is it that every so often a situation arises and one cannot decide which way to go? It's that 'tide in the affair of men'. Well, I didn't know what to do, torn as I was in all ways.

Chilham Castle. Kent, 2010

I went down to Chilham and saw them. Of course, it was all too lovely. They were nice English Jews, both in their seventies, dumpy and stout, English Jews. He had a huge beaked nose and she had piled-up white hair and soft, gentle eyes.

Sir Edmund and Lady Davis

I declared terms to Sir Edmund. "£3 a week."

"Very well."

"To be paid each week. And I don't want days off as servants have. I'll have my time free when Lady Davis is in London."

"Yes, very well," said Sir Edmund.

So that's what happened.

I took the job at Chilham and when Lady Davis came to London, I did too, and I'd ring Ray up at Harrods straight away, feeling terribly carsick (the Rolls always upset me) and I would meet him and we would have a lovely time for the next two days. I had lots of money and nothing to spend it on at Chilham, only the rent of the room at 45. Some nice new clothes, so there were theatres and dancing, watching cricket at the Oval or Lords, and days out in the country.

This was somewhat of a change to the poverty and lack of food I'd been having a few months ago. But I settled in very naturally. Except for the first night when, to combat the cold, I rolled myself up in a carpet and slept a fitful night.

They were a dear old couple, childless. He was a director of many companies with strong interests in Rhodesian copper; a wealthy man, very cultured and very kind. They were both about five feet in height, on the fat side, she with doe-like eyes, soft as butter and very generous, badly deaf and a somewhat bawdy humour.

I didn't have much work to do. I just had to be there to answer telephone calls, take people over to the Castle, arrange flowers, brush dogs and take them out (I didn't care for this) and pick up balls of wool and stitches. I helped with The Times crossword at which I failed her badly. And we embroidered and painted in oils.

There was one thing I had to do which was a real trial, and it had been so for Mildred and others before me. She being seventy and he seventy-five, they both went to bed at nine, and woke at four in the morning and wanted attention. A terrible loud bell rang in my room, right by my bed, and I had to get out and go into her room and collect her hot water bottle and make her a cup of tea. One would think there would have been some arrangement that it could have been made in her room but, no! I'd have to stagger off, sound asleep nearly and make this cup of tea in a sort of upstairs pantry which was literally a minute and a half away from her room around the hexagon shape of the house. Here at weekends, I would sometimes meet Sir Edmund, full of life and conversation, which I certainly was not at that hour. No, I was jolly cross!

Six weeks or so of this bell going night after night did something to nerves, and I used to long for a day or two of relief in London.

Monday to Friday, Sir Edmund lived in London. Lady Davis had this very high blood pressure and she could be in bed for several weeks, so bad sometimes, she had to have a nurse, which meant me giving up my room. I didn't mind in the least, since then the nurse had the bell to cope with. I usually moved to a room on the next floor called the Tower Room, which I liked very much as it had its own bathroom in a tower.

The house was most beautifully furnished - antique furniture, fine old linen-fold panelling and classic paintings and sculptures. But what really appealed to me were the eleven bathrooms. Most of the bedrooms had their own bathrooms but there was not one belonging absolutely to my bedroom, so I generally used the Parrot Bedroom one, which had a dozen

or so Degas drawings around it. Real, genuine Degas! During the week, Lady Davis and I were mostly on our own as Sir Edmund had a flat in London and came down on Friday evening for the weekend. When I'd get bored with the Degas bathroom, I used to patronise the others in turn.

Chilham Castle

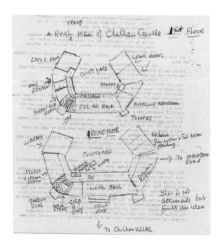

Barbara's sketch of the floor plan of Chilham Castle in 1937 drawn from memory
(drawn on reverse of manuscript with type showing through)

The Baker's Hall, 1924

The Baker's Hall with oil painting as it was in the 1930's

Dining Room, 1924 with the Canaletto on the left

View of Sir Edmund's Terrace. 2010

Terraces and steps with Sir Edmund's Summer House, 2010

The Norman Keep, 2010

My position in the house was a delicate one – half family friend, half servant. I saw that if I was going to be liked by the servants, I would have to be careful, so I never gave a direct order. When I had to get something done, I would say:

"Smith, Her Ladyship wants you to do this," or whatever. Then there would be no question and I kept a very reasonable relationship with them.

In order of seniority, there was Lewis – Miss Lewis, a stern, prim spinster hiding a heart of gold, who was Lady Davis's lady's maid and housekeeper and therefore she ran the house. She had been with them for forty years.

Smith was the butler and head house parlour maid, a very efficient person with twenty years of service. Some jolly queer people, with strange tastes, stayed at Chilham. Sure enough, if they came again, Smith would remember that they liked cayenne pepper with their coffee or such, which delighted and flattered them and possibly earned her a good tip.

The Under House parlour had twenty-five years service. The housemaids were Hurst, a cockney spinster of about forty, a nice old bird, the only way I can possibly describe her, with about thirty years service. There was another called Ruth, who had about ten years. And there was Mrs. Troke, who cleaned my room and Lewis's. The Trokes lived in one of the Lodges on the main gate and Troke butlered at weekends or when there were big parties.

In the kitchen department, which I did not have much to do with, thank God, was a miserable, dyspeptic female called Mrs. Smith – a spinster, but could she cook! She also had been with them a long time. I don't know kitchen maids, but there were eleven in all in the House.

Outside there were two chauffeurs. Mr. Kirkwood, Number One, was a dour Scot and had been with them longer than Lewis. He had once been a coachman and, my God, did he drive on the brakes! The agonies of car sickness I suffered in the Rolls, not so much with Sir Edmund as he just went off to sleep, and Kirkwood drove so fast from Chilham to town, I didn't have time. But Lady Davis insisted on his driving slowly and it was braking all the time. Yes, forty-five years he had been with them, so all in all it was a very settled household. The Davises were good and kind employers and everybody was fairly and kindly treated and they were loved in return. There were ten gardeners and there were gamekeepers and farm workers.

Ron Knight, gardener, 1937

I enjoyed the first few months very much until the luxury and glamour of it had worn off.

In the first spring there, I went to the South of France with them, stopping four days in Paris and staying at the Ritz – on the whole rather disappointing as they had most of their meals in their suite so I missed all the exciting people. Sir Edmund took me himself to the Louvre. This was his pleasure, to show people the things he loved. I stared with rapture at the "Winged Victory" and I looked long at the Mona Lisa.

Lewis and I were told to choose a theatre to go to.

"Barbara, you and Lewis better go to a theatre. Where would you like to go?" said Sir Edmund. "You have a look and I will get the tickets."

Lewis and I had a confabulation (sic) and came back and horrified Sir Edmund.

"Please, we'd like to go to the Folie Bergere!"

"The Folie Bergere! Good Lord!" I think that he was astounded and somewhat amused.

The prim Lewis! Of course, she would never have asked for this if it hadn't been me. "I'd thought you'd want to go to the opera."

However horrified, he got the tickets and we went and goggled at the nudes, Maurice Chevalier too.

La Fiorentina, Cap Ferrat

La Fiorentina, at Cap Ferrat, which Sir Edmund had bought form Countess Beauchamp, was beautifully placed at the extreme end of the Saint Hospice point of the peninsular, with a most lovely garden, each bedroom opening off to its own little hedged-in private garden with pools that had pots of white Arum lilies, where little emerald green frogs sat on flowers and croaked and chirped. Geraniums, wisteria trees and orange blossom…across the bay, a fine view of Monte Carlo and the Alpes Maritimes, snow-capped.

Gardens and view, La Fiorentina, Cap Ferrat

They had a whole set of rich friends, people who never came to Chilham, and Lady Davis would have one of her cousins. The women all brought their diamond necklaces with them. Each day a hairdresser would come to do their hair. Curiously, while the food at Chilham was very sumptuous, on the whole they ate simple meals at Fiorentina, sometimes almost sparse. Sir Edmund would carve one minute chicken himself and make it do for nine people. And sardines stuffed with spinach for lunch, this was very out of keeping.

Sir Edmund and his friends went off to the Sporting Club each night. Lady Davis did not, so my job was to stay with her. She liked her gamble however at the plebeian "kitchen" in the morning and lose her 50 francs.

Sir Edmund did take me once to the Sporting Club and gave me 100 francs to play with. I won, and each time I did, I went and cashed it, and when my 100 francs were all gone, I sat and watched the others winning or losing. Not very exciting! But what was good, when these rich people had a win, they would give me 100 francs and when it came to changing the money back to English currency, I surprised Sir Edmund by bringing him 700 francs in cash.

And they bought me a pearl necklace. I was with them while they were buying a pearl necklace for Mrs Amery (Leonard Amery's wife) and there were about six they were choosing from. I hadn't been thinking of myself in any way and was astounded when Sir Edmund flicked, with one finger, a single strand to me. "For you, Barbara!"

This is what they were like. It gave them pleasure to give and yet there were many who took advantage of this and got all they asked for. In the end I became disgusted and sickened by it. I never, ever asked for anything.

When we got back to England it was summer, and in the summer one rather suffered from an influx of her friends and relations and this is when the scrounging was at its peak. Her friends were mainly invalids, dull, aged and boring. His were rich stockbrokers, politicians, sporting, medical and opera singers. I was alone with her mostly in the summer as he went off to Africa or somewhere. The food at all times was good, plainer when it was just the two of us there. But there were usually people at the weekend. Fortnum and Mason things. Guernsey cream from his own cows. I fought that cream always and lost. I started to put on weight – no longer wraith-like!

And then there were the shooting parties at the weekend in the winter. I was allowed to go out with the guns in the afternoon while the old lady rested. After what I call a masculine lunch – say steak and kidney pie or roast goose and a trifle, with that dreadful devastating figure-destroying cream, or a suet roly-poly dripping with blackcurrant jam, we would all stagger out. I, in gumboots and an old mackintosh, nothing bright that would frighten the birds, would climb into the shooting bus followed by the men, hearty and happy, smoking cigars, full of lunch and port.

It was almost dark, the mist rising and a coming frost nipping my toes in their cold boots, agitated ducks, quacking and wheeling above, the thought of tea, Indian or China, hot teacake, foie gras or smoked cod's roe sandwiches, fruit cake, creamy cake and then a swim in the heated swimming pool with its Rodin statues at each end, then dress for dinner.....dinner, but I won't say more!

Indoor heated swimming pool, 2010 (without the Rodin statue)

As had been arranged, when Lady Davis stayed at the flat in London, I went to 45 and had my days off. This arrangement did work very well as it gave me a rest from that wearing bell, which really did harm me. One such time in my second year at Chilham in the summer, they were just off to France. I was not going with them this time, and Ray and I had planned to go off on a holiday. She had sent me up with an umbrella to be covered. It was pouring with rain. Ray met me at the station and told me he was going to Singapore. He got a job as Manager in the Grocery Department at the Singapore Cold Storage in three weeks time!

It was as if my whole world had dropped in, how I got to my room, I don't know, but I wept and wept and wept and as the day wore on, we arranged to get married – secretly. As he was going out on a single man's contract, we really had no business to get married at all, but I carefully read the contract through and there was no mention of the word "marriage" in the whole of it so I could see no reason why not.

I had accepted and taken him for granted up to this; he was always there in London to take me out, it was now and only now born on me, that I loved him deeply. We had a sad parting and I went back to Chilham and told Lady Davis, and she let me go straight away and I returned to London.

And marry we did. In secrecy, in three days, by special licence as Ray had to produce his birth certificate, he was so near underage. Maybe we were mad.

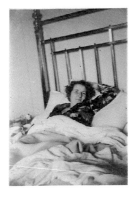 

Barbara and Raymond Everard, Grosvenor Hotel, 1937

Barbara and Raymond Everard, Kew Gardens, Wedding Day, 1937

The marriage was kept secret, except for my family knowing and the Davises, for nearly a twelve-month. We had a brief but sad honeymoon, that time that had been planned to be a joyous holiday. Ray got an old car and we went to Cornwall, visiting Looe and Newquay and Port Isaac and Padstow and then on to Wales to say goodbye to his sister, Betty.

Barbara and Raymond Everard, Honeymoon, Looe, Cornwall, 1937

We hadn't a lot of money and we lived mainly on fish and chips and we stayed at boarding houses each night, bed and breakfast. The weather was lovely and, of course, we enjoyed ourselves but over all was the dread of the coming parting…..

I have had two partings from my husband so far and each time the last I saw of him was going round a corner. The first was two weeks after we married, and the second, I'll be getting to later on…much later on.

We said our farewells and I leaned from the landing window at 45 to see him go, through pouring tears, till he disappeared from sight, away for years maybe, round the corner of Queen's Gate Gardens into Gloucester Road.

London was unbearable after he left. So I went to stay with Ursula at Emsworth, and when the Davis's returned from France, I went back to them at Chilham. Lady Davis had, of course, told Sir Edmund and he was most tickled with it and enjoyed the secret, which they kept well.

So I settled down to my luxurious life once more, indeed it was rather difficult to remember that I was married, except for my wedding ring to remind me, which I wore round my neck tucked away seductively in my cleavage. I was Miss Beard still, not Mrs. Everard.

So passed 1938, a restless year, not long after the Abdication and a war looming, and with me, with one thought on earth, "how to get out to Singapore?" Ray wrote to me fairly frequently at first and I started to collect clothes and linen and saved quite a lot of money. And life just went on. I started a stamp collection for Sir Edmund's wastepaper basket and also Ray's stamps on his letters. And then something dreadful happened. One morning early, I was awakened by Lady Davis.

"Barbara, don't be shocked but there has been a burglary."

"What! What!" I was half asleep and couldn't take it in.

"Come with me and I will show you." We went to the oak stairs and into the big hall.

"Edmund found it first this morning at about five. He couldn't get in to his study, they put these armchairs against the door," she said. "Just look, the Saskia is gone, and the Van Dykes and the Lady Clarges."

Saskia a sa Toilette

Lady Clarges

William Pitt

I was speechless with horror, the dreadful gaps where these three superb things had been.

"My God, how horrible, horrible." One could not take it in.

The aftermath of the burglary

Sir Edmund was in his study with detectives and he came out. He had somewhat gotten over the shock and was now rather enjoying himself. "Look, they've taken my Rhodesian mint coins."

The children of the then-Governor of Northern Rhodesia were staying with us and they had given him these coins. The thieves had also taken the children's cameras, which had been left in the flower arranging room. Apparently this had all happened in the early hours. It would have been thus as they all went to bed about nine, and I suppose the rest of the house-party were all in bed by eleven, at the latest. So there were, besides the Davises and myself, eleven servants, plus a house-party, all in the house. And Lady Davis, waking at four, only gave them a few hours. But that one night, and up to this she had been ringing for me pretty well every night, she did not ring, and Sir Edmund was late, too, getting up. What a shock it must have been for him, not to have been able to open the door, and then to see the chaos.

"Edmund was so brave and he had great presence of mind," Lady Davis said, as we went on staring at it and finding fresh things. "He didn't try to get in. He guessed something was wrong and went straightaway and phoned the police."

A thought occurred to me. "But think of the dogs. Why didn't they bark? They always bark, even if they hear the Lodge gates being opened so far away."

They had entered by the dining room window; they bypassed the beautiful Canaletto next door to the Long Hall. The police reckoned that at least ten men would have been on the job, as they would have needed four men to take the Van Dykes down which were very heavy. When they had to be moved, four men from the estate always had to be brought in to move them. So, assume four did the hard work, possibly two experts who cut the paintings from the frames. These were then rolled up and taken (we assumed) to a waiting car on the Maidstone Road. While all this was being done, there would have been several lookouts, probably one at the top of the stairs, just by my door! Oh, how I shuddered to think of this – but supposing she had rung for me!

The police thought that the four, after their part of the haul was done, just went through the rooms, lifting what they could of value, and taking the coins and cameras. The Governor's children and I had been playing Monopoly (which was just out) in the studio-sitting room the night before and they had a look in the box, to see if we were using real money, I suppose! But a gold statuette, an Aztec idol, had been taken down from its plinth, looked at and left.

"Perhaps they thought it was brass."

"As if Sir Edmund would have a brass ornament on his mantelpiece," sniffed the Inspector. "More likely they were superstitious. These chaps are very like that, you know."

Yes, there had been a previous burglary, years ago. At the time they were going to Buckingham Palace, and they got a ladder to her room, when they were all at dinner, everybody being concentrated in that part of the house. But they were disturbed by a servant going to the room, and when she couldn't get in. she ran back to them at dinner. But by the time they all got there, the thieves had got away, taking some jewellery and furs with them but leaving behind some fine, black opals, which were supposed to be unlucky.

It was a horrible feeling in that house for some time and we were all nervous. I was very frightened, making tea at four in the morning. I dreaded that bloody bell worse than ever and would switch on all the lights I could find on the journey.

But what I cannot understand and don't to this day, it was my job to let the dogs out for their run before nine each evening. There was, besides the miniature bull-terriers and the dachshund, Lewis's ghastly Skye terrier, Binkie, who would yap quite equal to the rest. And keeping himself to himself, a dignified Chow, and excellent and intelligent dog – not one of these animals made a single sound all night and no-one in the house stirred. Why was this? Just this one night? Were we all drugged? And, if so, by whom and how? All the staff had at least ten years service. I was the only new arrival and I was a sort of family retainer, having worked for Mildred and the Storeys, so it wasn't me.

Of course, the burglars would have been fairly safe in the early hours, that everybody would be asleep, but one could never silence those dogs. Someone, somehow, somewhere gave those dogs something, I am certain of that.

And I often think how easily it could have been me who showed the thief the house. One of my chief jobs was a conducted tour of the house and the old Norman Keep in the garden and, what with open days, I must have shown hundreds over it. The pictures that were stolen were to have been left to the nation- the two Van Dykes, Gainsborough's "Lady Clarges" and the beautiful Rembrandt, "Saskia a sa toilette." This last was a lovely thing and it had been a great joy to be able to go close to it and peer at it and the more one looked, the more wonderful it became.

Well, we had detectives all over everywhere and it was horrible. Lady Davis weathered it well and her blood pressure didn't go up but this was typical. Something catastrophic like this wouldn't worry her, but if some old body from the village told her some sorrowful tale, Lewis and I would have a job on our hands. We always made a point of never telling her any worry…ever.

It was £33,000 worth of pictures (1937 value). They were insured, of course. At last came a day when the assessors heard something. A little man had called in about the reward. He thought he could help with the recovery of the paintings so could he have the money.

"Oh no," said the assessors. "You show us where the paintings are."

So he tipped them off. Two of the paintings were saved but three were burned, lost forever – and one was the Saskia.

The Daily Sketch pictures of the recovery (photos 1 – 5 top from left)

Paintings returned to their rightful owner

To jump right ahead, some thirty-two years, only a few weeks ago, I read some news about this picture. Someone in America was offering a picture for sale, "Saskia at her toilette," some dealer or an auction. Even after this long time, the assessors were interested and made enquiries. But what I want to know is this: what was this Saskia painted on? Because Sir Edmund's was painted on wood. I know this because it made it very difficult to carry away and they used several fine carpets to wrap it in, and also Sir Edmund himself told me.

Well, we settled down again but for years after, things would suddenly be missing, car rugs and such and a fruitless search would take place and then, "the burglars took them!"

I went with Sir Edmund to Maidstone Assizes for the trial of the man who informed, and as it had turned out, he was one of the gang. He was a terrible sight, slashed with razors, and his hands couldn't open. When he was sentenced, a woman at the back of the court screamed and screamed.

And that autumn another horrible thing happened. Their priceless Guernsey herd got foot and mouth. We had the stink of their funeral pyre with us and I had a view of it, in the field by the ducks.

The New Year, 1938, came. I stayed up to see it in and wondered whether I would ever join Ray. I was having a lot of worry; he had become a shocking letter-writer, and it was sometimes months before I had a letter, which nearly drove me demented. Still, no-one at Chilham had any idea I was a married woman. And then, one day, I had a letter from him, saying he thought that I could come out in November. This was quite enough for me, something definite!

'Glenshiel', 1924

I booked on the Glen line, "Glenshiel," my passage costing £55. Well, I got more and more prepared and Hitler got more and more unpleasant. Chamberlain did his trip, complete with umbrella, and I got more and more worried, whether I would get away before war broke out. Ray wouldn't say "yes" and he wouldn't say "no." He just didn't answer the torrent of cables and letters I sent.

At last I could stand it no more, so risking everything - Ray's love, his anger, everything - I sent a cable to the General Manager, Mr. Potts:

"WHY NO LETTER FROM MY HUSBAND? IS HE EXPECTING ME TO SAIL NOVEMBER 12TH?"

I felt I had betrayed him. I felt terrible and terrified at what I had done. Later, I heard, arising out of that cable, there was much trouble. Head Office had had a meeting. It was touch and go whether Ray lost his job.

Writing this now, I do wonder what would have happened if they had sacked him. However, they didn't. They decided to keep him on and wired me:

"INADVISABLE TO JOIN HUSBAND FOR FOUR YEARS."

Words to that effect. I sat down and wrote:

Chilham Castle

Dear Sir,

I thank you for your cable. As I have given up my job, my room in London, and sold my furniture, my clothes are ready, my passage paid for and booked, I regret I cannot do as you suggest and shall be sailing Nov 12th to join my husband!........"

I did put in a bit more to soften the blow, but it doesn't matter. Head Office then went into another fuddle (sic) and gave in. But I don't think the Cold Storage forgave the girl who didn't give a damn for them.

Meanwhile, no letter from Ray! He, poor devil, he was having one hell of a time and was annoyed with me to say the least. He was perfectly justified but I was forced! Every instinct I had urged me to get out to him whatever.

It was great fun telling everyone my secret at last. I shook Smith's aplomb badly by going into her pantry and saying, "Smith, what do you think of this?" showing her my wedding ring, which I was at last wearing. She goggled.

"Yes," I said. "I am married. My name is Everard really. I've been married a year. Her Ladyship and Sir Edmund have known about it all the time.'

It was a surprise and I left her to tell the others. Her Ladyship herself gave Kirkwood a shock, most dangerous actually, when that old Scot was driving us back from Canterbury. She prodded him in the back with her umbrella.

"Kirkwood, what do you think, Miss Beard is MARRIED!" The car wobbled appreciably.

"Well, I never, my Lady. You do surprise me."

I had a letter from Mary Morey, a friend of Ray's, she turned out to be. She was in England and wanted to meet me. We met and I liked her, a little, bird-like woman, and young for her age, sharp eyes, downright in her speech. I told her what I had done and she took my misery from me.

"Damn the Cold Storage!" she exploded. "You have done the very best you could possibly do. Ray needs you, my dear. Get out to him as soon as you can. Just wait till I see that old Potts!"

Then the Munich crisis and that was plain hell, still nothing from Ray. I was frantic lest we should be at war. All this repercussed on Lady Davis. It was impossible for her not to know my worry. Indeed, everyone was worried for me.

So one day, bless her forever, she said to me, "Barbara, can one telephone Singapore?" I did not know. I had never thought of that. "Go and ask the operator, dear. See if you can."

One could, and I booked a call. It took three days to come through. One day, just before lunch, the phone rang and a pleasant male voice asked if I was Mrs. Everard.

"I just want to test your voice. Tell me, what sort of a day is it?"

"It's a nice day, cloudy and little bits of sunshine," I said. "I can't think of anything else to say!" (Lunch was just going in). "We're having chicken for lunch today."

"Sounds good. That's all right, Mrs Everard, you're through."

Then I spoke to Ray, hearing him perfectly. I did not lose my head, forget, bungle my words, or sob speechlessly for the whole precious three minutes. I went straight to it and asked him- one way or the other, what was I to do?

"Come if you want to," he said, which didn't sound very enthusiastic. Then I spoke of other things, private things, never mind if half the world overheard, but I did gather from the conversation that he would like me to be out there with him.

"Can I come then?"

"Yes."

So, all that worry was over. I really could go, and I did. The war clouds blew over. Hitler settled on his stolen properties and Mr. Chamberlain flourished his little piece of paper, "Lasting peace in our time," to a cheering people.

All was peace.

I said goodbye to Ursula and Ruth, now married, and to the Uncles and Aunts. And to Chilham and England with joy.

When I parted from Daddy, he was filled with gloom and wondered if he would ever see me again. He prophesied a world war soon. I have never forgotten when I told him of my marriage months before, he had then said: "Well, what does it matter? There will be a war, and you, Barbara, will be going out to live on a volcano."

What did I care? Ray was on that volcano. That was all I worried about.

Interlude – Journey One

This next part of my story, I wrote about twenty years ago (1960?) and the reason I did was for my elder son, Martin. I thought it would interest him later on to have an account of his parent's small part in one of the greatest disasters in this century.

The cargo boat 'Glenshiel' moved out of the Royal Albert Dock, London at about four o'clock in the afternoon. It was cold and misty, nearly dark. The only other sea voyage I had ever done was the one to the Channel Islands with Mrs D. H. so I was most interested in the docks and the seemingly impossible task for the tugs to get this enormous thing through the narrow entrance. I stayed on deck for as long as I could see.

It is strange that a woman will leave family, country, all she has ever known, without the slightest sorrow. I tried hard to feel some appropriate sorrow. I looked at dear London, wallowing in the November weather, and just felt glad, glad to be going. I was most impatient and irritated at the two hours delay and, even more so, when I was told we were to have two extra ports to call, Haifa and Aden, which would make us three days late arriving in Singapore.

A Mrs Prior was sharing my cabin. Quiet mannered, very kindly, I would say. When we had arranged ourselves in the cabin, Mrs Prior thought she would lie down, She had what I call 'seasick nerves'. I felt fine and went off in search of food and found out that I was to dine at the Captain's table. Why I was so honoured, I don't know. Perhaps it was my impressive Chilham Castle address but as there were only twelve passengers to choose from, possibly he hadn't much choice.

I learned to regret this honour as he, the Captain, had a dreadful habit of talking for hours after a meal. That is no exaggeration, except for breakfast. I can only think he had to go to work then. Apparently, it is not done to leave the table before the Captain does but, after a bit, done or not done, I got bored with it and got up and left him to his talkings.

On his left sat Mrs Yarrow, young, slender and attractive, bound for Shanghai. She didn't make an appearance for four days. Strange that I cannot remember her facially but for all that I can never forget her because of a remark that she made to me. I should explain, because I have jumped on a bit, that I was thought very odd by most of the passengers because I refused all drinks. I think my reason was good. I had only a limited amount of money, about £10, and I intended to keep it and not send it down the gullets of other people. And, even in those days, £10 was not a very large sum to have to get to the other side of the world. This eccentricity on my part caused much comment from the Yarrow woman.

"I wonder if you'll be the same when you return home!" she said, cynically.

"Of course she will!" Mrs Prior snapped in reply.

Somehow that has always stuck, plus the horror of drunkenness. That remark of hers is what made me dig my heels in and refuse drinks. Time and time again, so many people, men mainly, tried to make me drink stengah's or beer. No one ever succeeded! One reason is that I hate whisky, the main ingredient of a stengah, and another, what a waste of money! The idea in Malaya that one cannot possibly be enjoying oneself drinking a glass of water, I ask you! So many were to look at me in astonishment. Is she real? Does she mean it? A reaction when I have said: "No thank you, no really. I'll have a lemonade or ice cream soda."

Later, much later on and not in this part of my life, I came to like a gin, filled with orange and crushed ice to the brim....jolly good.

I had the lower bunk and we did not use the upper one except to put things on. Mrs Prior slept on the sofa. I now realise that this was a most large and luxurious cabin with a fan and two portholes. My fare incidentally was fifty two pounds. Mrs Prior continued to feel a bit ill, I was fine.

The steward brought horrible tea at seven and then I got up. We made an arrangement that one of us should rise first so that we would not be dressing together. But, this first morning, I had it all to myself, Mrs Prior feeling somewhat ill.

On deck, cold and windy, we were probably some way down the English Channel. 'Glenshiel' was not a P & O liner by any means. Her comfortable speed was twelve knots and that wasn't comfortable for us. She had tremors or vibrations, you might say. She would be going along when, suddenly, a sort of belch would be felt in her depths at three minute intervals, which I think upset Mrs Prior quite as much as the sea.

Bacon, Egg, Kedgeree, Sausage
Curry
Hominy Cakes and Syrup
Toast, Marmalade
Coffee, Tea

Breakfast was good and I enjoyed all thereafter. But how I hated the tea with its filthy-tasting milk!

No other female appeared for breakfast, actually, for some days so I had it all to myself. But it did get rough in the Bay of Biscay though perhaps in my elated state nothing could affect me. Wonderful sensation - to stand on deck, see a wave tearing at us and feel the boat take it, wallow and meet another. By Cape St Vincent, it calmed slightly and, when we turned the corner, the weather changed. I saw Gibraltar early one morning, perfectly glowing pink in the sunrise. By the time we arrived at Haifa, it was hottish, warm enough for a cotton dress. As it was just after the Jewish rioting, Haifa was interesting as, for me, it was the first sight, sound and smell of the East. We were allowed to go ashore. Shop windows had been smashed and soldiers were on guard. There were interesting palm trees and flowers, mainly those that I had seen already when with Sir Edmund and Lady Davis in the South of France.

So, after what seemed to me to be days of dawdling, we left Haifa and arrived at 'the gateway to the East', Port Said. I went to Simon Artz. Everyone does. I bought Turkish Delight and ate it until I could eat no more. Then, to the Suez Canal. I hated the slow crawl, past Ismailia – what a name that is, so feminine! We anchored out at Suez, doing nothing at all that I could see, which nearly drove me crazy, I was so very impatient. Then on to Aden, red everywhere and so little green.

At last we were in the Indian Ocean and another corner turned. It seems my life was bound by corners. Flying fish were pointed out to me, difficult to see until you know what to look for. And porpoise, lovely bounding things. Phosphorescence. There is nothing original in calling it blue fire but that is what it is, blue fire, sea fire! I found the Indian Ocean endless but at last the day dawned when, miles away on the horizon, Sumatra was pointed out to me. (now renamed as part of

Indonesia, I will point out here that I prefer to and will call these places by their old names)

"Now, we are getting somewhere" I said to myself.

Penang looked nice with a distinct change in temperature. I lunched at the Runnymede with Mrs Yarrow and some of her inevitable friends, who turned up at each port we called at. This was my introduction to 'tiffin' and I learned my first Malay word – umpat – four. I don't think that I went anywhere or did anything other than this lunch. The strain was beginning to tell and I was suffering rather.

Mrs Prior left the boat at Port Swettenham. I promised that if I was ever near Kuala Pilah I would look her up. Actually, I did meet her again, unhappily. I was sorry she was leaving the boat. She was very charming and I liked her best of all the people on board. Also, she had to a certain extent, protected me. I was the only one new to the East and so bridal as well, so I was rather teased.

That evening, the last before Singapore, Mrs Yarrow and her friends turned my cabin upside down. They were tight, of course. We then had a pitched battle, which ended with everyone getting soaked with water, and I fell down the stairs to the dining room, on my bottom, thereby collecting a magnificent bruise, which measured a full two inches. All very childish! There was much ribald speculation as to what Ray would say when he saw my injury. At last they all quietened down, I cleared up the mess and went to bed.

'Glenshiel' drew in slowly, passed little green islands on the right, on the left Singapore. I felt quite ill with excitement and apprehension. Every five minutes or so, someone would come along and pile on the agony, look at me as if I were a strange animal, ask me how I felt and then, sentimentally "Not long now!". Dreadful!

As 'Glenshiel' turned the corner – the last! – and the tugs took over, the town began to show. It seemed flat with one hill in the background, away in the distance. There were only one or two people waiting on the wharf but I spotted Ray. He was there with his sister, Lillian, and her husband, Frank, who was in the Admiralty, at Naval Base. Ray had the same dark hair, with its unquenchable kink, moustache a la Clark Gable but, even with the deck's distance between us, I could see he had changed. When I saw him last, aeons ago, he was thin and tall, now he was very large and tall. I wonder if I had changed. I leaned over the rail, all dressed in white pique and a Henry Heath panama – oh dear, my idea of a suitable tropical outfit – and called out to him:

"You're much too fat!"

It was sheer nerves that made me say anything so tactless. Later, Ray told me it shook him!

"What a greeting! You're much too fat!" So he was!

He came on board as soon as the gangplank was down. Lillian and Frank lingered behind.

Malay Glossary

This list of some of the most elemental Malay words is not definitive. Europeans, more often than not, spoke 'Mem's Malay', which was quite different to 'kampong malay' in many words and phrases.

Stengah	Whisky and soda
Umpat	Four
Jagga	Watchman, guard
Jagga baik	Take care
Jampan	Lavatory
Syce	Chauffeur
Amah	Nurse, usually Chinese
Krani	Clerk
Gagi	Salary
Tida apa	Never mind
Ada baik	All well
Bawa ana sini	Bring baby here
Sudah habis	Finished
Makan	Food
Kampong	Village
Apa makan	What food?
Telur	Egg
Hari raya	Feast day
Kebun	Gardener
Orang Nippon dating	Japanese are coming
Ulu	Jungle
Pergi	Go
Tuan besar, mem besar	Manager and his wife
Tuan kitchil, mem kitchil	Senior and Junior Rubber Assistants
Tiffin	A light meal, especially one taken at lunchtime

Book Two - Chapter Seven - Singapore

And one year and six months were accounted for in our kisses.

Ray took over control immediately. Lillian and Frank then arrived with George Holt, the assistant in the meat department at the Singapore Cold Storage. In later years he was to join up with Fitzpatrick and founded a rival to the Cold Storage.

"Where's your bar bill?" Ray asked.

"Bar bill!" I said incredulously. "I haven't got one."

"What, you don't owe anything?"

"No, I haven't had any drinks except lemonade and I paid for them, of course." Why he seemed so astounded, I could not think. George Holt told his wife and everyone thought it a great joke and then they all sat down and had a drink – at my expense! I thought this was all very odd as I was longing to get off the boat but I had to sit there while the men drank lagers. When at last they had finished and my luggage had been collected, we drove off in George's car.

Past the Post Office, over Singapore River, where the smell hit me good and proper for the first time. What a smell it is! Reminiscent of the baddest of all eggs, somewhere a sewage farm and a spot of durian – it defies further comparison. It was cool-ish in the car but it was the afternoon and it looked the hottest place that I had ever seen.

I then gave Ray another shock. I surprised him by knowing the names of most of the plants and shrubs growing along the Pagang – bougainvillea, canna, hibiscus, frangipani – all the most elemental tropical flowers that Sir Edmund had grown in his hothouses.

"Good God," he said, solemnly, "here I am, a year here and I don't know one and my wife knows them all!"

Not all. There was a tree that was new to me, very magnificent and crowned with a sheet of flaming red flowers, lining the pavement as the planes and poplars do in London. It was Poinciana Delonix Regia.

We turned away from the sea and were soon going up a long, straight road, with European and Chinese shops on either side, all spilling out onto the pavements. Orchard Road and there it was, with a winking neon sign saying, "S.G.S.", in blue and pink. A grey, squat, modern for then, building, a typical store with the second floor over the pavement supported by large, grey granite pillars.

The greetings were many, particularly for me, by blue and grey uniformed, brown-skinned, bearded, august gentlemen with joy, not that I understood a word that was spoken, but they were obviously greetings. Later, I learned that these were the 'jaggas'. They guarded the store night and day. The day jaggas did duty as door commissionaires; running errands, calling taxis, carrying the Mem's groceries. The night jagga slept on his string jagga bed, always blocking the door. This was his home, the doorway!

As I had arrived in the afternoon, the store was still open but I did not go in. Ray took me round to the back entrance and to the flat above. Actually, this flat was the bachelors' quarters, which my arrival had upset horribly, turning them out of the best rooms.

Lillian and Frank went off; I unpacked and showed Ray the things and presents I had brought with me. He was thrilled with them all and, I think, a bit proud of his newly dug-up wife but, I also knew, he was not pleased with me. "Up the pole," my sister, Ruth, would call it – injured male dignity!

We had dinner with two other men, Rafferty and Cockerill. They were both about to be sent upcountry, one to Kelantan, the other to Penang. Ray had champagne to celebrate, too sweet for my Chilham palate but lovely to have.

His 'boy' was an elderly Chinese. I don't know his name. I never did. I did not like him very much. He took away my good, blue Naval Home Industry suit, that I had been married in and which I would probably been wearing to this day, on the pretext that he thought that I had finished with it. Also, he spoilt Ray, even to putting the links in his cuffs!

That evening we kept off the subject of my high-handedness and we did not discuss it for several days, which was rather clever of us, as, by that time, we were so tickled to death with each other and so happy, it didn't seem to matter. Thus, what might have been very unpleasant was avoided.

Ray warned me that the flat was noisy.

"Dearest, our room is over the meat store. They start work at four a.m., sawing meat and so on. I sleep through it. I'm used to it."

"Well, I shall have to, too, shan't I?"

"Yes. And, just under our window, the vans for the early morning delivery of milk start loading…"

"All at the same time, Ray?" I responded.

I was wakened. Suddenly, as I woke, for a second, I couldn't place where I was. There was a terrifying noise. It was as if a thousand devils were below and shaking the bed. A drumming, vibrating sound that ended in a tortured shriek. The meat saw! Outside, engines starting up, backing, backfiring and changing gears, milk bottles crashing together in their cases, loud, agitated voices, in what chaotic language I knew not. All this going on and there was Ray beside me, as he had said, asleep. I never did get used to it.

Ray went off to his Provision Department at about eight, after a frugal breakfast of a cup of tea. I was very surprised, when I went down, to find the store so up-to-date. In general, I think that I had not realised that Singapore was so modern. This was 1937 but already there were milk bars, air-conditioning, super swimming pools, all very American.

Later, I readjusted this impression. Singapore is modern on the surface but take a look around you. Malay, Chinese, Indian, Tamils and other Indian peoples, Japanese and Javanese, all go to make up Singapore. Graft, corruption, dirt, cruelty, every conceivable evil, kongsies, eating houses, bed houses, brothels, dengue, rickets, overcrowding, stinks, heat, rubber and dollars. It is mostly Chinese and British owned with a sprinkling of Indians but never a rich Malay.

It is a city of contrasts, of expensive cars side by side with the coolie rickshaw; modern, beautifully built houses (Chinese women build them for a few cents a day) and in their shadow, the filthiest, darkest, atap-roofed hovels would sprawl with naked babies, lean dogs, rotting refuse, sewage in their drinking water a few yards from the house of a European.

The Singapore Cold Storage was simply planned with two departments, Meat and Provisions. Ray's also had a bakery, wines, drugs and a perfumery. George Holt's domain, Meat, also had fish, fruit and vegetables. In the back of the store were enormous cold rooms. The staff was mostly Chinese and Indian.

Later, we took a taxi, an open one as Ray liked them but I hated them. They blow one's hair about! He took me for a tour around Singapore, all of which looked very much the same. All the shops had Chinese characters on the shop fronts and I longed to stop and look. There was washing hanging out of the upper windows on long poles from either side and nearly meeting in the middle. There were raucous noises and the smells! All this made the streets seem identical and I knew that I would be hopeless out alone.

Four days later, Ray told me Mr Potts wanted to se me. Mr G. A. Potts, known as 'God Almighty Potts' to his staff and, Ray tells me, not just to them!

"Can't think why he wants to see you."

"When do I have to go?"

"Tomorrow at three."

Punctually, the 'awful' Mrs Everard arrived at Head Office down by the Docks' Gatehouse. I went all by myself, which was adventurous. I was completely reliant on the Malay syce to deliver me safely. I got there. I was told to sit down and wait. Mr Potts was a tall, thin man with a moustache, rather thinning hair and a seedy, weary look.

"Good afternoon, Mrs Everard" was his welcome. "Please sit down."

And he proceeded to tell me that it was unfortunate that we had married, that I had insisted on coming out, that we must live on a single man's salary. All so charming!

"Well, I suppose it can't be helped" he went on. "We must make the best of it."

"Yes, certainly I shall make the most of it." My only remark...

He looked at me very straight and that was all! Anticlimax! I still find it hard to believe that he had me come all that way just to tell me that. Could it be possible that he was just plain curious to see what I was like, who had in such an unheard of way, told him and his Directors what I was going to do? Whatever, that seemed to be all, so I left and returned safely with the syce to Ray.

"What did he say?" I told him.

"Good God! Dragging you all that way for that. I shall bloody well charge them with the taxi!"
And he did!

I saw quite a bit of Lillian. She lived further up Orchard Road in a really dreadful boarding house. Apart from that, I don't think Singapore suited her and certainly not Marshall, her eighteen month old baby. She told me all about the day before my arrival. They had all dined with Ray and saw him safely off to bed – before the great Event! No sooner had they left than Jimmy Hamilton, the Number One baker, appeared with two merry friends. He was horrified to find Ray going to bed and straightaway pulled him out.

"No, no!" they chorused. "Your wife arriving tomorrow! This won't do! We must celebrate!"

And, in true Singapore style, they had brought whisky with them. When that had all gone, they drank everything left in the flat except the champagne, which Ray kept hidden. The last thing Ray remembers about that night was propping Jimmy up against a chair. He does not know what he did with himself!

Next morning, Frank and Lillian appeared, horrified at the devastation, particularly to Ray. They tried everything they knew to pull him together as my boat was due in at twelve, albeit not that it arrived on time.

Then George Holt appeared and said, "Come and have a beer, old chap!"

And Ray said, "I think I will. It can't do any harm, anyway."

It was rather a case of the 'hair of the dog' as it seemed to do the trick, with George taking the credit. When Lillian told me all this, I realised why, to me from the boat, Ray looked so fat. He had a bad head and he was just bloated!

Just after Christmas, the Cold Storage decided they wanted to make more offices over the store. We were not sorry to move as it was an impossible flat being so terribly noisy and so public. We were never alone, always someone dropping in. It was the first port-of-call for all the upcountry bachelors, making whoopee. So we moved a few hundred yards up Orchard Road to a boarding house kept by an old German Jew, called Stern. He was exactly like all Germans are described - gross, staring prominent, blue eyes, fleshy nose and jowl, bald head with two great wrinkles at the neck.
He was pathetic in his desire to be British. I never knew his full story but someone did tell me they thought he left Germany rather hurriedly, poor devil. At any rate, he charged us two hundred dollars a month for two rooms, a balcony and a bathroom. The bathroom we had to share!

The months spent at Orchard Road were not happy for me. Ray was away for hours at the store. He was always late for meals, which made it difficult for me as I had to persuade old Stern to keep his meals hot. And ray would get cross if he didn't. Just as the servant boys were going off in the afternoon, with all the food and tables cleared away, Ray would appear. He couldn't help it and the boy, a Javanese who looked after us, had to remain behind and wait on him. Probably Stern paid them by the hour so, if so, it must have irked him.

And, then, I was lonely. Paying out two hundred dollars did not leave us with much more than five over and that just about covered Ray's drinks. So, I couldn't go anywhere but, indeed, if I had been able, I wouldn't have known where. Ray did not realize that I was a stranger in a new country, quite befuddled and bewildered with Singapore and knowing about six words of Malay.

I mostly sat on the balcony, embroidering or reading, but I was not bored. Far from it. Everything was new; everything interested me, from the houseboys to the ants on the floor clearing away a cockroach corpse or crumbs. Birds, butterflies, trees, sun, wind, storm, they were all new. Storms with the sudden cool and shade, and a wind rising before a rain that roared its arrival and arrived as a curtain. The storm drains, six feet deep, filling and overflowing within a few seconds, so suddenly that children, playing in them, were washed away and drowned.

Since we could not afford the usual amusements of the Europeans – swimming club, hotels, cinemas, cars, drinking, bridge – Ray and I walked a good bit and explored. On one of these walks, we were in Dhobi Ghaut and came upon an aquarium shop owned by a Chinese. He had tiny tropical fish that previously I had only seen in Paris when there with the Davises. I was very taken with them. Of course, Ray, always wanting to shower gifts on me, bought a pair of Black Mollies. We took them home, with much excitement, in a glass tank.

That evening, we went to the pictures. It must have been the first of the month as, otherwise, I can't imagine how we could have afforded fish and the cinema. On returning, the first thing that I did was to check on the fish and I was astounded to see a minute fish swimming about. One of them had had a baby! This was most satisfying.
We watched and saw two more. I had never before heard of fish bearing young alive before – viviparous is the correct word, I learned.
Ray telephoned Frank and Lillian and they came immediately to see the wonder. We caught the babies, seven in all, and put them in a jam jar, where they all died. I supposed of starvation as I did not know what to feed them on. But now, I was no longer lonely. I had the fish to study and it occupied me for hours. We bought more. A lot died at first through not knowing how to feed them until, at last, we found out from the old Chinese what he fed them on. He fed the grown fish on bloodworms. These were nauseous and quickly went bad and turned to black blood with a sickening smell if kept too long.

But the fish thrived on them and I hit upon the idea of squashing the worms up in my fingers for the babies and they then lived and grew. Very soon I had three hundred young fish, mainly Black Mollies, in three twelve-gallon tanks. These viviparous fish spawn every two to four weeks, with between thirty to sixty young. If not taken out of the tank, the parents will eat them. Gradually, we added others; guppies, rainbow-coloured; orange and moon-coloured swordtails, of which the male, with a wicked point to his tail, alternatively fights, slashing the others, or tickles his lady.

I had a pair of angel fish. Fascinating things with long trailers, they have a way of blanching when frightened. And I had a pair of Siamese fighting fish with turquoise, blue and purple trailing draperies. The male was quite peaceful as long as there were no others of his kind in the tank. He ignored the other fish, but two fighting fish will tear each other to bits. I needed to study when he felt like not killing his wife, when to put her in the tank with him. It was the only time they desisted from fighting and they were more interesting than the other viviparous fish in their courting.

The male wraps himself around the female and squeezes the eggs out. He would then dart after the eggs, while the female was recovering from being squeezed, gather them up in his mouth and take them up to a bubble nest in the weeds, which he had made a day or two before. And that was my clue as to timing! When the male makes his bubble nest, then it is safe for the female fish to be put in the tank.
This process was repeated several times after which he guarded the nest from the female who saw them as possibly on the menu. So I would take the female out of the tank.

From the time that I had these fish, I was well occupied. There was always a tank to be cleaned or a fish would become ill or baby fish or eggs would arrive or some other new and strange development. Ray lost interest and left me to it.

Lillian left Singapore in 1939. She had been poorly for some time so. One day, we went and saw her off on P & O. It was sad to see her go and I knew that I would miss her. So far, I had made no women friends except Mary, but Mary was so rich and lived far away on Bukit Timah Road in a most palatial flat, so we did not see her very often.

Two months after Lillian left, we moved and took a flat in Cairnhill Road, for D110 a month furnished. I got an amah for housework and washing. The flat was a slight improvement on Orchard House. At least it was a sort of home and Ray could have his meals when he pleased.

It was the oddest flat I have ever seen. Nothing cohered. The kitchen was downstairs with a batch of other kitchens. This meant trays and trays of food had to be carried up to the flat. The bathroom was two corridors away.

My fish moved well. The landlord was most interested in them and arranged for me to have them in the garden. This was fine. I had a hose from the kitchen tap to refill the tanks and, by now, I had even more varieties – zebra fish, neon fish, gourami – but my pets were the two cichlids.

Large when compared to the others, the size of a small goldfish, they had grey bodies with iridescent, turquoise spots on cheeks and tail. I put them in a fifteen-gallon tank to themselves, covered on top by Blue Water Hyacinth (Eichornia crassipedes), which is grown by the Chinese for pig food. Lillian had paid D2 for some, under the impression that she was buying an orchid when sold them by a Chinese at her door!

These fish were very interesting. They were very fond of a small, flat, light shell, which they would spend hours, taking it in turns, to drag around the tank. When a spot was found that they could both agree on, the female laid rows of eggs like little seed pearls. Then, they took it in turns to fan the water above the eggs for three or so days. The eggs hatched and the babies came out like little tiny inverted commas. Within a week, they had righted themselves and swam in a cloud around the parents' heads. But it was months before I reared any with success. In the end, I had around forty and game little fish they were.

We were at the Cairnhill Road flat when war was declared. Listening to the broadcast, it seemed impossible, unbelievable in un-warlike Singapore. There was no change in Singapore for some months to come, that I noticed. But some things must have, things that I would not have known, like censorship for instance. I had not been out there long enough to know. I felt very unhappy for my family at home but I also felt glad that I had got out to Ray when I did.

So, what can one write of war in Singapore when there is no war? As far as war was concerned, Ray and I, we had long ago decided if it happened, we would have a baby so that I would not be lonely should we be separated. This defence measure, we straightaway put into action. How strong the reproductive instinct is. Never mind that the world is about to embark on a most appalling war, one must have a baby! Never mind that the baby will be just one more to be bombed, drowned, starved, lost, maimed.

I suppose that even had I known all this, I would still have had a baby. And to think of all the babies that have been born through these years, as bombs crash down, in air raid shelters, under shocking conditions all over the world, women have also reared these babies most successfully.

So, I, too, would still have had my child. But, however, living in a fool's paradise, I had no forsense of these horrors.

Also, in this first week of the war, we bought a car, an old, ramshackle Essex Tourer. Ray gave about D40 for her, about eight pounds in English money. Her number was 7773 so we called her 'Tujoh, tujoh, tujoh, tiga', the number in Malay.

Ray beside 7773, the Essex Tourer

That car was a great joy to us. We gave up our walking tours and there wasn't a road that we didn't follow on Singapore Island to find out where it did or didn't go. Rather dangerously, I used to fish for barbells and wild tropical fish in streams by the roadside. Dangerous because of snakes and fevers and leeches, but I didn't realize this at all.

Ray was longing to show me upcountry and, so far, I had not been off the island except for a brief trip to Johore. Then he found out that he had a couple of days free, an unheard of occurrence normally, so we decided to go to Malacca and Kuala Lumpur. Great preparations! A dozen beers for Ray and a dozen Frazer and Neave orangeades for me, all arranged on a fifty pound block of ice on the floor in the back of the car. It was that sort of car; it didn't matter with what one filled her up.

Curry puffs, a pint of ice-cream well packed in freezing salt, bananas and a good fruit cake, luggage, camera, cigarettes and a box of chocolates for pig, me!

We left on Friday evening. It was dark so I couldn't see the countryside. As usual, we had no money so we could not afford to sleep at a Rest House, the proper procedure for Europeans while travelling in Malaya. But what is done or not done, never fretted me. We were utterly happy and slept in the car on the road just past Malacca, a road that I was to get to know very well.

Actually, Ray slept, I didn't. I agree that Rest Houses have the advantage but, then, Ray always sleeps. I spent most of the night covering my bare parts with mosquito oil and looking out at the night, which was noisy with insects and...Malaya! To every Malayan, who passed by, stopped and peered into the car, I would glare back in the dark.

I did not see Malacca except at night. I had an impression of ancient trees, fern and orchid covered, a lapping sea and a cool sea wind. Streets that were narrow, brightly lit with flaring shop lights and overflowing with people.

At four in the morning, Ray woke and we ate cake and drank orangeade, then drove on. It was cool, the best time of the scorching day that lay ahead. We sang at the top of our voices as we rattled along, his rich tenor and my flat voice. No thought of the war.....

7773 was behaving well. Of course, one never knew. She was always at her best on a long journey we found out, when we came to understood her idiosyncrasies. She would invariably fail on a single five or six mile journey, but tell her that she was going two or three hundred miles and she would just purr along. After all, she was an Essex <u>Tourer!</u> Anyway, that's what we fondly imagined about her.

At six, it became light. There were high, forest covered hills. Jungle, jungle on either side of the road and a loud humming in the trees. Then, low-lying padi fields and water buffalo with small, naked Malay boys riding them and the white egrets following. Dull stretches of rubber trees, all in neat rows, deadly looking trees with large sombre leaves. I was bored with their sameness.

We arrived at Kuala Lumpur at about nine a.m. and already it was jolly hot. Kuala Lumpur is a bit warm; it hasn't Singapore's saving sea breeze, lying in a bowl surrounded by high hills. What I saw of the town, I thought, rather fine, well spaced, some lovely buildings. But, there for only two hours, I didn't see very much. Of course, we went straight to the Cold Storage and saw Cockerill, who was in charge there. He gave some avocados. We were given breakfast at the Singapore Cold Storage bungalow and, after refuelling, we headed back for Singapore.

Soon, it became very hot to drive and Ray began to get sleepy. He found my orangeade kept him awake a bit. I am always nervous when he gets sleepy. Back in England, he had fallen asleep while driving and crashed the car he had and we were <u>still</u> paying off a large bill for that.

So we stopped in a bit of shade and he went to sleep. And, for half an hour, I sat listening to his breathing and to the monkeys calling in the high, Jackwood trees above us. This was the first time I had seen the real jungle and it was very thick on either side, still and green, yet noisy and humming from the insects. The Malayan jungle is some of the deepest in the world. I admit, I felt very much by myself and rather nervous and what on earth would one do if a tiger bounded out, or a python….

Ray woke and we arrived safely back in Singapore late on Saturday evening, and that was my first journey upcountry.

A day or so later -

"Barbara, Potts phoned me. He wants to see you at Head Office. Don't ask me what for, I don't know."

So I went to Head Office, this time with more confidence. I could command the syce this time in Malay.

"Oh, good morning, Mrs Everard", Potts began. "I just wanted to speak to you about a little matter that has come to my notice. You went upcountry this weekend, did you not? Where did you stay for the night?"

"We didn't. We slept on the road" I replied.

"Yes. Not very wise. There is sometimes malaria about and it is not suitable for the position of Europeans."

"We were covered with mosquito net and I used up a bottle of oil. I don't see that we did something wrong."

"Nevertheless, it was not a wise step. I want you to promise not to do it again."

"I can't promise," said I "but we will try to save some money before we go and then we can afford the Rest House."

After that dig, which I hope went home, I left. Later, a notice was issued, telling the European staff to ask permission before they left the Island.

Two o'clock one morning, we were woken by George Holt. The Asiatic staff had gone on strike. We were not to know then that this was the first of many strikes. The Harbour Board, later, had a nasty one. Writing now, I realize that I didn't understand anything that was going on as it was all so new to me. And I had only been in Singapore a few months and never spoken to any of the Asiatics, a conversation that is. So it is best I keep to my facts, just as it all happened, otherwise I might be untruthful.

Undoubtedly there was unrest and it was due to the war in Europe although, some say, fifth columnists. Had we all thought and looked around, we might have learned a lot from those strikes. As it was, all we did was carry on; the Mem to her Bridge, mah-jongg, Red Cross, dress fittings, tea and tiffin parties; her husband to his work, earning dollars, the cricket club, stengah's; the Chinese to his dollars and kongsie; Malay and Indian coolies, they all went on living their own way. Malaya sent her rubber and started a Patriotic Fund. What else could be done? Half the world away from the war, the phoney war, and a great Naval Base to defend us from Germany's ally, Japan, should they be so foolish to dare…

And whatever I don't know, I do know this. No one was more stupid, ignorant and unthinking than I. I just went on in my own little rut, wrapped up in my own affairs. Ray got up….and I…turned over and went to sleep again. At about ten, I walked down to the Singapore Cold Storage, thinking to see the trouble would be over, and was very surprised to see a large and very agitated crowd of Chinese around the entrance. I got through them and went to the Provision department. The place was empty except for four miserable-looking Chinese kranies.

The Chinese girl, whom I called Miss Phang Wang because it sounded like that, was the only person I recognized. She was on duty behind the perfumery counter. I imagine a female counted as nothing to the Asiatics. It did not matter whether she struck or not! The whole of the Asiatic staff had gone on strike, for better pay. I must say I sympathised on this point if their pay averaged anything like the Europeans'. I felt it was a pity the Europeans couldn't strike as well but that would never do.

The Singapore Cold Storage had retaliated by sacking all the strikers, a grand gesture, but there would have been a lot more strikes in Singapore but for this firm action. And the Chinese outside were all surprised to find themselves unemployed.

I looked round for Ray but couldn't see him anywhere. Then the Branch Manager, Mr Monk, came down the stairs and, seeing me, nodded.

"Morning, Mrs. Everard, this is a bad business, isn't it?"

"I had no idea it was so bad." A thought occurred to me. "I suppose I can't help at all?"

"Oh, no, no!" he said rather undecidedly and then, with inspiration "You can! Go in there and do what you think best."

So I took over the Grocery, wines, bakery, perfumery, and tried to get things sorted out. Luckily there was one faithful storekeeper, who knew his stock and where things were, as without him it would have been very different and difficult. The four kranies, I found, had only just been taken on and only knew their manager's name was Everard – Everlard even – so all four decided, 'Ah, here is our Manager to help us!'

And for five days, I was their Manager. I signed the most important documents during those days. For months afterwards, Ray had to deal with queries over my signature. During that morning, there was a rush of people to deal with but somehow each problem was met and overcome. Mr Potts came and embarrassed me by saying he was 'most grateful'.

Soon after, other Cold Storage wives turned up and they went and worked in the Meat department.

I saw Ray in the afternoon. He was in a mess, no shirt but wearing a strange sweater, covered with filth. His trousers were coated to the knees with a mixture of mud and blood. He had been butchering at the back for six hours and then had taken a delivery van out. He hadn't had the time to worry about what I was doing in his Department. I suppose he saw that it was more or less functioning and seemed to take it for granted.

The management had the sense to close the store at five instead of the usual eight o'clock. The other wives left when the store closed but I stayed on. They were surprised.

"You staying on?" But aren't you tired?"

If those wives had only known that, all through the night at the Cold Storage, I've seen cold rooms taken out and new put in. I've seen a department repainted, turned upside down and put straight all in a night's work when Ray had to be on duty. It was the rule because the Asiatics were so dishonest and would thieve, that, whenever given the smallest chance if workmen were in the store, then a European had to be on duty. Not that it stopped the thieving a bit!
So, if there had to be alteration work, which had to be done overnight, the Europeans took turns and very often when it was Ray's turn, I stayed there with him. I hated to sleep; indeed I couldn't, knowing he had an all night session at the store. We used to play Six Pack Bezique, make coffee, cook a nourishing meal at about two in the morning, cheer on the coolies with jokes and chat with the jaggas guarding the door, not sleeping for once. Jaggas are always asleep when they should be awake. Then at four o'clock, it was time to watch the sausages being made, being poured into their skins and twisted expertly and the meat saw, noisy as ever, and the great blocks of ice rushing down the chute into the waiting vans, loading up for the milk delivery. Then, at eight, the European for the day would relieve us and we would go home to breakfast and a long sleep.

So, it was anything but remarkable for me to stay on with Ray. I had a look around, helped myself to the squashiest, creamiest cake that I could find in the bakery case and went to offer my services to Rafferty, who, all alone, was cutting up beef steaks for the Naval Base order. I wrapped up eight hundred for him. Mr Potts came in while I was working on the steaks and was overwhelmed to see me there. He really was winded and, for once, I believe, favourably impressed.

After the steaks were dealt with, I cleaned down the counters in the Meat Department. I didn't make a good job of them, they were so greasy and bloody, and the fish counter was nearly too much for my stomach. They all needed scalding water and there wasn't any. At about eleven o'clock, when I was thinking all was nearly done, Ray asked me:

"Have you done anything about the Christmas Island order?"

I hadn't nor had I ever heard of Christmas Island before. It is a small island, dependent on Singapore for all its provisions, where a boat calls in once a month with mail and food. So this meant returning to the Provision Department and opening it up again to pack up the order. Ray also found that the Naval Base orders for the following day still had to be done. So, thereafter for the next few days, each night Ray and I, when all the rest was done, went back and packed Base orders and coped with anything else that needed doing. I suppose we did sleep sometime! Things did improve and were better when coming on duty at eight o'clock.

There were some more new staff taken on, all dumb and frightened. They had to have police protection from the most annoyed dismissed staff, who ranged around outside, waiting to get their hands on them. Police buses took them to their homes each evening.

One day, Mr Potts happened to meet Ray, coming off one of the vans, in an even worse state than the first day with two days beard and his mass of hair on end.
"Where have you been, Everard?"

"To the Mental Home, sir," was his response.

This was quite true. He had been there to deliver food but, as Ray said it, it had a double meaning and Potts turned to Monk, standing near him>

"Give them all one day's holiday, starting with Everard tomorrow!"

So it was that Ray had the only holiday he ever had in three years, that is a day off when he should have been working. I had one too! This holiday, being such an unheard of thing, we decided to really make a day of it. The best thing about Malayan weather is that one can always decide the night before or even weeks or days ahead what you want to do and be nearly sure of the same blazing sun!

We thought we would have a day at the Selatar Grange, a sort of Road House on the Naval Base side of the island, with a large, shady garden, quiet and secluded, overlooking the Johore Straits. No one was there except the two of us. I spent half an hour irritating Kringa ants, the dreadful half-inch long red ant that has leaf nests that they sew together and fight you if you touch the leaves. They rush around in a frantic rage, standing on their back legs, defying you. And they can bite!

We bathed in the pagar before we had lunch, great fun as the water was undisturbed. So I swam quietly and chased little shoals of minute fish. It goes without saying that I had prawn fritters for my tiffin - enormous, great prawns, almost the size of langoustines, fried in batter with thin bread and butter – unbeatable! Ray had curried chicken and sambals. Sambals are chopped tomato, banana, coconut grated, baked cucumber in coconut milk, ground nuts, papaya, mango, all sorts and all important to a curry.

The English idea of curry is one big joke compared to the real thing. The idea here is that it has to be hot so as to make it practically uneatable, to say the least, unpleasant. Made in Malaya, basically, it is only mildly so but chilli is ground up into a paste and served to those who like eating fire! We always intended to take with us home to England the ingredients and educate our relations to a real curry but we never did.

After the prawns and curry, we had Gula Malacca. This is a most gorgeous pudding and so simple. Plain, boiled tapioca, drained and put in a mould and then turned out. Take coconut milk, thickened with its own flesh, ground for hours into a pulp and the sugar from the coconut, rather like maple syrup, very thick and brown. Pour these two sauces onto the tapioca. And there you have it. This sap, when fermented, makes toddy, wine of the coconut and the ruin of the Indian. But tapioca, with these two sauces from the same tree, is one of the very best things I have ever eaten and after a large plate of curry, takes away that blown out effect.

After tiffin, I wouldn't let Ray go to sleep but we got a boat, crossed the Straits and explored a little river. I was interested to see lungfish in the mud, very repulsive looking. We had a hard pull back to Seletar against the tide and, after a cup of tea, returned to our flat. We had dinner at Raffles, which we signed for, and then went on to the Cathay Restaurant, newly opened and having icy air conditioning.

It was now the thing to go to the Cathay Restaurant on a Saturday night. Everybody went.

When the Cathay opened, Ray had noticed that on a Saturday morning, women would come and ask for their silver fox furs and mink whatnot's to be taken out of cold storage and then back they would come on Monday. After a few weeks of this going on, he was mystified. Then we went to the Cathay and there were these furs draped round their owners against the chilly atmosphere.

Next day, we were back at the store. The strike was still going on but things were a little more orderly. There were some amusing incidents that I should record. Allen, the accountant, took it into his head to take a break from accounting and sold a cake. He very successfully sold a birthday cake. Later it was returned with the message that it was uneatable. It was a wooden model! And some dumb krani sent a woman to the bakery for sweetbreads!

The fifth day, the strike ended and Ray returned to his kingdom and I was needed no more.

The following day I had a letter from Management, formally thanking me, with a cheque for D50 and a personal note at the end from Mr Potts:

'May I add my own thanks for a job of work so cheerfully and willingly done?'

This was very nice of him. The other wives were given wristwatches as I suppose D50 would have been rather superfluous. Ray, also, had a letter, bless him, and D50. So did all the Europeans. The Asiatics that had been faithful were also rewarded but I forget how. Any way, we all felt duly surprised, gratified and thought that the Singapore Cold

Storage had behaved very handsomely. Ray and I experienced an unaccustomed feeling of wealth.

Chapter Eight - Event

A month or so after the strike I really began to think that we might have our baby. I went and saw Dr Elder and he said there was a possibility. We decided that we could not stand the Cairnhill Road flat any longer. We were given D25 a month for a house allowance so I said, 'Very well, we'll find something for that.'

Rents in Singapore at that time were anything from D85 to D200 a month, but we heard that the Municipal Improvement Trust was building modern flats and some were nearly completed. This Trust was building with mainly Asiatics in mind in order to improve their housing conditions. There was no bar, however, to Europeans taking one, provided they were married and not intending to take the flat to keep some little girl in!!! On the other hand, the one drawback was that Europeans would be too afraid of what their friends might say about their lowly dwelling.

However, as I have said before, I am not given to fretting what people say and I thought, as we looked over the plans in the Municipal Office, that here was the very thing. They were not quite completed, the block that we were looking at, that is, and we had to pick and choose the middle top floor, which had a wide balcony with a concrete seat all around and the most wonderful view of Singapore. I could see what an ideal place the seating would be for the fish tanks.

The flat had two rooms leading off the balcony, our bedroom, a living room hall, a servant's bedroom, kitchen and European lavatory. Only six of the flats had this luxury, the others having elongated chins bowls let into the floor. Asiatics find it easier to relieve themselves, squatting. There was also a tiny shower room, the only thing in it being a tap. Walls, ceiling and floor were all concrete, cream-washed. The doors were a single slab of wood and there were no ledges anywhere.

I quite thought the Singapore Cold Storage would object when they heard where we were intending to live, that, even if one only had D25 house allowance, you must still keep up appearances but, no, nothing was said. We enjoyed furnishing the flat; this being really our first real home and we spent our strike cheques on furniture, mostly rattan. We painted it all pale grey and apricot. No curtains as we were very high up and no one overlooked us. I cannot see the reason for having curtains in the tropics as they only provide nesting places for chechas – lizards.

The pearl grey colour scheme we took right through the flat so that everything was interchangeable. I felt ill during the painting and almost gave up. It's no easy job, painting rattan. It turned out I had dengue. It's a malaria-like disease, contracted from the mosquito's bite. The temperature jumps about and after four days a rash develops. It is not serious but unpleasant and lowers your spirits.

When I recovered from dengue, I started being sick. And was I sick! <u>Morning</u> sickness! My God! I was sick constantly, morning, noon and night, everywhere and anywhere. The house boy – we had got rid of the amah that we'd had at Cairnhill Road and Ray thought he would try his old boy of the first flat days – was told to hold back half of my meal. So I ate the first half, was promptly sick of course and, momentarily recovered, managed to eat the second half.

But the sickness got worse and I was really suffering. Dr Elder said, "Keep flat if you are very sick."

And I did, sometimes for three or four days. Another thing that had me worried were my teeth. I had four vital teeth that my plate hung on. My plate was gold and we reckoned that losing one of those teeth would cost more than having a baby. In those days, one had to pay one's own dentist and doctors. My teeth had always been very queer owing to the fact that my father had been so anxious that I should ride to hounds and carry on the hunting tradition of the Beard family. He had a little trap pony, back in 1913 just before cars arrived, and he fixed up a saddle chair on her. Something happened to upset the pony and she reared and I fell into the road and cut my upper lip. I was three then. When my second teeth came through, they were crooked and as a consequence, I bite on the roof of my mouth. Gold is, or was then, the only thing that would stand up to it. I told Dr Elder the situation.

"Take one pint of milk a day and six calcium tablets for six months," he said, "and then increase the milk to one and a half pints for the remaining time."
This was going to be very expensive because nothing would induce me to drink powdered milk... I had to have Singapore Cold Storage milk form 'contented cows', proper English cows, which were kept in great luxury as Bukit Timah and so, milk was very expensive!

"How much will it cost to have this baby, Dr Elder?"

"My fee is D150."

"I can't afford that. The S.C.S...we haven't a large gagi." I tried to explain. He quite understood.

"That's all right, Mrs Everard. I think the best thing is for you to see Dr. English. He's Professor of Midwifery and you can attend his clinics at the hospital each month. Mind, if he personally has to deliver you, it would cost you D250 and he will not attend a normal case. The sisters are there for that. But you will see him each month for him to see how you are getting on."

I thanked him. Such a nice man, I was sorry I could not afford him.

Just at this moment of financial stress, the Singapore Cold Storage thought this a propitious moment to cut the European's commission because of the thieving by the Asiatic staff. If the losses exceeded D2000, it had to be deducted from the commission and, as it always did, it was a foregone conclusion that there would be no commission. I was very annoyed over this and would have liked Ray to leave but he would not on account of me. Poor Ray, it was a difficult time.

Luckily I sold a few oils of flowers and, with the money, I bought baby things until I had a simple layette. Babies do not need much in the tropics. After four months, I got over the sickness but there were roads in Singapore, which were forever remembered for some disgraceful happening – 'I was sick just there!' And I shall never forget going into Raffles Hotel for dinner and only just composing myself during the last few yards before we arrived. It was nerve wracking for Ray.

I made a most exciting discovery. It was a boy. My father, years and years ago, taught me a trick of how he used to find out the sex of pheasants eggs. A wedding ring, tied to a bit of cotton, is held pendant over the eggs. If it's a male, it will swing straight back and forth; if female it goes round and round. I don't know why it does it but it does, over anything male or female.

I found out that, over my fat tum, it went straight but all over the rest of my body it went round and round. The conclusion was obvious, after which I never worried any more. It was a boy.

Ray had been very trying and unhelpful about names. When I asked him to be serious, he would say, "Why not Everard Everard?"

"Oh, don't be such a fool. Think seriously!"

"I am. What about Anthony Paul?"

"Ray! Don't be horrid! A.P.E." I retorted, spelling out the initials. "You're hateful. You don't help a bit."

And so it went on. That was all that I could get out of him. However, one day, driving up Killiney Road, I suddenly said: "Martin!"

"Martin," said Ray. "What are you talking about?"

"Martin, of course! Martin, that's a lovely name. We will call him Martin Raymond. That makes M.E., I am B.E and you're R.E. I think that's good."

"I think you're nuts." said my dear husband. All the same, I didn't bother about any more names. He was Martin.

1939 went by, seeing us playing at war. France fell and maybe some in Singapore read the significance of that disaster. Certainly I didn't. To me Singapore seemed just the same in some ways, dancing and dining out and parties.

"The Japs won't touch Singapore!"
"Won't dare!"

"Terrific fortifications!"

But, as I have said, I can't judge truly. In my state, I did not go out a lot and I know few people who really knew anything so what I write is how Singapore appeared to me. So much has been written about people dancing etc., but there was dancing, in London, even while the bombs were falling. No, Malaya had a reputation of 'whisky swilling' planters (God help them at D10 a bottle!) and women just out to enjoy themselves, which takes a lot of killing out. But many women volunteered for Red Cross work. Many women worked long hours at the Hospital. The Singapore Royal Artillery Volunteers put in a great deal of time. Ray was always volunteering. He was a very keen Volunteer, too keen, I thought sometimes, I was so lonely.

But, it did seem, that everything went on pretty much unaltered. There was no rationing. Rice should have been rationed from the start. It was later, much later, together with petrol.

And nothing was done about identity cards except at the very last moment. In fact, all was very 'tida apa' and the war seemed miles away. But the 'tida apa' attitude cannot be completely laid at Singapore's door. Singapore, remember, was governed from Whitehall by a body of people who in 1939 and '40 had not, I think, looked properly at Singapore's position on the map and could only think in terms of naval bases. It was all very well to try and lay the blame somewhere and it is too easy to write 'this should have been done' or 'why, on earth, didn't they do that?' The awful truth is that we are all to blame, every single British person, for the second war ever happening and the consequences. But one fact remains. Singapore was lethargic, unthinking.

And the Singapore Cold Storage was more unpleasant than ever. They capped it all by taking the commission away to everyone's disgust.

One evening, in early July 1940, I was bandaging Ray's foot. He had Singapore foot. An insect, fungus or parasite, I am not sure which, gets under the skin and burrows and is very unpleasant and itches. This had been annoying him so I dabbed Listerine on it, a sure cure but it would smart a bit. He made a shocking fuss, saying he was in agony, that he would faint. He must have made me hurry and, in moving my somewhat heavy self rather quickly to get him a bandage, something happened inside me, a most queer sensation of something breaking. Seeing this baby was quite three weeks overdue and Ray had spent much time driving over some of the bumpiest roads on Singapore Island, all to no avail, it seemed that at last something was happening.

"Oh Ray, I think something has happened."

"No, not really! Darling, are you O.K.? I'm going to go to the hospital to find out when you should go there."

In is excitement, Ray had forgotten simultaneously a cold, a pain in his stomach, that he diagnosed as appendicitis and his foot trouble, and dashed in 7773 to the hospital to ask whether to bring me in then and there.

"No need, Mr. Everard, not just yet," he was told. "Let her wait till the pains are down to every twenty minutes."

After all that age of waiting, it was a relief to know that something was going to happen. I was at home all next day. About four in the afternoon, I told Ray I'd better be going to the hospital. But before I went, there were a few things to be done.

I took the cichlids, parents and the forty babies to Dhoby Ghout for the fish-man to look after. I didn't feel like leaving them to Ee Moi's tender mercies. She was our new house amah, a fool, if ever there was one, but Ah Chung, my baby amah, would not come to me without her and as we wanted a house amah, I had to have the pair.

I went to the library and got out some books and then called in to the Singapore Cold Storage and terrified Jock Taylor, a new arrival, by telling him that I was about to have a baby at any minute. I might have been a piece of high explosive judging by the horror with which he looked at me. The Asiatic portion of the Cold Storage staff had been very interested in 'Tuan Everlard's baby' and Ray had spent the last two or three months, daily answering questions about my health. The last two weeks had been hectic. He told me, "I'll have to have a bulletin board for you, darling."

"Why?"

"I don't get any work done. All I do is answer questions about you saying 'no change, my wife is just the same' to all my clerks and customers, too."

"I didn't know I was so famous."

"You are. People daily open their Straits Times to see if Mr. Everard's baby has arrived!"

"They must have given it up as a bad job by now, a month late!"

We returned to the flat and collected Chung and the luggage. All through Saturday I had pains, unmentionable pains. Sunday, I don't remember anything much about. Ray was with me most of the time, sort of meeting and helping me with each pain. Nobody, except Ray, took any interest in me. Dr English did come and look at me and in the middle of a most excruciating pain, shook me by my leg and said, "There must be something Scots about you. You don't want to give up what you've got."

I was very annoyed with him and, in a breathing space, said, "Do you mean to tell me that with all the medical science they can't do anything to help me?"

Ray tells me that he felt helpless, so sorry and so upset when I said that. Sunday evening, Sister Rintoul began to show a little interest in me and told Ray to bring me to the labour ward. It took some time to get there, having to stop every minute for pains that by now ran into one another.

Ray was left outside. The Sisters then forgot all about him. Ray tells the tale that he waited outside the ward for some time, no one came, and so he went back to my ward and read the paper for three quarters of an hour and then picked up a book. He got a bit worried; up to now his nerve had been pretty good. The Sisters changed duty at nine and, when Sister Rintoul at last emerged, she was met by a raging, infuriated man.

Sister Keir calmed him. "You go home and have some supper, Mr Everard, and come back at ten and we will have your baby for you."

I found Sister Keir was more helpful.

"Come on, Mrs. Everard. I've just promised your husband to have that baby by ten."

I looked at the clock and I thought, 'by God, only three quarters of an hour...I will....I will!'

Nine fifty, he arrived. July 7th, born on a Sunday.

> 'The child that is born on the Sabbath Day,
> Is happy and blithe and bonny and gay!'

Ray, for once, was punctual and, at ten, I heard dear tujoh, tujoh, tujoh, tiga roaring up the hospital drive. He kissed me and said:

"Thank you, thank you!"

"Go and have a look at him," I said.

I don't think that he could see much of him. He was a nine pound baby, with red hair. I felt marvellous, gloriously tired mentally, physically, but I felt that at last I had achieved something. Ray left. He had had to have Special Leave for a Volunteer Camp, which had to be extended all over the weekend until his baby arrived. So, the Volunteers were waiting as were all the Cold Storage staff and the whole of Singapore! So I was wheeled, a delightful journey, back to my bed, where I slept, and I have never before or since experienced such a sleep. It was my first real sleep in six months.

The next day, I spent cleaning myself up, hair, face and nails, and admiring Martin privately. There must have been something the matter with me as whenever I looked at him, I overflowed with tears.
Flowers began to arrive. Magenta Vanda Miss Joachim orchids from the Holts with:

> *'Congratulations to Everard and Co.*
> *Quality good but service slow!'*

Flowers came from the Cold Storage staff and a colossal basket of fruit arrived from the Chinese stall holders in the market next to the Cold Storage building. Ray managed to get to the hospital each day to see me but, of course, regular visiting hours were not for him! He upset the whole routine of the place, as his Volunteering did not fit in with the hospital hours. In the mornings, I always had to be bathed first of all 'in case Mr Everard would come.'

Mr Everard also distinguished himself by exploding a box of matches and burning his fingers. Sister Rintoul, who I believe rather loved him for blazing out at her, said she would give him first aid. A nurse appeared with some pearly liquid and he was told to put his fingers in it. He did so and his fingers immediately stopped hurting.

"This is a wonderful cure! Wonderful. It's stopped completely. Well, I must get back to the Volunteers. Good-bye."

And he went. Three minutes later, along comes Sister Rintoul with a nurse carrying the first aid box.

"Where is your husband, Mrs. Everard?"

"He's gone, Sister. His fingers were all right and he says it was a wonderful cure."

"But that was only soda that I gave him to clean off the cigarette stains with."

We all laughed.

"Well, he went off cured and happy." I said.

On the fifth day, I was allowed visitors. Fifi, Mrs Fugler, one of my few friends came and Ray brought Jock Taylor, looking rather like a fish out of water in a maternity hospital. He was to be Martin's godfather. It was really rather pleasant, listening to the admiring remarks about my efforts.

On the tenth day, Ray took me home and I had to stay incarcerated in the flat for ten days with only Chung and Ee Moi to talk to. I was not allowed to go downstairs because of having to climb the stairs back up. So I was really awfully bored as the amah was able to take Martin out in his pram but I couldn't. And no one came to see me so all I could do was watch the unending life of the Chinese families around me, listen to the Mah-Jongg squabbles that broke out, the endless bamboo stick tapping of the restaurant boys getting out orders, and the cries of the Chinese street vendors.

Ray returned from camp on my birthday and we had both forgotten that it was my birthday. He was only home for ten days before he went away for more volunteering. Singapore was beginning to wake up a bit. All the young men were conscripted into the Volunteers at about this time, and not a moment too soon either.

Mr Monk lent Ray a small, seaside native-built house for me to go to for a change. It was at Changi, on the beach. This was fine as Ray could get night leave. It was really lovely with a cool breeze and right on the sea's edge. Both amahs came as well and Martin thrived. I just lazed around, paddled and caught fish, and did some water colour landscapes. Then Ray, in the evening, might take me for a drive before off early to bed as there was nothing else to do - only lamplight and very primitive, and nice to listen to the chichas in the atap roof.

Martin was quite an ordinary baby, a good, strong baby. I fed him myself, which I didn't like doing, for four months. Then I had another bout of dengue and tonsillitis and Dr. Elder said 'wean'. So I gladly did and I put him on Lactogen and he did even better. We had him christened in October, with Jock Taylor, godfather as arranged. George Holt was proxy for Cecil, my sister Ursula's husband, and Lillian was his godmother.

Jimmy Hamilton was thrilled to get the order for the Christening cake. He told Ray, "I have been waiting ages for this order!"

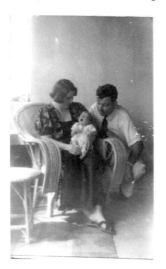 

Barbara, Ray and Martin, at 6 weeks old

Martin was christened in the Cathedral, which had been built by convict labour. I think that is rather terrible. I feel they were forced to build it and I don't think that men should be forced to build a church. Surely it should be built for the love of the building just as a picture is painted or a statue is carved. Maybe I am wrong, perhaps it was a penance. Anyway, I never liked the Cathedral. He was christened in the family christening robe, which, a family conference had decided, should be sent to me as it would be safer with me because of the bombing in England.

I don't think that I have mentioned Joe Giles yet anywhere. I should have! He arrived at the Cold Storage about a year after me - so young, so ignorant, so full of himself with lank, fair hair; little, close-together, suspicious of everybody eyes; a tight mouth with a few, fair whiskers for a moustache. I, personally, didn't see much of Giles as he was sent to the Kuala Lumpur branch.

Then he fell in love with a girl called Hetty. I can't remember her other name, it doesn't matter. She was eighteen; sweetly pretty with long, wavy, black hair and small features. The only trouble with Hetty was that somewhere she had coloured blood. And she has no brains, just beauty. Since our marriage, the Singapore Cold Storage took good care to insert a clause, stating 'No Marriage' in their contracts.

Giles deliberately married Hetty. This was too much for the Singapore Cold Storage. They sacked Giles straightaway.

A week later, Ray was told to go down to Head Office. We knew what was coming. I can't say I felt any sorrow, only regret that we hadn't got out a year back. Ray refused to give them notice because of the Provident fund. Had he done so, we would only have got the money we had put in.

"I'll not give notice. I'll let them sack me."

And when he came back:

"Well was it?"

"Yes, damned amusing. I kept asking Potts for his reasons. Of course, he couldn't give any, just that work had not been satisfactory."

"Of course, they have no reason that they can give," I suggested. "You can't give a reason that you are sacking a man that has married, when they've let you work as a married man for two years. You are too popular for that. Having sacked Giles, they are getting rid of you as well."
But the real cause was I. I knew it would come to this in the end.

"I have the choice," Ray continued, "of going home in two weeks and they will pay your passage."

"I am sure they will, just to get rid of you," I replied, "but I wouldn't like to risk Martin on the sea right now."

"Then I'll have to get another job here. I'll start looking around tomorrow." said Ray, "Potts wants a list of all bills. I expect he'll be surprised to find only my old ones and not much of them."

Since I had been in Malaya, whenever possible, we had been paying off a car bill for the car Ray fell asleep in and crashed, and we had it down to D500.

"We've about D500 Provident to come and a month's gagi. Potts insists on paying all the bills."

"What a cheek!" I said in fury. "I suppose he thinks we won't pay them."

"Probably not. I don't care. He can pay them if he bloody well wants to, for all I bloody well care. All that worries me is getting another job."

Getting another job did not turn out so easy. He had several good probables during the first week but somehow they all fell through. I had a feeling that the Singapore Cold Storage did not want us in Singapore. As it was, quite a few people were horrified that a man with a wife and six month old baby could be dismissed so, apparently, without reason.

We began to feel pretty hopeless but were quite decided that we would not risk taking Martin on a voyage home, whatever.

I said, "I shouldn't worry. If nothing comes along, you can always join up."

"But you would be just a Private's wife, living in married quarters."

"It wouldn't kill me. I wouldn't mind so don't worry on that score."

That evening, I was waiting in the car for Ray, just outside the Singapore Cold Storage. Mr Monk came out.

"Good evening, Mrs. Everard. I hear you are leaving soon."

"Oh no, Mr Monk," I retorted, "I shan't leave Singapore. I don't think it's safe to risk a baby on the water just now. Don't you think I'm right?"

I continued, bringing out the big guns into action. "I must say it seems very difficult for my husband to get anything in Singapore. Every time there seems to be some drawback....something. So, I tell my husband and he agrees, if we can't get anything, he will go into the army as a Private...here!"

Clearly this had gone home as it was intended, and he retreated into the store. Then Ray appeared. I bubbled over.

"Dearest, I've just told Monk you're going into the Army! I bet you he's ringing up Head Office and I also bet you they'll want you there tomorrow."

I'd have won that bet. Sure enough, they began to take an interest in Ray's future. They offered an introduction to a rubber estate upcountry and Ray said he was interested. Head Office, there and then, rang Guthrie's, Kuala Lumpur and fixed an appointment for Ray to see the General Manager in three days' time. Why on earth couldn't it have been done before?

The next thing that happened was the appearance of Giles and Hetty. All bridal, at our flat, much to our horror. And Giles was swanking. Swanking over our jobless condition. Oh yes, he had been taken on by Guthrie's on Malacca Rubber plantations. We wished him luck and I thought, 'My God, are we going to be haunted by Giles?' Poor devil, if I had known then what I know now, perhaps I would not have disliked him. He was killed, we believe, by the Japanese, somewhere in Sumatra.

I did not go to Kuala Lumpur with Ray for his interview. He wanted me to go but I thought he'd get on better alone. Later I had this letter:

"I saw Thorn at nine and was ushered into the presence of Mr. Hartman, the big noise, who was very nice and offered me a job on a rubber estate, subject to my reference being in order, at the following rates: six months probation at D225 a month plus D20 per month servant allowance plus D20 transport of ten cents a mile. Free house, furnished. After the probationary period, if satisfactory, the same salary and allowances for the first two years, dating from the time I joined the company with, however, a bonus payable on completion of the second year, which as they stand at present, are pretty good….."

This read to me very well. So different from the contract that I read three years ago. It sounded fair and giving something. Also, the fact that Ray was a married man was quite acceptable. I cannot understand the marriage bar of some firms in Singapore. Married men are far more contented and settled than unmarried men, who only get involved with Chinese and Eurasian girls and end with keeping them. But the firms can turn a blind eye to that and they have not got to pay their passage home.

Well, this letter gave me great joy. I could hardly wait till he returned to start to make arrangements. The relief to know all was well and no more Cold Storage. After what seemed months but was only days, he returned.

"Well, how's my wife and how's my baby? Hallo, Ah Chung Ah! Ada baik?"

"Baik, Tuan."

"Tell me all about it, Ray."

"I want to see Martin. Bawa anak sini, Chung."

"No, don't. He's asleep, don't wake him!"

"I'll have a look at him."

When he came back: "Do you know? He's grown! After all it is four days since I saw him. Well, darling, we are rubber planters now. Do you think you will like a rubber estate?"

"Yes, love it." I enthused. "Anything's better than this. What estate?"

"Malacca. Bertam Estate, Malacca Rubber Plantations."

"What! Giles' Estate!"

"No. Giles is on Asahan. Same firm but 40 miles away."

(Later, Madge Ross told me there was much comment among planters about the 'butchers' M.R.P was taking on!)

"How awful," I said. "Still, perhaps we shan't see much of them. When do we go?"

"Two weeks time. And we don't need any furniture so we'll just take what we want and sell the rest."

We went on discussing and making plans. I asked Chung and Ee Moi if they were coming with me. Chung, however, did not feel equal to a rubber estate and that went for Ee Moi as well. And I was not sorry. They weren't a bad pair except for Chung's infernal unpunctuality, but better to make a clean cut, servants and all.

"Look here, Ray, we must get some money from the Cold Storage. I want some new clothes and so do you."

"It's no good. Palmer won't let me have the money until we leave."

"Palmer? Who's Palmer?"

"R. P. Palmer, the company secretary."

"But, wait a minute, we can get round it. Why not go to the bank, tell them the situation and see if they will give us an overdraft."

Brains of the women! We straightaway went to the bank, saw the Manager and he spoke to Palmer and asked if there was any money due to us. He said there was money due to us and we came away with an overdraft of D300.

"That's D100 for you and D100 for me," said Ray. "And the other for anything that crops up."

Later when the Singapore Cold Storage had paid all our bills and we literally did not have a cent in Singapore, and the time was getting near for us to leave about five days hence, we began to wonder when on earth we would get the remainder of what was owing.

"I can't think what they are keeping it for and they have no business to. There can only be about D500, I reckon," said Ray. "I'll go and see Palmer."

"Yes and I'm coming too. I am fed up with this. I'll see Palmer with you."

And I put on full war paint for my last visit to Head Office. Palmer wasn't a very pleasant looking man. I preferred, on the whole, Mr Potts. But why was it they all looked so horrid?

He stared at me nastily and told us to sit down. 'Interfering women.' I could see him thinking. Ray then asked him, "Now that the bills were paid and accounted for, what money was owing to us?"

Mr. Palmer called a clerk. "Get me Mr. Everard's account." The clerk returned shortly with a sheet of paper.

"Well, provided all is clear here, there is D556 to come to you. But there is the question of an overdraft on the Hong Kong and Shanghai Bank, is there not?"

I was watching him and, tapping lightly on the table with my finger, I now said:

"But that is purely a private matter between our bank manager and ourselves and is not the concern of the Cold Storage."

He was furious and um'ed and ah'ed.

Ray then asked, "As everything is settled, is there any reason why we should not have the remainder?"

"And we do need some money to get out of Singapore, you know," I pointed out.

"Mrs. Everard, I think it is quite unnecessary for you to have any say in this matter. Any business can be discussed with Mr. Everard..."

I did not get quite what he was saying with the noise of the typewriters clicking behind me, so I said "What?" and made him mad, and he repeated what he had said, very slowly and distinctly as if he were speaking to a dolt.

"No, it may not be my business according to you but to me, it is very much my business and both my husband and I wish to be clear of the Cold Storage."

He then started saying that there was no need for me to be so antagonistic; everybody was trying to do everything for our good.

"Well, Mr. Palmer," I retorted, "if that is the case, the best way we can be helped is for us to have our money."

I did not make any other remarks as I didn't want to annoy him too far. I listened to them arranging it. In the end, he gave in and said we could have the money in two days' time, which would be Saturday, as we were leaving Singapore on the following Monday. I believe that what he really wanted to do was to hold it over in case any bills turned up. Which only goes to show, they didn't know me!

I loathe and detest owing any money and certainly would not have left Singapore owing a cent. One of the things I have against Singapore is the chit signing habit. I think it is very bad and I don't suppose I signed more than half a dozen in all so the Singapore Cold Storage were fussing about nothing. They could, quite comfortably and without calm, have given us the whole lot. Anyway, Ray was to come and collect it. I wonder Palmer didn't add 'alone'.

When in the car, Ray said: "You know, you are a little bitch, darling!"

"Well, these blasted people annoy me. They think they can do everything the way they want and I don't like it!"

The next day, Friday, Ray heard he had to attend a weekend Volunteer Parade. One would have thought that, seeing he was leaving the Singapore Volunteers to join the Malacca Volunteer Corps, they would have exempted him. He asked them, but no!

"No, I've got to go. I'll be back Monday morning. You'll have to get everything ready."

An awful thought dawned.

"And who is going to see Palmer tomorrow?" I wailed, "Oh Ray, I can't, I won't. He won't give it to me. He said he wouldn't do business with me. Oh, why was I so awful to him? What shall I do?"

"I can't help it. You will have to see him. You must."

I was in a state. We had quite a row over it and, what upset me further, Ray went off to camp and we were still quarrelling. I got in a taxi and went to Fifi Fugler in desperation. Ray had given me a note to Palmer but that didn't seem to be much help. I felt sure he would be nasty to me and refuse to give me the money. I don't know why my nerve had failed, but it had.

Fifi promised to take me in her car and hold my hand. Feeling slightly better and resigned, I went on from Fifi's flat to the Cold Storage. George was on duty and I told him the calamity.

"I tell you what. I'll get Palmer at his home and you can tell him that you have to come and get the money." He looked at his watch. "He'll be in a good temper, had a couple of stengahs by now."

I don't know what George actually said to Palmer. If I ever meet him again, I'll ask him, but I spoke to Palmer and he was charming.

"Of course, Mrs. Everard," almost purring, and he went on and on. I cannot remember accurately, but he said that he was 'sorry things were a little strained at our first meeting and he did not wish to be unpleasant.'

I put down the receiver, speechless with surprise and not a little winded.

He actually got up and gave me a chair when I came in, gave me the miserable dollars, asked me when we were going, and hoped I wasn't antagonistic any more.

"Well, I and the Cold Storage have never seen eye to eye, you know," I said warily.

"No, no, the whole thing has been rather unfortunate, hasn't it?" he said. Really, I thought, he was rather nice, after all.

I got up to go. Just then, Potts came in. He only said "Good afternoon, Mrs. Everard" and I replied similarly. That was all. I never saw him again but I heard of him later. I shook hands with 'Reggie' Palmer and he asked me to wish Ray luck. I think that in another half hour we would be firm friends, such pleasantries being exchanged. I rejoined Fifi in the car.

"Well?"

"All's well. That's suda habis Singapore Cold Storage. Finished with them, thank God."

I had for the next few hours a very busy time. I gave my fish to Agnes Ferguson as I could not possibly take them with me. I have forgotten to say but my precious cichlids had died while I was in hospital. The fish-man, when I went to collect them, presented me with forty dried corpses. The parents had a tragic end also. Quite a few months ago, I had been disturbed by a flopping sound in the night but it did not wake me sufficiently to realize what had happened. In the morning, I found Mamma cichlid had jumped out of the tank. Poppa spent one month roaming round the tank, refused all food and died.

By eleven on Monday, I had the car all packed so all that was wanted was Ray. Being me, I was ready hours too early. I am the sort of fool that arrives for a train an hour before it is due, and I ran true to form on this auspicious day. It was a dreadful tension, waiting.

We had thought to make a start about four in the afternoon. It may seem a strange time to start on a one hundred and fifty mile journey but it wasn't so queer really. We were considering Martin; give him his six o'clock feed in the car and put him to sleep on the car's wide back seat. We reckoned on making Segamat Rest house at ten o'clock and staying the night there, doing the journey in two stages. It may seem nothing nowadays, but it was quite a business especially with a young baby.

All the china, linen and one or two pieces of furniture such as my precious camphor wood chest, bought in Tangs for D16 in 1937, had gone on by rail but for all that, the car was pretty tightly packed. First, Chung and I had made up Martin's bed on the seat and, great forethought on my part, with his mackintosh pram cover. I left space for me next to him. His potty, slop pail for dirty nappies, spare clothes just in case, food, bottles were all laid on the floor and arranged just so.

Ray's Volunteer kit and all the last minute things would have to go on the front seat by Ray. And I left him the job of securely tying the cot on the back of the car. I gave 7773 a good fill up of water, pointing out firmly as I did so that this was not a trip round Singapore, so no funny business!

Ray arrived back, late of course. We had some tea and Chinese makan fetched by Ee Moi from the restaurant below. We couldn't cook anything ourselves, all our possessions having gone on before. Ray told me he had been up been up for two nights and had had no sleep…!

"Oh Lord! That means he'll be sleepy, driving!"

I was always so nervous of this after the crash he had had before I came out. We said goodbye to Chung and Ee Moi. They looked rather pathetic standing there, not that I think they had any feelings one way or the other at parting. They were going straight to another job. I often wonder what happened to them.

We got away at five, which wasn't bad, and were so thrilled to be going. I felt no sorrow leaving Singapore. Of course, I had enjoyed being with Ray, yes, but what with the Singapore Cold Storage and the thankless, long hours Ray had worked and for so little money, no, I was glad to be gone. I don't think I ever had a chance to enjoy Singapore. It was a place where one must have money to spend and, if you haven't, you must pretend you have, so Ray said.

I remember Ray saying, when I had only been a week in Singapore, that it was very artificial. "You must pretend to be what you aren't."

"Now, look here. I have never in my life pretended to be what I am not and I'm not starting now. People must put up with me as I am."

And Ray had said that it will be difficult, but it would have been more so the other way, I think. It is possible that, in writing this, I have been unjust to Singapore and maybe, even, to the Singapore Cold Storage…and to Mr Potts. Other people found them a wonderful firm and management. We had started on the wrong foot, so to speak, from the very beginning. Palmer put it very well. "All very unfortunate!"

And I don't feel fully qualified to criticize Singapore. I don't know and I didn't understand what was going on. What I write is how things appeared to me but it is worth recording as it will be of interest to Martin later on. And I remember it now. In twenty years, maybe I won't.

Notes added later: Probably written in the 1950's.

Mrs Phyllis Fugler: answers to Fifi. One of my lifelong friends. She got out of Singapore on the Empress of Japan. Her husband was the accountant of Robinsons, Singapore. He died a few years ago. She, disastrously, remarried a man working for the Singapore Cold Storage. Went out to Malaya for the third time and things didn't go right. The marriage was dissolved. Has recently been severely injured in a road accident. Her son, Edward, is in Singapore, with the RAF.

Joe Giles: My husband knew him before Singapore days as he was with him at Harrods. He was the errand at the Staff Shop and came to the Singapore Cold Storage about a year after Ray. Rather an unfortunate, pathetic person. Married a Eurasian, who, I suppose, is alive and, if so, there is a child. Joe died terribly in Sumatra as a P.O.W. at the hands of the Japanese, poor devil.

Chapter Nine - Malacca

Over the Causeway, we ran into a heavy rainstorm. No rain is **NOT** heavy in Malaya. The Causeway road is so open….and so was our car! I got soaked as I took the full force of the rain on me, keeping it off Martin, who was asleep on his bed beside me. We had fed him, as we had arranged, in the car at six o'clock and he had obligingly been very good and gone to sleep.

It had been pleasantly cool, being soaking wet, but I estimated that I would dry off in a couple of hours. I had to keep an eye on all our impediments to see they stayed in place. Then, on the other side of Johore town, when nearly dark, I saw the car veering towards a deep ditch. Ray had gone to sleep at the wheel. I woke him just in time.

I knew it would happen, and after that I kept up a continuous chatter to keep him awake. However, Ray says, I insisted on him singing for the whole eighty miles or so. He sang every song in his repertoire and was prodded in the back and asked if he was asleep every time he paused. This may well have been so, all I know is that I was very worried sitting in the back seat.

We would stop at every kampong and Ray drank iced, black coffee and walked around the car to keep himself awake. It really was a nightmare. Each stop woke up Martin. He was delighted at the bright gas lights. The kampong women milled around to see the strange sight of a Mem and her baby and in such a dilapidated old car, so strangely packed.

We discovered that the hood had been badly torn in the storm, crossing the Causeway, and at one village we had to have it patched. It would have been disastrous to have to face another storm minus the hood. It wouldn't have mattered if I had got wet but it would never have done for Martin. I can't say I enjoyed myself, what with holding portions of luggage in place, my damp condition, and keeping up a bright and persistent conversation at the top of my voice with Ray.

So, it was late, well after eleven o'clock, when we arrived at Segamat for the night. The houseboys quickly untied Martin's cot and the luggage needed for the night. I went in, carrying Martin under one arm, and two planters, who were drinking lagers, looked up as I came in. They were so surprised, one would have thought they had never seen a baby before, and said, "What a lovely baby to be up so late at night."

The 'lovely baby' was put in his cot as soon as I could get him there, and then we had a bite of something cold. My poor, tired husband dropped into bed.

The next morning, we left after a good breakfast. This time, we packed ourselves into the car differently. Martin and I sat in the front seat as, being daytime, Martin wouldn't need a bed. He loved riding in the car and, if he felt sleepy, he could sleep resting on me. He did so off and on but became a little fed up by midday when we reached Malacca Town and were held up in one of its narrow streets by an endless Chinese funeral for twenty minutes.

To me, this is one of the silliest things I have ever heard. The more imposing and lengthy the funeral is, the more the wealth of the dead person. This funeral was led off with a brass band playing dance music, ahead of a large studio portrait on a sumptuously decorated lorry. This carried the dead person on it. On top, surmounting the gold and silver tinsel and Vanda Joachim orchids, stood a model dragon, signifying a male. If a female, it would have been an eagle. The lorry was drawn by hand, priests in front, dressed in yellow, the colour of mourning, and carrying umbrellas.

Traditionally, following the lorry would be the paid mourners in sackcloth, weeping very realistically. Then, children in sackcloth; decorated lorries, subscribed by rich friends; relations on foot; another band, in a lorry this time and playing different, martial tunes. Then might come hundreds of men, carrying emblems and lanterns, followed by another band, on foot, playing Chinese music. It's total cost might have been D10000.

This particular funeral seemed very large and the noise of the various bands, playing different music all at once, was chaotic.

"Will it ever end?" said I. "What are all the empty lorries for?"

"That's to take them all back to the dead man's house for a feast."

"A marvellous Chinese makan, I suppose, costing dollars and dollars."

"Yes. Shark's fin, bird's nest soup, crab soup, fish. Did you know, if you want to tell a rich Chinese, give him a fish and see where he eats it.

If he only eats the head, he is a rich and well educated Chinese. You see, he's so rich, he can afford just to eat the head and throw the rest to the poor!"

"Oh no, I can't believe that!"

"It's perfectly true. And after the fish heads, they will have prawn fritters, chicken, pigeon, duck; boiled, fried, roasted, beaks, feet, claws that is. All a great luxury. Pork, everything they eat…except the squeal! Much whisky, neat with just ice, so, consequently, they all go under the table rather quickly. Ah, this looks like the end. Lucky it's not a big one or we would have been here for another hour."

"You mean this is a little funeral."

"God, yes! Add about nine more bands, three times as many people, and a couple of dozen cars. Here's the end," Ray said, starting up the engine. "I'm going to the Cold Storage here to ask our way to the estate."

The Malacca Cold Storage clerk, delighted to see Ray, was one of his old hands and still trusted Ray as if he was still his boss. He directed us, "Straight on over the bridge and when you come to the railway, cross it. Go on until you see the estate notice board."

Very soon we were going along the very same stretch of road that, to Potts' horror, we had slept on when we had taken our trip upcountry. Little did we know then that we would be living on this road. We crossed the railway line as directed and, four miles further on, we saw the white board the clerk had told us to look out for.

MALACCA RUBBER PLANTATIONS LTD.
BERTAM ESTATE, DURIAN TUNGGAL DIVISION.
MANAGER A.E.BENNETT.

I thought, "Here we are at last!" Martin was getting very bad-tempered and he needed attention that I could not give him in the car. We turned in, off the main road and up a red road, the laterite of Malaya. It was cool and shady with deep trees.

Presently we emerged from the trees into the blazing sun and the road climbed a bare, steep hill. It was all cleared rubber. Ground that has been cleared of old rubber trees really looks dreadful, as if some hand had smashed the trees down and the trees lie dead, flat on the red earth, being chopped or burned to make way for the new, young rubber trees to be planted.

On the summit of the hill, there was a bungalow with one large tree growing beside it.

Ray stopped the car and got out, leaving me and Martin in the car. Martin fidgeted and 7773 came off the boil. I could hear her saying, "Chobble, chobble, chobble. Fancy ending up in the boiling heat, up a hill like this, chobble, and at my age too! And nearly dry!"

Ray returned after ten minutes, ten very long minutes it seemed to me, trying to pacify Martin and roasting hot under the hood.

"This is the wrong place. Our division is eight miles away on the other road. We shouldn't have crossed the railway. Man named Mitchell lives here. He says will you come in?"

"Must I? Can't we go on? Martin is so tired."

"No, come in for a minute, just for a minute."

Needless to say, Martin wetted his sofa, but he was a nice man and he didn't seem to mind very much. After Ray and he had had their drink, the inevitable drink – why must men always have drinks? – we, at last, started off again and got onto the right road.

It had been arranged that we stayed with the manager for a week or so as the bungalow, that we were to have, had someone living in it and they had to be got out before we could move in. Eventually, after passing little Malay kampongs and alternating rice and rubber planting, we came to another white notice board.

"This is it, this time!"

My first impression of Mr Bennett's bungalow was the wonderful Congia clematis cascading in a sheer, pale mauve mass, smothering a Cassia tree out of existence. The bungalow was enormous, wooden and perched on high pillars like the Durian Tunggal bungalow. Mr Bennett came down the stairs to welcome us. I thought he looked very nice, a Scot, about fifty with a grizzled moustache and bald head. He was tall but very stooped. He had been waiting for us for some time and wondered why we were so late. I can't think what he must have thought of our equipment and me as I emerged, with child, creased, pee-ed upon and sweating!

"Hah!" said Bennett, "Here you are at last! Beginning to wonder what had happened to you. What's this? A baby? First white baby on this estate for years."

He looked at the car and contents. "Bit packed up, aren't you? All your crates and boxes have arrived. They are over there under the bungalow. Come along in. Come and have a drink."

I left Ray to drinks. Martin was a much more urgent necessity. I went straight to our bedroom. It was colossal. Our entire Tiong Bahru flat would have fitted nicely into it. There was an adjacent bathroom. Mr Bennett's cook-boy got the cot unpacked and I bathed and changed Martin and put him in it and, wonderful child, he slept.

I had a shower. Glorious! There was no real bath, just a large, Shanghai jar full of clear, cold water, as cold as it can be in Malaya, that is with a pan nearby to sluice oneself with. I think there is nothing so refreshing as standing on the stone floor and dashing pan after pan of cold water over your heated body. Your mind wakes and you live again!

We had tiffin on our own at three o'clock. I felt very apologetic and thought that we must have put Mr Bennett out. I soon learned that I needn't have worried. Tiffin, in the bungalow, was served at any time between one and six o'clock.

Not having an amah, I had my hands full with Martin and I didn't see much of anything the first day. I was not free to myself till after seven in the evening when Martin was settled down for the night and his washing was finished. Martin aroused a great deal of interest. Mr Bennett's boy and his wife in particular were most thrilled. When we were changing for dinner, Ray said, "I think I am going to like this. I like old Bennett, anyway."

"That's a good start," I replied. "What about our bungalow?"

"We can't get into it yet, not for a month. There's another planter belonging to another estate renting it and he's leaving at the end of the month. The bungalow isn't very far from here. We passed it on the way here."

"I'd love to see it."

"I daresay you'll be able to in a couple of days. There's no furniture in it. We are to have all new furniture."

"Lovely, Ray. I must have an amah."

"Won't it be difficult to have an amah here? Surely, you had better wait till we are in our own place?" Ray asked.

"But that means a month of me doing Martin completely. That means I'm tied down. It's all jolly fine."

"Yes, I know, darling, but I gather he doesn't like amahs. You will have to manage. But he doesn't mind if we get our own boy now as that would help his boy with the extra work of us here."

I wasn't very enthusiastic with this prospect, not that Martin was much trouble. He was a very good baby, and I had never left him to Chung completely so that I had no control or understanding of him. So many women left their children far too much in the care of the amahs. But to a woman in the tropics, washing clothes was a hot, hard job and, as for the ironing, that really was torture. There weren't electric irons, only charcoal ones, and these were difficult for a white woman to handle. First, one had to get red hot charcoal from the fire bucket, put it in the iron and fan it until it was the right temperature. Often, it was either red hot and scorched everything or wouldn't get hot at all. Or it dropped bits of fiery charcoal in its wake and burned holes in everything. And it was so hot!

Martin was just six months old and was just starting on pureed foods, which meant I couldn't go anywhere or see anything with Ray. And everything was so new and interesting.

The morning after our arrival, Ray was hovering around, wondering what he was supposed to do. "Shall I wait for him, do you think?"

"I don't know," I said. "Why not go and have a look around and come back in an hour?"

"You are right. That's what I'll do."

Then he came back. "I've been everywhere. The dresser showed me round. Have you seen Mr Bennett yet?"

"No, I've been too busy to see anyone. Ray, do come here and see Martin. He's in his pram just here."

The pram was under the window and he was going and blowing delighted bubbles at a great, red double hibiscus flower that Ramaswamy No. 1 had fixed to the hood. There were so many Ramaswamies, to distinguish one from the other, they were all given numbers.

"He likes it, doesn't he? What do I do now?" as he turned away from the window.

Then, Mr Bennett did appear, and he and Ray went off to the office. Martin tired of watching the hibiscus and fell asleep, so I was able to have a look around.

There was one main room, fully forty feet in length. The colour scheme was white and a heavy, dark grey paint; black stained, shabby furniture with ultramarine covered cushions and some nice brass pieces on shelves. Flanking this room on either side were the bedrooms. A covered way led to the kitchens, the boy's quarters and to the electricity generating room. Our bedroom looked out on to the Congia and beyond to a dried-up lawn and beds of enormous cannas, and, beyond that, to the rubber trees. On this part of the estate, the rubber was in production, being tapped.

Underneath the bungalow, Mr Bennett had his dining table, the usual place to sit as it was the coolest spot. Interesting for me were the massive pots grouped about and some hanging up. There were several varieties of maiden hair and orchids, one of which was flowering and had a purple spray like a flight of small birds. This was Dendrobium phalaenopsis. There were great hibiscus bushes in pots really like roses. One intrigued me as it had double red, white and yellow flowers all growing on the same bush. I had never seen a graft before. There were violets, yes, real violets, pinks, chrysanthemums, petunias, powder blue plumbago, coleus, several deep green velvety aroidea with their immense leaves, and a good few more that were new to me.

There were lots of squirrels in the cassia trees. I had never seen anything like them before. In the Botanical Gardens in Singapore, when feeding the horrible spider monkeys, that lived there, I had loved watching the tiny red squirrel no bigger than a dormouse. But these had a long body and a ratty tail, which was not the luxurious one I am accustomed to seeing on squirrels. On the sides of their rust-red coats, they had stripes of white and black. They chattered about mostly in the cassias, but sometimes came in through the windows or got in under the roof and chased one and another all over the bungalow rafters, making a rattling and roaring sound. I would have liked to watch them for hours but Martin took up a lot of my time.

Ray said he would take me to see our new bungalow. It was only a mile away but on a separate division, divided from the Home Division by padi fields and a two-mile stretch of road. Bertam consisted of five divisions; the Home Division with the Manager's bungalow, factory and office; D Division with our future bungalow on it; Krubong, four miles away; Malaka Pindi and Durian Tunggal, which was eight miles away as the crow flies but sixteen by road and was the one at which we had first arrived. There was a short drive through the jungle to the bungalow called Eighth Mile bungalow because it was at the eighth milestone from Malacca.

It was at the top of a slight rise in the ground. I saw it first at noon. It was blazing hot and the glare so bad that, had I not got my sunglasses on, I couldn't have opened my eyes against it.

There were no trees, as in Mr Bennett's garden, just a clearing in an ocean of rubber trees. In the middle of the drive there was an attempt at some gardening. It was a large mound of earth, which put me in mind of Stonehenge. It had wooden posts around the edge with Vanda Joachims curling up them, waving their untidy, spidery trailers about. Now, I am very fond of all flowers but there is something about Joachim that I don't like. Perhaps it's their crude magenta or possibly because they are used for bridal bouquets, wreaths and displays in vases. I don't know but there they were.

The bungalow had no pillars but it sat, sprawling and squat, on short piles and looked badly in need of a lick of paint. Two fearsome Alsatians leapt at us from under the bungalow, barking. We introduced ourselves to the planter. He did not offer to show us over the bungalow as I had hoped he would. I would have liked to have had some idea of what the inside was like so as to choose the furniture. No, we all sat down and they had a drink. Martin was fidgety. It was furnished very badly, with heavy stuff and the colour scheme was excruciating with sandy-yellow, painted walls, generously picked out in a strong leaf-green and badly mildewed.

I felt rather depressed as I got back into the car.

We went into to Malacca to choose furniture. It was a dreadful business, coping with Martin and buying D450 worth of furniture at the same time. I just sat in the car and examples of furniture were brought out and displayed to me by Ray and the shopkeeper. The free exhibition attracted quite a crowd of onlookers, who murmured approval at each article. When it was all done, I hadn't the faintest idea what I'd ordered. Not my ideal way of buying furniture at all but I felt with that colour scheme at Eighth Mile, it didn't much matter.

Furniture dealt with, Ray drove us round Malacca. A charming old town. I saw the place by daylight, where we had stopped that night on our weekend, and there were certainly beautiful old trees, great things, with ferns and orchids, Dendrobium crumenatum, the pigeon orchid, growing on them. I would say they were several hundred years old. By this quick drive, I saw that Malacca had little of Singapore's modernity. The streets, full of Chinese and Indian shops, were narrow and winding. There seemed to be many interesting china shops with their wares spread all over the pavements. Gradually, over time, I had a nice collection of rice bowls and spoons, bought from these shops for a few cents, painted in gold and turquoise, gold and orange, blue and white, and decorated with flowers, dragons and birds.

Mr Bennett always went to Malacca on Saturday evening. Everybody did. One Saturday he said to us, "You haven't been out since you have been here. You should. Why don't you go and have a good time tonight?"

"But how can we?" I cried. "We can't leave Martin."

"He'll be all right. I'll look after him. You go along and don't worry about him," said Mr Bennett. I looked at Ray in horror.

"But supposing he wakes up."

"He won't wake up," said Mr Bennett, and, then, to Ray, "Go on. You take her out and enjoy yourselves."

So I put Martin to bed, dressed myself in my new, black dinner dress while he was dropping off and left him, hoping for the best. I didn't like the idea at all and was anything but happy about it.

We went to the Resthouse. It was an ordinary Government Resthouse with a broad verandah with tables and chairs. A cool breeze blew in from the Malacca Straits across a lawn dotted with clumps of bamboo. We had decided to have dinner there, but Mitchell, who was having a drink, got up as we came in and we sat at his table.

"Have a drink, Mrs Everard. What'll you have?"

"I'll have something soft, please."

"Soft! Really?"

"Yes, I always do," came my signature tune of a reply. "I'll have an orangeade, please."

"Does she really mean it? Everard, what's yours?"

"Stengah, please."

"Is this your first night out in Malacca?" Mitchell asked. "Where are you having dinner?" We said we thought here. "Why don't you come and have a Chinese makan? I always go to Foo Lounge in Banga Ayer. They do a good Mee Hoon if you like it."

I'd never heard of Mee Hoon, but we both love Chinese food. So we went along, going down the brilliantly lit little streets, assaulted by the raucous music and crowded with people, babies still crawling around with the shops all open and doing trade even though past nine o'clock. We stopped at a Chinese hotel, which had swing doors like those in cowboy films through which people are thrown out. It was ugly and bare with torn table cloths, notices in Chinese and mirrors with advertisements on them. There were private cubicles for those who wished to dine away from the public gaze.

Mitchell ordered the Mee Hoon. It turned out to be a kind of spaghetti with large prawns, onions, cabbage, pork liver and chicken, all mixed up and seasoned with soy sauce. It was very good. When we had finished, Mitchell said, "Would you like to see our one and only dance hall? Don't expect anything wonderful, will you?"

But it wasn't so bad, a humble copy of the Singapore Worlds. There were the same dance hostesses, perhaps not so beautiful and certainly no Anita. Anita was a fascinating female, who had been the Sultan of Johore's mistress or concubine. She was a great attraction at the New World. One night a soldier said something she didn't like and she threw a plate at him. That started it and, in ten minutes, the place was a shambles. However, these Malacca hostesses were just the same, sitting at their tables, collecting their tickets. All had the same carved, enigmatic, slit-eyed faces, faultless hair dressing, and wearing shimmering, sheath-like dresses with the same deep slit at the side. They walk well; there is only one woman, who carries herself better than the Chinese modern girl and that is, of course, the Indian.

The floor was good, what there was of it, and the band seemed all right. I can never see any difference in dance bands. The only way in which this place was not like the Singapore Worlds was the size.

All the Europeans knew each other, which made for a rather pleasant social feeling, unless, of course, you wanted to be alone. Indeed it was impossible to spend an evening alone in Malacca. Ray and I have tried but sooner or later, the table would have six or seven people around it.

We did not stay late. I was worrying about Martin. Back at the bungalow, Mr Bennett was drinking a stengahs.

"Not a sound. I went in and had a look at him. Have you had a good time? What do you think of Malacca? Where did you go?" We told him. "Well, now you have done Malacca and, having done Malacca, there's nothing else you can do, whenever you have an evening in Malacca."

He wanted Ray to stop and talk. He was lonely. He seemed to like Ray and would talk for hours into the night. I went in to check on Martin, who was sound asleep but very wet. That was too much to ask of Mr Bennett.

We thought it wise to get our house boy while we were still living in Mr Bennett's bungalow. It would help his and get ours a bit used to us. He was a nice little chap, cheerful, eighteen years old or so and took the deepest interest in everything. His name was Ba Hing Tee and he spoke fairly good English.

I was still not allowed to have an amah, but Ba Hing fetched along an amah for me about three days before we moved into Eighth Mile. She was twenty-eight, we learned, rather sulky-looking and had a gold tooth right in the middle of her upper front teeth. I never did find out much about her as she spoke no English and, at that time, I spoke little Malay. Conversation was not easy but I usually managed to make myself understood. If things became too difficult, Ba Hing would interpret.

It was a relief to have an amah again. I could go out with Ray a bit and see the estate. The furniture had arrived and was waiting at the bungalow and the planter was moving out. The boy was delighted to be moving at last. He was most anxious to be in his own establishment. Previous to us, he had only been a number two boy, under a cookie boy, but now he was to be number one boy in his Tuan's bungalow. He had already cycled several times on his bright, blue bicycle to look around.

An estate lorry was detailed to collect our crates and luggage, the unopened crates that Ba Hing was itching to investigate. When the lorry was all loaded up, we followed in the car, Martin and I in the front, the amah in the back. The boy scorned a ride in the car even though we offered to tie his bicycle to the back.

We said goodbye to Mr Bennett, thanking him for his many kindnesses. Off we went, Ba Hing tearing along in front, trying to race us.

The lorry was already unpacked when we got there, and about fifteen Tamil coolies were waiting around for orders. I wanted Martin's room straight first so we unpacked the playpen and plonked him in it. Then, Amah and I fixed his cot up and his room was done! The bungalow was the same layout as Mr Bennett's, the same 'aeroplane' shape that is shown on all maps of the estates, but only smaller. One bedroom was mosquito proofed so we gave that to Martin, making the wire partitioned part his night nursery and the rest became his day nursery. It had a deep verandah, a bathroom and a little room for Amah.

While Amah and I were fixing up Martin, I kindly gave Ba Hing his much-longed-for job of unpacking the crates from Singapore. I am afraid he was somewhat disappointed if he expected fine silver, crystal glass, fine linen and such! Ray had bought most of our household stuff, all together after much haggling, for about D50, before I came out to Singapore. So, plain, cheap china and a most modest selection of pots and pans must have greeted his eyes.

I didn't see Ray for some time but that he was doing vitally essential and important jobs, I could be sure; things quite too advanced for me such as directing the fixing of the kitchen chimney to the cooking stove and getting the electric light generator to work, as delicate a feat of engineering as any. Checking to see if the water tank was clean, he had to climb up to see for himself and then get fresh water pumped up. One of the best things about Ray was that I could always be sure he would be doing something so entirely essential and usually something that I would never have thought of. An estate bungalow is a very isolated place and has to rely on itself entirely for water, lighting, fuel and sanitation. Even so, these Bertam estate bungalows were considered close to town.

When Martin was absolutely in apple pie order and Amah was looking after him, I started sorting out our furniture. Such a job as it had all been dumped in our bedroom, the whole D450's worth, still in its packing. It all had to be manoeuvred around to get the bits out that were not for the bedroom. I had nine of the coolies working on it. At last, amid an ocean of packing material, we got the living room stuff into the living room and our bedroom furniture into its place. Ba Hing had cooked up a meal somehow. Ray was persuaded to leave whatever job he was doing, probably inspecting the boy's lavatory, which was a wooden hut over a deep, deep hole in the earth, or maybe the rubbish pit, another enormous hole, for flies!

I could hear him calling me. It must have been a new sensation to have to call to find me. I know he was very pleased with the bungalow, ant-eaten and untidy though it was. I was in Martin's domain, mushing up his dinner.

"Well, family," said Ray, "what do you think of your new home?"

"I think it's lovely."

"I say, the boy's got some tiffin for us."

"Right! I haven't got out to the kitchen yet," I said. "I haven't had time and I must get the linen unpacked and our mosquito net unpacked."

"Yes, well, when I've got it straight outside, I'll come and give you a hand."

"Thanks. Ray, how dirty it is! I shall wash all the walls down. I don't think it will get the mildew off but they will be clean."

"Later on, let's get in first. Macdonald has left his dogs here and three cats and a hen with chicks."

"Those awful dogs! I hope he takes them away," I said. "I don't mind the cats. One is Siamese, isn't it? What about the hen?"

"I don't know. I'll find out for you."

Towards evening, after hours of solid, sweating work, we were a bit straighter. Remember, all this was done through the heat of a tropical day, during the hours when doing even the simplest work brings one out in a sweat. Martin was in his cot, ready for sleep. His cot seemed so very small in such a vast room, and the room seemed such a long way from ours.

I had a walk round with Ray outside and visited the kitchen and was appalled. It was quite black, both walls and ceiling, which was draped with horror film-like cobwebs hanging from the rafters. There was an unused antique brick oven taking up most of the space. A 'modern' iron stove, burning rubber tree wood, would be what Ba Hing would cook on.

I learned that it was best for Mems to keep out of the kitchen. Bungalow kitchens are something that the white woman cannot work in though, many years later, I did do the cooking in an estate bungalow on an open brick fire, with eyes streaming from the smoke, for several weeks, achieving the peak of accomplishments by making a lemon cheese cake meringue in a kerosene tin for an oven.

Outside the kitchen, by the door, was a huge Shanghai jar, which was connected with a tap, and, standing beside it, a washing-up drying table. Servants never dry up. After washing crockery, they place it in the sun on the table, which is like a horizontal plate rack, and the hot sun dries it. Ba Hing would do most of his food preparation here, squatting on the ground, peeling, cleaning vegetables, washing rice, grating coconut.

Next to the kitchen, were the boy's quarters, and I made sure he was comfortable by giving him a pillow and a sheet. I had given Amah the same as I was most anxious to treat them fairly and equally. There can be so much trouble between an amah and the boy. Our two seemed to ignore each other, indeed I rarely saw them even speak to each other. Possibly Amah did not speak Hylam, being Cantonese; Ba Hing, a Hylam, did not speak Cantonese. It is quite common for two Chinese to talk together in Malay or English while not understanding each other's dialects!

The next room was the kebun's into which I did not investigate. Next department was the boy's bathroom, but it wasn't there as it had blown down.

The cats, which were sitting around, were ordinary kampong cats with the twisted or bumpy tail of Malay cats. Why do Malay cats have bumps in their tails? It is something that I never found out but there is a lovely story about it.

A princess had a cat, which she took to the river when she bathed. The cat would sit on the bank and she would thread her rings on the cat's tail for safe keeping. One day the cat was attracted by a fish in the water and dived in after it. All the rings were washed off in the water and all fell off its tail. After that, when the Princess went bathing, having put her rings on the cat's tail, she tied a knot in it!

One of the inherited cats was a lovely little animal, with cream fur and light coloured paws, but a dark brown tail and ears. Later on, I named him Mr Thai.

The dogs were tied up at the back and barked madly.

"They are staying here tonight and Macdonald is calling for them tomorrow," ventured Ray.

"Also the hen but you can keep the cats," he added.

I saw the 'garage', which was just a lean-to with an atap roof, but tujoh, tujoh, tujoh, tiga looked happy. It must have been a few years since she was under her own roof. Once upon a time, the bungalow had two tennis courts but now, one had the generator house and the other the garage. We walked over the ground, which had been the garden and which I could have wept over. It was just one mass of secondary jungle, Lalang grass, Allamanda and sheets of Mimosa pudicas, the fascinating plant that closes its leaves immediately when touched. I wasn't a bit fascinated with it. It is horrible and, when thick, it can graze one's legs badly.

This garden was completely surrounded by full grown rubber. There was one ancient rubber tree in the garden, so old I should think it was part of the original Hevea brasiliensis brought from Kew. Apart from this, the garden was derelict and hopeless. Of course, there was the dreadful Stonehenge with its spidery Joachims waving in the air.

Then, we heard excited chatter from Amah and went to find out. She had disturbed a green and black snake in Martin's bathroom. We called out for flat-footed Ramaswamy No 2, who was officially an estate weeder but had been allotted to us by Mr Bennett as our gardener and chopper of wood. He killed it. Everyone said, "Oh, very poisonous!" but I don't know if it was. The black snakes are the ones to avoid.

After a dreadful night due to Macdonald's dogs' barking incessantly, peace only returned when they broke loose and ran away. Ray was out and away by seven-thirty to the Home Division and I did a lot more jobs. Ramaswamy No. 1 arrived with a fine bunch of cannas, flame of the forest and Congia from Mr Bennett's garden, which gladdened my heart. After that, he brought me flowers each week until I had some growing of my own and so I made some good flower arrangements.

Ray came back at around ten, full of a tale about the estate doctor. It appears this was his day to visit Bertam and he was with the dresser, chatting with Ray, telling him what a wonderfully healthy estate it was and so on, when two men, tappers, came in. Ray asked, "Ah, what is the matter with them?" One had a little ache, the other had leprosy! Ray roared with laughter.

While he was getting through three fried eggs and a mound of chipped potatoes, he said, "What do you want Ramaswamy to do, darling?"

"What don't I want him to do! I want that awful Stonehenge taken away. I want all that jungle and grass cut down…"

"He can't do all that, poor devil," he interrupted. "He can hardly walk, he's so flat-footed."

"And he's not exactly intelligent. " I finished my coffee. "But if you would tell him to just take away some of those posts and when he's done that, I'll come and look and think what to do with the garden."

"Right, I'll get a couple of weeders over to help him clear the jungle. How's Martin?"

"Fine. Asleep. Don't go and wake him."

"No I won't. I'll just go and look at him."

I could hear him talking to Amah in Malay so I went along to find out. "Well, what is it?" I asked.

"She wants a bolt put on this door," as he pointed to a little, side door to her room, which opened onto the garden where the garage was. "She doesn't feel safe without it."

"Yes, of course. And while you are about it, Ray, you might ask her, please, when she wants her day off."

There followed a torrent of Malay from Amah.

"Darling, she wants two days off for the Chinese New Year, in three days time"

"Oh, hell! What a nuisance! Just when I'm so busy. She'll have to have it, I suppose, and the boy will want it too. We had better find out. I'm going to have a fine time doing Martin and the bungalow for two days!"

But no, the boy wouldn't. We offered him a day, told him to take a day. But he wouldn't leave Mem at all just now. "Too much work for Mem!"

"Good," said Ray, pleased with him. "Good, you shall have the days later."

And I felt very grateful to him.

Gradually we settled down. Amah returned from her junketing and was soon into her immovable routine. The Chinese are very much creatures of habit and so it was with her, once she had Martin's daily routine fixed in her head. However, if there had to be an alteration, as there was bound to be, she was quite lost for a day or so until she had the hang of the new way.

Life revolved around Ray and Martin. After a cup of tea with Martin crawling around on the bed, while we got up, Ray would go off to his rubber trees at about seven-thirty. Amah took Martin for a walk in his canopied pram. I liked to see them setting off, Martin dressed in a fine embroidered dress and nappy; Amah with well starched, high-necked white tunic, black silk trousers and clop-clopping wooden sandals. It could hardly be called a walk, not further than two hundred yards to where there was a green patch of open grass and a coconut grove. Here she would sit and hold court, with Martin always the focal centre of local interest.

While Ray and Martin were out, I arranged flowers, saw the boy about food for the day and pottered in the garden. At nine, the mailcar came with letters, papers and fresh milk from the Malacca Cold Storage. I did not get many letters, and letters from home, when they did arrive, were weeks old. Around nine-thirty, Ray would come rushing up the drive. How the sound of that old car tearing along made me happy! Ray, full of breakfast thoughts and well justified, walking as he had been in the rubber since seven-thirty!

"God, I'm hungry! Apa makan, boy?"

"Telur, Tuan. Flied."

At ten-thirty or so, he would take himself off again. Sometimes, I would promise I would walk over later to watch the latex being weighed. This was always in doubt, as the path to Home Division lay over Malay padi fields, and, if the water buffalo were there, I wouldn't pass because they don't like the smell of Europeans and can be nasty. Also, I am afraid of them!

Martin, after his breakfast, was put in his playpen where he played and crawled until he fell asleep, curled up in a corner. He was usually awake when Ray returned for breakfast and Amah and I would hold him up to see the car, which he loved.

Mid-morning, the bungalow was quiet and the boy would close the shutters to keep the heat out. It was too hot to garden so I mostly read or sewed. I found time hang heavy until Ray returned again, and I never knew quite when that would be, maybe one or three-thirty. More often than not, just as he was finishing latex weighing, Mr Bennett would ring down to the office and ask him to go up to his bungalow. Ray couldn't refuse so, with luck, he might get away by four and Martin would come and join us for tea and we would all play together.

After tea, when it was cooler, we sat in the garden. Martin had his bath and Amah would bring him to us, ready to be put in his cot. First we would carry him around the garden to see the night lilies open. I had them growing in pots. They are wonderful flowers, Ipomea bona-nox, big white convovulus that rapidly open their ice cream cone-like flowers just at sundown. We liked to help them by blowing gently down the opening. Then Ray would carry him to his cot, followed by me.

"Night, night, boy," chanted Ray. "Night, night, Amah. Night, night, cats. Night, night Daddy. Night, night, Mummy!"

Then we had a hot bath, which would have been cooking on the stove in a kerosene tin all afternoon, and change for dinner. This might be followed by a game of six pack bezique, our great standby against boredom, and then I would go to bed about eight-thirty and Ray not much later. There was nothing to stay up late for. There were always the mosquitoes biting and the eternal flickering of the electric lights. However, it was preferable to have the parp, parp, parp of the generator than the hissing of the kerosene lamps that some bungalows have. The only nice thing about the evenings was that we could have the fan on. If I had the fan on during the day, it meant having the lights on as well.

The powerful generator might have burst a blood vessel if it only had to run for the fan.

I would spend time before settling down to sleep, diligently hunting for mosquitoes in the mosquito net. One thing I cannot stand is a mosquito buzzing around me all night. It was impossible to sleep until the generator was shut off in its shed close to our bedroom window, making a dreadful noise. I said, "Thank God that row has stopped!" when Ray at last called the boy to 'tutup engine' and it spluttered into silence. After that, all that could be heard was the boy catching the cats and turning them out for the night.

Lastly came the noises of the tropical night - chichas, the little house lizards, chick-chicketting from one end of the bungalow to the other, the eternal hum of the cicada and our two tic-toc birds warming up.

I believe they are a kind of nightjar. I have never seen them, though I knew they roosted in the day somewhere in the garage. They used to emerge from the garage at dusk, that much I knew. They fly with an owl's silence and they used to sit on the drive and call 'toc-toc-toc…..toc….toc-toc…..toc-toc-toc-toc-toc and so on, all through the night. It is rather trying at first and if you start listening closely, you begin to count the tocs. People have been driven mad by them, I am told. I can quite understand this because if you do start counting, it is so difficult to stop. The Chinese, who will gamble on anything, have bets on the number of tocs and the one getting it right collects the winnings. Tropical roulette!

There may be or there may not be a cool, night breeze through the rubber. The nights upcountry are cooler than in Singapore, a degree or so, but what breeze there is will last until morning.

I learned quite a lot about the estate. Bertam had Malay and Tamil labour, men and women. They started work at daybreak after muster. Each tapper had about three hundred and fifty trees to tap. Having tapped his (or her) tree by slicing off a thin strip of bark with a 'v' shaped cutter on a slant round the tree, he would place an aluminium cup at the lowest part. The latex would run down the groove and into a spout and drip into the cup. The tapper would leave this and then go onto the next tree and on until he had done his allotment of trees. That finished, he then goes back to the first tree and tips the contents of each cup into a pail or bucket.

One of these cups was to serve me for many years as the container for my paint brush water, dipping them from time to time as I changed the colour or watered it down for a wash.

In the meantime, Ray would be walking round with the overseer, the 'kengany', inspecting the trees and the tapping. The trees were tapped every other day, doing one field and then the other in rotation. At eleven o'clock, they would bring the latex to the factory. With the clerk, Ray would weigh the latex or susu, ('milk' in Malay), dipping into each pail a mysterious instrument called a 'latexometer' to check the rubber content. And but for this rubber content, latex could be a food! Straight from the tree, it hasn't much smell but is sweetish and sticky. Leave some to coagulate a day or so and it has a most revolting smell.

The tappers all stand around until their pail turn is called. The Tamil women, so dark-skinned with their black hair in heavy buns, wore gold earrings, nose-rings and thick silver bracelets on their ankles. Dressed in a bright sari, or would be if it were cleaner, these women were cheeky things, bold and handsome, with fine bodies and that walk.
There was a particularly attractive devil called Maryai, who was quite a distraction on the lines, the huts where the Tamils live. An expert abortionist, there was always someone fighting over her, always talk of her in the ditches. I asked Ray what he would do if he came upon a sight as embarrassing as this.

"Chew them up, tell them to get up and dock their pay. But they are too damn clever to be caught mostly."

But one morning, Ray came upon seven or eight nude women! There was terrible embarrassment all round! Apparently they had all been resting after finishing their tapping and had sat on an ants' nest and, just as the Tuan appeared in his car, they were shaking out their saris!

All the latex is then poured into great aluminium tanks to which acid is added and then left to coagulate in strips by being partitioned off with aluminium sheets slotted into the sides of the tanks. When coagulated, the strips are taken out and fed through a rolling machine, which flattens and stretches them with a pretty honeycomb pattern all over. The slabs are then dried in the sun over bamboo poles, then put in the smoke house and 'kippered' for eight days. After this, it is baled into wooden chests and sent down to Singapore, quite likely off to England to help the war.

After the war, the bales were no longer put into chests, but each slab of rubber would be folded around another until forming a large cube. The slabs were stuck together using a sharp spike. Some of the rubber strips would be put though a series of milling machines until they were as thin as crepe paper and were dried in long ribbons.

I hate the smell of rubber in all these stages. When fresh, it has a sweet, sour bad smell; in a cup that has been forgotten, it is one of the worst smells ever, even equalling the durian fruit. When smoked, it has a bitter, acrid smell.

After the weighing, the tappers would have finished their work for the day and the mothers would go off and collect their children from the estate nursery. There, while their mothers tapped, in an open atap shelter, a dozen or so babies were left in the charge of a frightful, old crone. Ray would go to the office for a while with Nair, the clerk. If it had been a day when the buffaloes were not around and I had walked over, I waited about for him or we went up to Mr Bennett's and had a drink with him.

Sometimes, there were days when no tapping could be done.

This would be whenever there was a heavy rain and when everything was dripping wet or it had rained early in the morning. Deluded, at first Ray would rejoice as he would not have to get up so early but we discovered that there was a snag to this. The tappers could be called out to start tapping later when the trees dried and then it would be very late before the day was finished.

Then, there was PayDay! In the old days, when estates were miles away from anywhere, perhaps two days journey by river, the planter, arriving back from town, made PayDay a wild and drinking orgy. But, now, with cars, the distances were not so great and PayDay was not such a gala day. But Mr Bennett was from the old brigade and he had definite ideas how PayDay should be conducted. He and Ray would disappear all day and return in the late afternoon, definitely the worse for wear!

As soon as I could get to it, when the bungalow was reasonably straight, I started on the garden. I found the kebun, if he could be called such, disappointing. He had set ideas about certain things and either thought that I knew nothing about gardening or that it didn't matter what I thought. I explained as best I could in my poor Malay where I wanted plants put, and then to make, I thought, for clearer understanding, I'd tell the boy to repeat the orders in Malay. Then I would go away, returning in a couple of hours to have a look and there would the plants be all planted but not where I had said. Furious, I'd make him pull them all up and replant them where I had said.

This was a regular procedure, and it was quite two months or so before Ramaswamy No. 2 realised that I expected things done as I wanted them. His places for the plants may well have been better though I doubt it, but, as with a child, had I given in to his way, I would have lost my authority over him.

The Vanda Joachims were removed and we put a small round border on top of the mound. It still looked dreadful. We also made a border edge round the drive, planting it with lemon and orange African marigolds, coreopsis and coleus. Each day I gardened until I was driven in by the heat. My pet plants were in pots, positioned by the house where they got the morning sun but were in the shade at noon. My pots were a humble imitation of Mr Bennett's but, as our bungalow did not have the lovely space underneath it, I could not have a display like his.

The kebun was tasked with making a vegetable garden at the back. Everybody had been asked to try and battle with the elements and grow food, so this was our war effort.

The boy was most interested in it and worked harder than the kebun. He was a good 'boy' and I admired his keenness. The tomatoes were his chief joy together with loofah gourds, better known in England in bathrooms. They were very bitter. We grew a vegetable called kangkong and papayas; chillies, grown for the kebun; mint in boxes, which grew well and rapidly if kept in the shade; miserable lettuces, which were a perfect nuisance as they had to be shaded from ten in the morning and four in the afternoon and watered copiously; and large pumpkins, quite tasteless, which Ba Hing ate. Sugar cane, pineapples, ginger, bananas and all the tropical fruits grew with no fuss.

Ba Hing was a good cook. I'm not bad but, if I showed the boy a new dish, he would improve it and make it next time far better than mine.

Sometimes, if Ray could not take me into Malacca, I would send the boy on his bicycle. One day, on one of these journeys, he bought a cockerel and a white hen, which were supposed to be for tiffin. I decided not to kill them and so we kept them. After the hen laid eighteen eggs and went broody, we set her and she hatched eight. We got so fond of her. She became so tame, she would perch on my shoulder. It became our habit to feed them after tea. We had to or they would come into the bungalow and demand it.

When the young birds themselves started laying, they were very trying. Ray had spent hours making a set of three nesting boxes with little legs set in rubber tree cups, which were filled with disinfectant to stop the ants getting in the nests. All tables in Malaya had to have their legs standing in disinfectant for this same reason. But these stupid hens would not go near them. Oh no! Every morning, there would be a frenzied clucking of three hens nearly desperate with the urgent demand to lay their eggs. They came into the bungalow. One always tried my writing desk, fancying, for some reason, the little pigeon holes. Or they would try behind the cushions. At last, as a very last resort and hounded there by me, they would go to the nesting boxes and lay their eggs. But all three, in the same box! The white hen had more sense. She would just go off and lay hers in the rubber and that gave the kebun a bit of a job, looking for them.

After the egg laying performance was over, there was peace from the fowl except that, in the afternoon, they made a point of having a dust bath under the bungalow, just at a spot beneath where my bed stood. And then the rooster would rend the air with his crowing so I would call the boy to move them, and that disturbed him.

A small, Malay boy from school came each afternoon to give him English lessons. Ba Hing had ambitions though for what I don't know. I taught him a bit, making him write all the lists, grocery and laundry. But he was funny with his English. Once, I was saying something about our cups and saucers, calling them 'china'.

"No, Mem," said he, "not China, Japanese."

It beat me. I couldn't explain. I got Ray on to it and he got a bit mixed up. I am sure the boy was insulted to have Japanese-made crockery called 'china'.

The afternoons never seemed to be quiet for long. If it wasn't for the hens being a nuisance, then it might suddenly dawn on me what was this 'munch, munch' sound.

"Boy! Boy", I called leaping up. "Kebun, quick, cows!"

The boy, with the kebun well in the rear, would rush round the bungalow to chase Ramaswamy No. 1's cows from my marigolds. In the end, we had the garden wired in, which deterred them a bit, but nothing would keep the goats out. They belonged to the kampong and we would catch them if we could and tie them up until Ray came home. Then he would send Ramaswamy No. 2 off on his flat feet with a message to the kampong, telling the owner to come and collect his property. When the Malay arrived, Ray would deliver dire threats if the animals were ever found affronting our garden again.

We had a few horror moments in the garden. Martin and I and Amah were out in the garden after tea one day and I saw a small, black snake close to Martin. We got him away and Amah took him indoors, quickly. I called the servants. The boy came tearing up with a stick. Even though it was a very young cobra, it spread its hood and spat at the boy, who killed it. We carefully hung it on a stick to show Ray and also to confound him. Only a few days before, he had stated, in answer to my question, "Cobras! Oh, no cobras on D Division. Nothing to worry about."

Ray did thoroughly eat his words because when they cleaned a disused patch of rubber near the bungalow, they found six cobras. We did have another one, which was quite small but big enough to kill. The only big cobra I ever saw was on Krubong, when I was walking there with Ray. Suddenly Ray stopped, putting out his hand to stop me. Then, some four feet of black, shiny death slid across our path.

There were centipedes, red ones, four inches long, dreadful things. I never saw a scorpion near the bungalow though I don't doubt there were some. Mosquitoes and ants we had in their millions, and red and green locusts, which the cats ate with a sickening crunch.

Amah was always nervous of snakes. She never got over the one in Martin's bathroom but, in general, she settled down very well although I never got on with her as I had Chung.

Chapter Ten - Volunteering

Ray took up his volunteering again in the Malacca Volunteer Corp, which was a Machine Gun Company, Fourth Battalion, Straits Settlements Volunteer Force. Volunteering was held two nights a week. I went with him more often than not and did the food shopping. He was allowed petrol for parades, so this saved us a bit. It had its drawbacks for me. It meant waiting hours for him outside the M.V.C. and watching the rapid dusk go and then sitting in the dark, bored, and slashing out at invisible but audible mosquitoes. Of course, most women would have gone to the Club or Resthouse and waited there, but this did not occur to me.

At last, Ray would emerge, always the last it seemed to me, but, as we trailed home in our rattley, old car, the back seat laden with groceries and market produce, my irritation would vanish.

When we had been at Bertam for only four months, I had a reminder that we were at war. The Volunteers were going to set up a Camp, which meant Ray would be away for two months. What horror! I was very upset. Just before it came about, Giles and Hetty arrived at the bungalow. Of course, there was something that they wanted.

Giles had come to ask if we would have Hetty to stay with us for the two months as she did not want to stay on Asahan by herself. And it would be nearer for him to have Hetty at our place. I didn't want her but I couldn't say no. We had to make a sort of bedroom for her on Martin's verandah.

We were stupid, however, and made no arrangement over money except that Giles would pay D45 for Hetty's food. This would have been all right but, as Giles had been made a cook sergeant, to Ray's disgust as he only had one stripe, it meant that Giles could get away whenever he liked. So he was always at the bungalow and I had to keep him on D45 as well.

Eventually, Ray was made a sergeant in the Stores. He did get away at the weekends but Giles slipped away whenever he could and I got fed up with it when they went out night after night to Malacca and I was left just on my own in the bungalow, feeling very lonely.

One Saturday evening, however, we did go in to Malacca with them. I insisted on going in our car as I had had experience of Giles' driving with one arm round Hetty. We went to the Dance Hall. Giles had great difficulty keeping Hetty to himself. Any European woman was in demand there and, certainly if she was young and presentable.

A beauty like Hetty, with her long, black hair and lemon, lacey dress was besieged. Malacca was now full of Australian soldiers and they made a bee-line for her. It amused Ray and me to see Giles getting madder and madder. In the end, as soon as the band started, he would jump up and dance off with her.

While Ray was away, everything seemed to go wrong. The estate had a visit from the Engineer, who he took a look at the electric light generator. Prior to his arrival, it had been going quite well but he must have upset it somehow. Nothing would induce it to go and the bungalow had to be lit by lamps for a week.

Then another calamity! While we were having tea one day, there was a dreadful storm. All storms are severe in Malaya. I heard it coming and hurriedly helped the boy to get the shutters closed. The rain was pouring down and just when the rain was at its worst, there came a terrific gust of wind. Suddenly, the room became a sheet of water. The wind drove the rain under the lattices. We were all so soaked; we could just have been outside in it. The suddenness and noise were frightening, with thunder crashing and the wind all round, creaking the bungalow and the rubber trees.

And then it was all over and the rain just fell. Everything in the bungalow was wet, and we put Martin in his cot while I helped the boy swab up the floors. The boy came and told me that the garage had blown down – on the car. That the garage should be blown down didn't surprise me, but I was worried rather about 7773.

When the rain stopped just before dark, I went out –wreckage everywhere and trees down. The rubber tree carries a heavy weight of leaves and they have very light lateral roots so, when it rains, they get waterlogged and top heavy and, if the wind blows while it's raining, they topple and fall over. I was horrified at the destruction. I had never seen really bad tropical rain do so much damage before.

I persuaded Giles to take me to Mr Bennett to tell him of the disaster. He didn't want to leave Hetty. I asked him what the hell he was afraid of: "another storm or an Australian!" After which jibe, he gave in. Mr Bennett wasn't a bit impressed. He had heard the rain, however, but I couldn't make him understand how damaged his estate and the garage had been. The dresser would tell him next day.

The following day, Mr Bennett came to see me. Our division had eighty trees down. It had been a cyclonic storm and had cut a clear path right across the estate and our bungalow had been in the centre.

I showed him the pathetic plight of the car and he said he would send the estate carpenter to make a new one. The walls had collapsed inwards and the central beam, the tic-toc birds roosting place, was being held up by the glass of the 7773's windscreen. Why it was not broken, I don't know. The car hood was torn to ribbons. Mr Bennett said he would write to Guthries and tell them of the damage to our property.

Guthries wrote back later, saying, 'Though Mr Everard should have been insured for such contingencies, they were very sorry and would allow D20 for a new hood.'

I thought this very handsome and told Ray, "One thing, the Cold Storage would never have given us a dollar. Much more like they would have charged us for the cost of a new garage."

Soon after this, Ray returned, the camp being over. He had the job of clearing and counting all the fallen trees. He hated to see them smashed to the ground, all good-yielding trees and meaning quite a loss in rubber.

I don't think that Hetty and Giles enjoyed the last weeks of their stay very much. I was so disgusted with them and I had great difficulty in getting any money at all out of Giles. He seemed to think I ought to like having Hetty with me and thought me most unreasonable. But I could not afford to keep them. The truth was that he was hard up as he had just bought an expensive car and had to pay for it. Ray got the miserable money from him at last and they went back to Asahan. And we settled down again.

We didn't settle for long. One day, Ray told me Mr Bennett wanted to see me.

"Me?" I said, "What for?"

Well, Mitchell is leaving Durian Tunggal and Bill Ross is taking over but they can't leave the estate they are on for another month. So Guthries want me to go there and Mr Bennett wants to know if you can pack in three days."

"Good Lord!" I exclaimed.

So, I saw Mr Bennett and he asked could I do it.

"Yes, I think so. It isn't much really, only Martin's things make the most palaver."

"You really can! In three days?" I don't think he could have moved in six months.

"Yes. I must have a lorry and some coolies though and will you see my cats and chickens are looked after?"

"I think that you are a wonderful woman!" he actually said and went of in a wonder.

"It's marvellous." Ray said. "It's all replant on Durian Tunggal. I shall be able to learn a hell of a lot."

So I packed all the china, food, linen, Ray's clothes and mine, and all Martin's things. When it was all assembled, together with the boy's and Amah's things, Mr Bennett came and viewed the collection.

"Must you take all that?" he asked.

"Every bit," I said, firmly. "That's what I want the lorry for. It's Martin's cot, pram and playpen that make it look a lot, you know."

Once more we packed the car. This time the boy went on in front in the lorry with his bicycle. So once more, we arrived at Durian Tunggal and soon unpacked. It was rather fun. The bungalow on that high, open hill was delightfully cool and had fine views over the rubber.

With the replant going on, this was the plum bungalow to live in, and it was the second best bungalow on Bertam, being the Senior Assistant Division. I amused myself in various ways, going about the estate with Ray a lot. It was very different to the other divisions as Durian Tunggal, being all young rubber, the trees only in the main twelve feet high, had some fields being just replanted. Ray, for some time, had been growing a seed bed at the factory for replanting and, now, he was to be actually planting the trees he had sown. He was thrilled. I couldn't get him away from his six-inch high, baby trees. He was out in those scorching fields from ten to four.

I began to be afraid that he would get sunstroke and persuaded him to wear sunglasses. If he wasn't out in the field, he was in the Durian Tunggal, off having endless talks with Mr Bennett on the telephone.

Mr Bennett rang through a lot. I believe he missed us, particularly Ray. He liked to talk to Ray over a couple of stengahs – or more, even. Ray's six-month probation was up while we were away from D Division, and Ray signed his contract. We heard that Giles had also signed his. How happy we were and how we loved Durian Tunggal. This estate was Malaya at its best.

There was a 'chickoo' tree in the garden, Chicku – Achras zapota – a fine, old tree laden with the honey-tasting fruit. They look just like potatoes. I love them but much to Ray's and my sorrow, they were not ripe. We were so anxious as to whether they would ripen before we went back to Eighth Mile that the boy climbed the tree every day to see how they were getting on.

The great excitement while we were at Durian Tunggal was the Visiting Agent's visit. This is a most awesome event on the rubber estates; even the Managers get in a flap. But not our Mr Bennett with thirty years planting experience behind him.

Ray was told that Mr Bennett and the V.A. would inspect his planting. Ray was very pleased. It meant, he explained, that Mr F. might notice him and the fact that he, a raw Junior Assistant, was in charge of the replant. We got a bottle of brandy and one of whisky in his honour; and he sat under the bungalow for a quarter of an hour and had a glass of water! I felt I knew what it must feel like to entertain royalty. Then the two went to inspect and took Ray as well.

"Bloody good of him," said Ray. "Most managers wouldn't take their Junior Assistants with them on a V.A.'s visit."

The VIP, rather a nice man I thought, went back to his lair, or to worry some other estate, and we stayed one more week at Durian Tunggal. Before we left, Mr Bennett told me he was going to be allowed to have the Eighth Mile bungalow repainted. Oh, was I pleased that the awful yellow and green paint was going.

"What colour do you want?" asked Mr Bennett.

"I'd like white, like yours, Mr Bennett. And pale grey."

"Why not battleship grey? Best colour you can have."

"No. I'd like grey, a pale, pearly grey."

"All right, all right, have it your own way." He gave in.

So we returned, Ray having absorbed like blotting paper a wealth of new rubber planting knowledge. We had a huge basket of chickus, the boy having climbed the tree on the last morning and pretty well cleared it. They did ripen in time. I couldn't get rid of them for ages. I tried making them into jam but they must contain a high rubber content, as they made a strong, rubber-like goo when cooked. I have tried many fruits for jam. My successes were pineapple, guava and lime, which made a great curd. My failures were banana, papaya and, of course, the chickus.

Amah brought a durian with her back to the bungalow, and the stink was so fierce even after I told her to take it far away from the bungalow. Durian is supposed to be marvellous to eat if you can get over the smell. It's very good for the reproductive organs. There is always a good crop of babies after the durian season. The smell is difficult to describe. Bad onions and some rotten cheese and cabbage with a dead rat in it might get somewhere near the smell of the durian! I brought back with me new cuttings and plants for the garden.

Two days after we had unpacked, the painters arrived. They painted for two weeks and the confusion was awful. We had another storm while the paint on Martin's verandah was still wet. The wind came first, as usual, and I noticed there were a lot of flying ants, beetles and mosquitoes in the air.

I did not think of the paint until next morning when I went to see if it was dry. It seemed to have a grey appearance and, looking more closely. I found millions of mosquitoes and insects stuck on the paint. They were interesting as they had managed to lay their eggs there. The boy said, "Don't touch them. Let them stay there." Next day, he brushed them off and all were gone except for an isolated leg here and there and some eggs. The boy and I tidied up after the panting was finished and the bungalow looked very well.

Mr Bennett said he wouldn't mind coming to dinner now. He told me that Madge Ross was having all new furniture at Durian Tunggal and that I could have the pick of the things that she was turning out. After me, Mr Bennett would have some, and then the Clerk.

"Why don't you have first choice?" I said. "It's your right."

"Oh, no. I don't mind. You make your place nice."

So I had a few pieces of furniture from Durian Tunggal and had them re-polished to match mine. We had the chair seats covered and added cushions of royal blue, like Mr Bennett's, and lemon and grey. It looked cool, restful and very pleasant. Our car seemed to worry Mr Bennett and, one day, when we had driven up to his bungalow, he leaned out of the window.

"Why the hell don't you paint that car?"

"I've got no paint and I've got no money, sir," returned Ray, grinning.

"Och! Use the paint from the bungalow. Paint it battleship grey!"

So we did. We scraped off the rust and red earth of Malaya and at last came to the actual car. When the painting was done, 7773 looked restful and subdued.

About a week later, when everything was looking clean and tidy, Mr Bennett turned up.

"I can't think what you will say," he started to say.

"What," I said fearing some disaster, "what is the matter?"

"I really don't feel I can ask you, after all, you are all settled again."

"Not Durian Tunggal <u>again</u>?"

"No, not Durian Tunggal." He then explained. "The manager at Serkam Estate has had to go into hospital and Guthries wants your husband to go over there. It will be about two weeks. How soon can you do it?"

"You know my usual, Mr Bennett," I said, "and the arrangement as to transport."

This time Ba Hing and I had everything worked out like clockwork. Mr Bennett again came and gloated over the assembled paraphernalia. Ray said, "I'm Acting Manager this time and it's all useful. There's lots of factory work and crepe-ing done at Serkam." So he was pleased.

I didn't like the Serkam bungalow as much as Durian Tunggal or my own. It was open, that is, the verandah had only chicks, and I never felt safe with only blinds down at night. The furniture was massive, funereal and antique. But the garden was promising. I saw a wealth of seeds and cuttings for my own garden.

We were there for only three weeks and that was our last move for a while. My garden had profited from the three moves and I had pot plants coming along rather well. The problem of what to do with the middle border, the one that had been Stonehenge, also was solved while at Serkam. The bungalow there, identical to ours, had a beautiful round of well kept grass, with a slightly raised border in the middle. When I got back, I had the mound flattened and, immediately, it looked much better.

Ba Hing was rather overpowered by this last move. Continually moving around Malacca interrupted his English lessons. As I have said before, the Chinese love to go on, year after year, doing exactly the same each day. Ba Hing had had enough change and variety in the last two months, he didn't know where he was. Amah was no different, really, except she had the baby, up to a point. Amah was just about the most punctual person I have ever met. Tell her to have a day off, tell her to be back at a certain time, and, sure enough, on the tick, that neat person, dressed in black and white, appears!

I suppose, in their Chinese hearts, they thought that I was hopeless, inconsistent and unreasonable, with a screw loose somewhere. Yet they seemed happy. They had been with us nearly nine months, which speaks fairly well. The boy does all the housecleaning, cooks, superintends the vegetable garden, and bullies the kebun. He was delighted that I chose a Mee Hoon for my birthday dinner, my thirty-first birthday. That his Mem should honour him on her Hari Raya! Ray also gave me a square, gold amah ring so Amah should have been honoured as well.

When we returned to Eighth Mile, we found we had a new kebun, Mutandy, a great improvement who seemed to know something about gardening.

One day, Ray told me that Mr Bennett had recommended him for a raise and commission for his first year. This apparently is very good and is up to the Manager to decide. So, he had a further D25 a month. I then heard that there was to be another camp.

"Am I to have Hetty again?"

"Not if you don't want to."

"I don't. I'd rather be by myself." And then, later,

"Darling, Giles rang me today. He wants us to have Hetty. She's not too well and he doesn't want her left alone."

"Oh Ray, damn! It's not fair. Must I?"

And then I knew I would have to. However, this time, the camp was to be in Singapore so I wouldn't be worried with Giles continually around, and Hetty wasn't so bad, I didn't really mind her. Giles brought her along and, after many fond farewells, Ray and he went to Singapore. Typically, Hetty had a flow of letters, whereas it was days before I had one from my husband. When it did come, this was it:

'Dearest,

I arrived safely after a miserable journey. Seven and a half hours in a blankety train that went backwards at every station for about a mile to three. Why? God and the railway alone, knows.

Well, how are you and Martin? Both well and happy? Has Mr Bennett been looking after you properly? As

I have forgotten to bring any khaki trousers with me, would you be good enough to send me one pair c/o Major Pharaoh, SVS. V.F. Headquarters, Singapore.

Why haven't you written, you little bitch? Here I have been for the last two days and no letter. I am very disappointed. You are getting your own back, aren't you? Your letter to Fifi, I have been unable to deliver as I have no suitable clothes to go in to Singapore in so I have to stay in camp all the time.

Well, angel mine, I don't know when I will be back but I shall hear in a day or two and I will write immediately and let you know.
All my love to you both, your very devoted husband,

Ray'

I sent him the desired garment and later had another letter, which afforded me silent satisfaction.

'Dearest wife, (and only wife),

Two of my letters seem to have gone astray so I'll try and write a long one. I hope to be back in about two weeks time from now on the morning of the 29th DV (God willing). Then we'll have a lovely time. Well, we should have anyway. It seems our life is one long separation with a few months together occasionally but we are very happy when we are together, aren't we, my pet?

Dear one, is there anything you want in Singapore. If so you will get it if it can be got. Send a p.c.

Last Saturday, I had dinner with the Fitzpatricks, very quiet, just talking. I saw George Holt and he was very fed up with everything. Mr

Monk sends his chin-chins and hopes we will be happy and successful in our new venture.

Scandal

Mr Potts went to Cameron Highlands for his Christmas holiday and Cole (his nephew) went too. Cole quietly informs Potts that he has been married to an Eurasian girl for the past fifteen months and she is now very far gone. Potts was, of course, furious. Told Cole he could no longer work for the S.C.S.

The wife was sent to Australia at Potts' expense. Can you imaging Potts an uncle to an Eurasian? Bron has given notice, Monk is being removed to God knows where. Allen gave provisional notice, if he can't do what he wants, then he's going. So it looks as if the Cold Storage is cracking up. Thank God, I hope it goes bust.

I enclose D10, which is all I have got at the moment as there's a balls-up about payment. I have received one week's pay so far.

Your devoted husband,

Ray'

I'm a swine, I know, but I couldn't help gloating and feeling that it served Potts right. I felt I'd got my own back.

Hetty began to be rather a worry. She started being sick and I was a bit suspicious. After some tactful probing into her married life, I thought she was pregnant. I persuaded her to see the Estate doctor. He saw her; she was, about three months. She panicked and wanted to get rid of it. She braved a glass of gin to see if that would do it – Hetty, who hated alcohol. She wrote to Giles, who came immediately. He made matters worse by saying he didn't want them to have a baby.

"Well, you'll have to now," I said to him.

"Oh, no!" he said, "We'll get rid of it,"

"How?"

"The doctor."

"Don't be such a fool." I retorted. "No decent doctor will have anything to do with it. It's against their rules. Doctors don't take life, you know."

"Oh, well, we can't have a baby. I don't want a baby. Something must be done."

"It's no good, Giles. Hetty's got a baby and you will have to go through with it."

He carried on and they fussed and flapped. Then, the news reached Mr Bennett and he told the doctor, and the doctor spoke to Giles and told him to be a man and that she must have it. Giles accepted the inevitable and Hetty likewise, unwillingly at her sickness and the encumbrance to her dancing and little pleasures.

I got awfully tired of this day after day, but I did feel sorry for Hetty. I believe that she would have, after getting over her first fright, been quite happy to have the baby but Giles, being so selfish, hardly encouraged her mother instincts. She was only eighteen and all she asked of life was to have a good time, the rarest thing one gets in life, I reckon.

But I was sorriest for the baby!

When the camp in Singapore broke up, they were all quartered in Malacca for a week and on the last Sunday a large tiffin party took place; Giles and Hetty (not that Hetty could eat anything), Mr Bennett, two British soldiers, two Australian and, down from Kuala Lumpur, Jock Taylor, who was staying the weekend with us.

The boy made a good curry. He used three chickens, followed by Gula Malacca. After tiffin, Jock Taylor left, taking the two British Tommies with him as far as Malacca. But Mr Bennett, Ray and the two Australians all settled down again, drinking and talking. Four o'clock came and went and there were no signs of them leaving. A steady service by the boy and Mutandy was maintained between the village store to supply the beer. I had tea brought in as a hint but they still kept on with the beer. I got fed up as I always did with men sitting around drinking, and went and joined Martin in the garden.

The rubber nuts were cracking all around on the trees in the hot sun. They were ripe. What Ray told me the day before sprang to mind. He had been seeing to his seed nursery with the assistance of the tappers. Suddenly, in the hot, quiet afternoon, there was a veritable fusillade of nuts cracking. Ray looked round and said, "Ho! Orang Nippon datang!" This appealed to their keen sense of humour.

"Ha, ha, ha! Tuan, very good! Baik! Baik!"

When the Australian soldiers first came to Malaya, we were all asked to open up our homes to them, and we did. But, in the end, one had to give the idea up. They were so expensive to entertain, and so difficult to get rid of. They never knew when a party was over. I, for one, was very nervous of having them sty on after a tiffin party. We had a bill for D20 after that Sunday party, and we could ill afford that.

On another occasion, Ray and I were resting. Ray was asleep and I heard a different sound, different to the usual noises of the hens having their dust baths. I looked out of the window and then drew back hurriedly for, clad only in a delicate nightgown, I was exposed to the view of three sweating and crimson Australians. I woke Ray, who, in his sarong, invited them in. They had been dropped from a lorry somewhere near Durian Tunggal and told to find their way to Paya Rumput. They were delighted to discover that the kampong close our bungalow was it. But they didn't stay long.

However, let no one think that I run these Australians down. As Ray said, "Whatever they are as guests; whatever nuisance they are in camp; whatever shops they smash up; whatever they do or they don't do, by Christ! They can fight!"

These men were my principal reminder of the war. There was more in the papers about the Japanese, but I did not worry much. I had always been told how safe Singapore was, and, not knowing anything about anything, I believed and never questioned what I read and was told. Since those days, I have learned my lesson and now I never take anything on trust.

Of course, Ray being always away at a camp or volunteering was a reminder. Food was more expensive, and there would be sudden shortages of things like cigarettes and lipsticks.

The boy always seemed nervous of the Japanese. He had more vision that we had!

"Ah, Mem, if Orang Nippon come, I go to Pahang and hide in the ulu."

I laughed and said, "Don't worry, boy. They will never dare."

But there was more talk and more talk of Japan, and yet more talk; talk of evacuating women to Malacca.
I went and saw the person with whom I was supposed to be billeted in the event of an attack. At the same time, Fifi and I had been having considerable correspondence on the subject. If Singapore were to be attacked, she would come to me.

My beautiful, little world crashed about me on quite an ordinary, tropical afternoon. I had been resting for an hour after tiffin and heard our car tearing up the drive. I could always tell, by the way he came, whether Ray was anxious to be back or had important news. This time he was fairly tearing 7773 along. I ran out to meet him.

"Darling, the Volunteers are MOBILISED! I have to pack and go to Malacca at once."

"But, what is it, Ray? The Japs, are they coming?"

"Good Lord, no! Just a precautionary measure. Come on, I must be quick. We shall be leaving for Singapore soon."

"Oh Ray," I began to cry. "What shall I do? Here all by myself! How shall I manage?"

Everything seemed to bear down on me. The horrible, horrible thought that Ray was leaving me and I would not see him for months and months, marooned on the estate.

"It's no good, darling, I shan't be here," Ray said. "You must fight for yourself. You can't depend on me any more."

It was true. I did depend on him and went to him for advice and opinion on every little matter - for him to take me to Malacca; for him to help me pay bills, order food; for him to talk Malay for me; for him for friends; for companionship, for everything. This disaster seemed overwhelming. I felt bowed down.

I helped him pack his Volunteer kit. He told the boy and Amah, reassuring them, and then said to the boy, "Jagga baik Mem!"

"Baik, Tuan." came the reply.

In an hour he was gone. I think that he did not like it ruining all his rubber plans, but he was also very excited. I spent the rest of the day in floods of tears.

In the evening, dear Mr Bennett came to see me and did all he could to help me, putting his syce and car at my disposal for shopping in Malacca. I think he felt rather keenly the responsibility of having us on the estate and, unusually, I had never felt nervous before being in the bungalow, but this night I was. There was an eerie heaviness and silence, and I felt things were looking at me from the night. I had to go and look at Martin, asleep in his cot, to reassure myself, several times during that night. What it really was, was that I was alone and I realised it. The one white woman, ten miles out from Malacca.

I thought of Madge Ross, alone on Durian Tunggal, and Hetty, even worse, right out on Bukit Asahan, near Mount Ophir. I don't suppose they felt very comfortable. I survived the night and later that afternoon, I heard the music of tujoh, tujoh, tujoh tiga's engine coming up the drive. I rushed out and we clung together.

"Is it all right?" I asked. "Why have you come back?"

"I thought you would like me to." He said and then, "Don't you want me then? I'll go back if you don't! No, we've got night leave. We go to Singapore any day."

Oh, my God!

"Let's go and see Mr Bennett, Ray. He'll be so pleased to see you. And let's take Martin with us."

In the morning he went again, and I went with him and saw the camp and his hut. He told me that, if I came in the afternoons, we could meet.

And, of course, I did, and on the following day. Every possible minute that I could get with him was precious and I took every one. Then one day, he told me they were entraining at Malacca station at six in the evening and that I should come and see him off.

I went to the camp in the afternoon, and we sat in the car until he was called away to issue something. At five, they began getting into the lorries, and I told the syce to take me to the station. It had begun to rain, a steady, drip, drip like English rain and it seemed odd rain for Malaya, too gentle.

All the Volunteers were at the station. All seemed so cheerful and someone said to me, "Don't you worry. We'll be back in three weeks."

In the road outside the station, they got out of the lorries and marched into the station. Ray had told me to look out for him, a C.Q.M.S (Company Quarter Master Sergeant) would be at the end. It was nearly dark and they all looked alike. I panicked that I should miss him and he would go without a final goodbye. Then I saw a man making a sign to me, a tall man, it could only be Ray.

"I thought I'd never find you."

Then they marched on to the platform and all the Malay Volunteers climbed into the carriages. I and the other wives followed them on to the platform and, when Ray had finished arranging his men, he came to me. We stood on the platform for about half an hour, feeling miserable but with a forced cheerfulness prevailing around everyone.

The rain poured down. I felt it was only drawing out the agony more, and Ray and I have never gone in for long partings. Furthermore, I hate seeing him go, so I said, "Shall I go now and not see you off?" I looked at him, remembering when he left England. "I didn't the last time, you know."

"Well, I think that we shall be ages here, dearest. Let's say it and you go home to Martin. Take care of him for me."

I left him and somehow found the car. I cried. I cried my heart out in the car. I ran up the steps of the bungalow, straight to Martin. He was asleep.

"Tuan, pergi, Mem?" Amah asked. I nodded. I could not speak. Then the boy came. He knew without asking.

"Lock up, Ba Hing." I said. "Turn off the electric light. I go to bed."

Mr Bennett came to see me next morning. He was more worried than before. The estate was unsettled, there was trouble already. He had lost both his Assistants, and he was old. I doubt if he could have controlled them, had anything serious arose, respected and liked though he was. The Asiatics are an uncertain quantity and when panicky or frightened or if they think control is loosened or weakened, they might take advantage or, then again, they might not. I doubt if he could have controlled them, had anything serious arose, respected and liked though he was.

I saw what a liability I was to him. I thought, "Why shouldn't I go to Singapore?"

"Are you sure you would like to?" he asked.

"I might as well. I'm not much use here, though I could look after D Division for you."

"You couldn't manage the Division."

"Couldn't I? Will you let me show you? I know more about this estate than you think. However, I'd be out of your way in Singapore. You wouldn't have to worry about me here and I might see Ray."

It seemed a wonderful idea to me, so I went back with him to his bungalow and got to Fifi on the phone.

"Come whenever you want, Barbara. We'd love to have you."

So I went back and told the boy. He wanted to come with me.

"No, you must stay here and look after the house, boy. I will come back soon."

I packed in about six hours. I packed two suitcases to take with me, just what I would want for two or three weeks as I had been assured by that person on Malacca station. I took, however, my sewing machine because it was new and I thought that I might make some dresses while in Singapore. I took my dressing case and Martin's cot and pram. I packed Ray's clothes, our linen and all our things carefully into some wooden rubber packing cases and wrote 'R.W.Everard' on them myself. They were to be out into the rubber store, where, I presume, they were subsequently blown up.

My mother's jewellery, her beautiful, wrought silver dressing table set and our wedding presents, what few we had; my christening mug and the very old christening robe, which had been sent out to me when Martin was christened after the family had had that conference and decided that it was safer with me than in England with the bombing; all was put in a strong wooden box, sealed and nailed down, and given to Mr Bennett to put in the bank in Malacca.

It never got there. Mr Bennett hung on and didn't leave until the Japs were only an hour away from the estate, and then he had to just go and leave everything. He saw the Malays walk into the bungalow as he left. Our bungalow was gutted.

I gave cheerful instructions to the dresser about the cats. In the vent of the outbreak of war, they were to be killed and the boy could do as he liked with the chickens. Amah, I and Martin went in Mr Bennett's car to Tampin station, with 7773 following behind with Ba Hing and the luggage.

I said goodbye to the boy, enigmatic, brave little chap that he was; told him to look after everything and gave him 7773's ignition key, with the hope that he used her to take him back to his jungle.

I got onto the train.

It was seven-hour journey. I had never been on a train in Malaya before and never want to again. It was very uncomfortable. I was restless and anxious to get across the Causeway. I felt that something was after me. Some instinct told me, and, I realize now, that I did not feel safe until I had crossed from the Peninsula and was on the Island.

I was weary and I was ill. I had an attack of tonsillitis coming on. I had felt it coming on when I was saying goodbye to Mr Bennett and I knew it was going to be a bad one, probably due to the terrific strain I had been undergoing during the last week. Fifi met me at the station. She looked neat and smart. I felt awful, frumpy, dirty and very ill.

So, I came back to Singapore on December 5th 1941.

Chapter Eleven - Orang Nippon Datang

Fifi had a top floor flat in Meyer Mansions. It seemed so strange to be in Singapore again and, so far, Ray had no idea that I had arrived.

I felt that Fifi really didn't have enough room for the three of us and had turned her husband, Fugie, out of his bed for me. I did think this was a bit hard and, next morning, I begged Fifi to let me sleep on an amah bed in the kitchen with Martin. She was horrified, but I said it would be easy, Martin in his cot and I in a folding bed that could be put in a corner during the day.

I spent most of the morning of the sixth of December trying to get in touch with Ray. There was much hush-hush. After two hours fighting secrecy, I got through to him. He was surprised but glad that I had come to Singapore. I felt a great relief that I had spoken to him and that he knew where I was. My tonsillitis was very, very bad. My earlier attacks had been child's play to this. I could not eat except in agony, and I know I had a rip-roaring temperature. Martin, however, was wonderfully well, and Fifi and I enjoyed comparing him with her eight-month-old boy, Edward

But I felt so ill that I got quite worried and I had Fifi's doctor to see me. He said "Tonsillitis - severe attack", of which severity I was already quite aware, and told me to gargle.

Ill as I was, I had to admire the night. It was so calm and velvety. After dinner, Fifi, Fugie and I sat on their verandah and watched a great, gold moon rise over the Padang. For some reason, we all remarked in that moon, with the sea so calm and the moon cutting a path across it and the palm trees outlined in its track. But its beauty was treachery. If I hadn't felt so bad, I'd have been happy. I was in Singapore where Ray was.

The moon lost its gold hue and became as other moons. And we went to bed, Fugie to his rightful one and I to my camp bed and Martin, in the kitchen.

I was woken by being thrown backwards and forwards. The amah bed was rocking. There were explosions and guns going off very close by.

Half-asleep and silly with surprised fright as I was, Martin woke and was screaming in terror.

Then the sirens wailed an alert. Quickly, I picked Martin up. Fifi came running out of her room.

"What is it? God, what is it?" I shouted

"Must be practice."

"Practice or no," I said, "I'm going downstairs."

It was difficult to think clearly. I couldn't find my clothes for a few minutes. Fifi decided to come along as well. Being the top flat and divided from the lift shaft by a concrete bridge, my one idea was to get to ground level. I just threw clothes on and, with Amah following, went down the stairs and round the lift shaft. I didn't know what Fifi was doing. She was delayed as she couldn't find her clothes.

Out in the street, it was all quiet, except for a few people coming out of their houses. I asked a Malay A.R.P. Warden what was the matter. "Air raid, madam. Japanese."

"What?" I said, "What?"

"It's still on, madam. You must get off the street."

The street lights were full on and there was an early tram running. It was just on five o'clock in the morning and Martin, in my arms, was crowing with joy at the lights. I could not think where to go. I heard a most unusual noise, which I did not like, a sort of droning 'comer, comer, comer' – planes of course, bombers.

To one side was the Cathedral, and I thought of going and sitting on the grass for want of a better place. Straight in front of me was the Adelphi Hotel, and I remembcred a photo I had taken at a dance by the A.R.P shelter. I went straight over to the hotel, where there was a crowd of people at the entrance and some half dozen in the shelter. They all stood talking together, confused, stunned. No one understood, but we all knew that something had happened. That something was war. My father was right. The volcano was awakening.

Singapore - impregnable, formidable - had been bombed!

Then at last, the all-clear sounded and we returned to the flat. I wasted no time. I got the big bag packed with the things I did not want to lose and prepared myself for the next air-raid. It was difficult to think coherently or make sense of what had happened.

To know that this news was spinning out to the world, and that at home they would be hearing of it, horrified, shocked, angry. I was scared stiff and fully expected a visitation from the Japs at any minute. I tried to tell myself not to be a fool. People, my own family, were going through much worse.

The papers, though I may not be word accurate, ran headlines like: 'JAPANESE BOMB SINGAPORE. LANDING AT KHOTA BAHRU. FIERCE FIGHTING.'

Amah then began to be a bit of a nuisance. She wanted to go back to Malacca. I was mad as I had just paid her a salary but, if she felt like that, it was better for her to leave. So I sent her to catch the mail car with D5, telling her to 'pergi scaran lekas!' – go, now, quick! Poor devil! It was only natural that she should want to go back home. If I hadn't been so worried myself, I might have been more understanding, but it was so serious to have her fail me at such a critical time and I was so ill. But it was just as well to be rid of her if she was going to be unreliable.

Then Marian Humphrey arrived, surprised to see me with Fifi. She was also a bit nervous. Her husband had been conscripted into the Volunteers and she had been all alone in her little house on the Bukit Timah Road. She had come to ask Fifi to come and stay with her but, of course, she hadn't reckoned on me being there. If Fifi went, I would also have to go. She asked us both therefore. Fifi and I were in such a flap we couldn't think straight. All we could think of was that the bombs had dropped in Raffles Square, not a quarter of a mile away. Too close to be comfortable and that the flat was at the top. And I was so frightened. It takes a lot to frighten me but I really was.

So clever of the Japs to drop their bombs in Raffles Square, the heart of Singapore. Incidentally, Guthries' Singapore office had one right through it. So we decided to accept Marian's offer. As it happened, it was a great mistake. If only we had been braver and remained in the flat, we should have been much better off. But, in the great crisis like this, it is only when it is over that one sees clearly what should have been done. Fifi got her things packed; cot, playpen, clothes, her amah's stuff, and I got all mine reassembled. Marian went to get a taxi, no mean undertaking. They had to be bribed.

Singapore was in ferment with cars and lorries loaded with furniture and people going in every possible direction. There were crowds standing about. Marian returned eventually with a taxi, an open one. We packed it high with all our things. Then we went back up the stairs, as the lift wasn't working because the men who worked it, hadn't turned up, to bring the children down. Just as we all got in, the siren went.

Our hearts turned over and, getting out hurriedly, leaving all our things to the mercy and honesty of the taxi driver, we went to the Adelphi shelter once more. Nothing happened. An hour later the 'all-clear' went. The taxi and all our things were still there, so off we went; Fifi, Edward and dog in front with syce; Martin, I and Fifi's amah high up on top of the playpen, cot and the rest.

Now, the day before, had two Mems journeyed through the streets of Singapore thus, Indians, Chinese, Malays, Europeans, all the people that make Singapore, would have stared, not believing their eyes. But, today, everyone was too occupied saving their own skin. No one had eyes for us. There were too many such cars piled high. Driving was dangerous and we had several hair-raising escapes, especially on the Bukit Timah Road, death trap that it was even on an ordinary day.

But we did make it safely, and paid the exorbitant price asked for by the syce. Then there began the job of fitting three women and three babies into two bedrooms, and such tiny rooms too. Fifi and I were sharing a bed in one little room with Edward and Martin in their cots. We were all so squashed up and all trying to attend to our babies all at once. And, we were all waiting for the next air raid.

In the night, Fifi had wakened. She was holding something dark. I asked her what she had there.

"It's Fugie's coat", she said, and I laughed.

"I've got Ray's sarong!"

But it was all so frightening, I was quite frightened. I didn't sleep. I kept an eye on the window all night, I think, half expecting a Jap to appear. A horrible thought, but I didn't fancy the Bukit Timah Road either, it being the main road over the Causeway and to the North. I imagined Japanese soldiers marching along it at any minute.

Marian decided to dig a shelter as indeed were all the inhabitants of Singapore. The house was too crowded, so Marian suggested that I stayed with a friend of hers, a Mrs Parsons, two avenues along. I agreed. I was sorry to leave Fifi but we could not have managed the way we were.

I went to see Mrs Parsons, who seemed pleasant, if a little morose, but forgivable in the present situation. I left Martin with her while I went back to collect what I could of our things. I took one of her amahs with me to help as I wasn't able to get all our things back, just the two suitcases of the necessary clothes. Goodness knows how I would get the rest; there was no hope of a taxi in the Bukit Timah Road.

I had to walk back to Marian's house, a tidy way on a hot Singapore morning, with my raging tonsillitis. 'Mosquito' buses, crammed, whirled by, cars piled high, taxis full. The pace of the traffic was alarming. The Asiatic is a wild river at the best of times but now they were suicidal.

I collected the two cases and the amah and I started on the return journey. I had not liked leaving Martin with a total stranger but what else could I have done? What I should have felt if the siren had gone again, I can't think. Mercifully it didn't. We did get on a 'mosquito' bus. I had never travelled on one of these before, it being considered 'not done' by Europeans. However, but was I not pleased to do it now!

Marian promised she would fetch the cot and the other things along, but they never came. In the end, Mrs Parsons' neighbour went and fetched them in her car.

It was better in Mrs Parsons' bungalow but I decided that, as soon as I could, I would move into a boarding house. I hadn't seen Ray at all. Everything was so upside down, chaotic, but I left a message for him at the S.S.V.F Headquarters, telling him where I was.

And, all this time, I was so frightened and Mrs Parsons was frightened. On this very same day, we heard of the disaster of the 'Prince of Wales' and the 'Repulse' – quite unbelievable.

Mrs Parsons had had a slit trench dug, which she showed me. I was not overly impressed. It was five feet in length and quite deep with an atap roof covering. What I didn't like about it was that she had it positioned plumb under the north wall of the bungalow.

The siren went at about seven that evening, and we collected the babies out of their cots and went down into her trench. Mrs Parsons was a large woman, larger than I. She went in first and made herself comfortable in three and a half feet of her trench, leaving the rest for me to share with two amahs and a kebun. I got the most excruciating pins and needles in my legs through not being able to move, so I thought even less of her trench than before. Luckily it was only a short 'Alert' and the 'All Clear' went very soon. It was a sort of warming-up for what was to follow.

The all-clear ended and we came out into the bright moonlight, covered in deep red earth with the babies crying. I said I thought it would be better if I left her to her trench and I would risk it under the dining table. I did not put Martin back into his cot but straightaway onto a pillow under the small but solid table. During this interval that lasted three-quarters of an hour, I got the mattress off my bed and readied it to put over the table with my bag under it, ready with Martin.

Then the siren went. Mrs Parsons and her servants went to the trench. I opened all the windows and the front door. I did this all at top speed, not knowing then that there was a few minutes grace before all these Japanese air raids. Then I crawled in under with Martin, who was sound asleep. It was squashed and uncomfortable and I had nowhere to put my head. I could hear the droning coming steadily nearer and, from under the table round the mattress, I could see the searchlights.

This turned out to be a much heavier raid. And there was heavy gunfire. Shrapnel rained down on the roof and, hearing that, I was a bit worried for those in the slit trench, which, to me, seemed nothing but a death-trap. The noise was dreadful - the planes, the gunfire. I heard a man say, "I can see them! Look, there they are! Right overhead!"

If I'd been frightened before, well, it was nothing compared to this. I was literally paralysed with plain stiff fright - the searchlights, the guns and above all the 'comer…comer…comer!'

Then a most enormous cockroach appeared on the underside of the table top and ran, crazed with fright, backwards and forwards within an inch of my nose. It would see one bright light and make a dash and then rush wildly back, only to see another and rush wildly back again. I could see its long, horrid antennae waving. My attention as completely held by this cockroach. I didn't want it to fall on me or Martin.

Then came a 'crumping-crump' sound, which I later learned, were the bombs' falling. There was a bright, red flicker in the sky and the cockroach was more of a nuisance than ever before. Up to this point, I had been beside myself with fear but, suddenly, I was afraid no longer. I was brought to my senses by the cockroach. If I, in the middle of an air raid was worried more over an insect, then….! I have never been stiff with fright since, not panic stricken, nervous, yes, and in nastier raids than this one.

We gradually began to understand the raids. They were Asiatic! - seven to twelve at night and nine to one in the day.

This was the one redeeming feature of existence at that time, the peaceful afternoons, which turned out very convenient when at last I got in touch with Ray and told him where I was. And he said I could come to his camp each afternoon – how wonderful! It was only a week since I had last seen him but it seemed months. I was still very ill with tonsillitis and a high temperature, but I couldn't give in to it and go to bed because of Martin and the air raids. So I just had to battle on.

Having no amah, I took Martin with me to the camp, which I did not like doing much. The airport was so near the camp and in such a vulnerable spot. When, on the first afternoon that we met, Ray set eyes on me he straightaway rang Dr Elder and asked him to come and see me at the bungalow in Bukit Timah. Ray was very busy but we sat and talked for an hour.

"I'm glad you are in Singapore. You did the best thing," he said.

"I couldn't stay there. I was an awful nuisance to Mr Bennett. Ray, isn't it awful, the air raids? How did you get on in the first one?"

"I never heard it at all! When Abu Bakar told me, I couldn't believe it!"

"Do you think everything's all right? I mean, shall we hold them?"

"Yes, up north."

"When do you get leave, darling?" I asked, already leave having become the most important of things.

"I'll try and get a night's leave. Come tomorrow, won't you, and I'll tell you then."

"I'll come every afternoon from now on," I said. "I'll have to bring Martin. I have no one to leave him with."

"Will it be all right for me to come to Mrs Parsons' place?"

"Why? She expects you. She'll be glad to have a man around. Have you any money?"

"Well, not much."

"I haven't enough for taxis here all the week as it is. Still, don't worry, I'll get here somehow."

"I'll draw my pay at the end of the week and you can have it then," Ray said. "Well, my family, it's time you went. Take care of yourselves in these blasted raids."

I had told him of my procedure for coping with the air raids and he approved. I also told him that I would like to move to a boarding house, if possible, so he said he would try and fix it for me.

Ray did get a night's leave and it was wonderful to have him back again. So much had happened, so much to discuss, but now my voice had completely gone and I was speechless! There was an awful air raid on this first of Ray's night leaves, but I felt quite safe. Let all the Japs come, I had Ray with me and all was well.

Dr Elder did come and see me. It was good of him to bother as the Singapore doctors were very busy. The bad 'cockroach' air raid had badly damaged Alexandra Hospital.

"Dear me, that's a nasty throat," said he. "Very painful. You must gargle. Let me see, you had tonsillitis before, did you not?"

"About a year ago."

"Of course, while they are infected, it can't be done, but I think it would be better if they were removed."

"I couldn't possibly have them done now, Dr Elder. I couldn't leave the child in these raids. Also, I have no amah."

"No," he said, slowly. "Unthinkable just now."

When your world has been turned upside down, one's mind is all a jumble. I cannot, try as I might, think coherently about that first week. It was a week of adjusting ourselves to danger. It was a scramble; for food, for taxis, for shelter from the air raids. The Japs had penetrated deeper; the word 'infiltration' crept in. The air raids were regular, unpleasant and steady. Singapore was only such a small island and we always knew we were for it, somewhere, each time the siren went.

I received a nicely written letter from the boy, asking me what he was to do with the eggs the chickens had laid. I wrote back, printing very clearly that he could either eat them or sell them! Mrs Parsons gave up her trench and took to sheltering under her bed. She could not make up her mind whether to return to Australia.

Then, it was Christmas, which was unbelievable. Mrs Parsons got a turkey somehow and Ray got night leave. We ate it in semi-darkness in the 'brown-out' on a small coffee table, ready to run if the siren went. We gave no presents. We had no time. No one felt Christmas-like, except for a few, misguided people. It was not the time for frills.

Again, the Japs got closer.....Ipoh. We were all sure they would be held soon. Cockerill arrived from Kelantan Cold Storage, having lost everything he possessed except for the shirt and shorts he had on. Bread was rationed, potatoes were expensive and in short supply. The chief difficulty was getting in to the centre to get food. The Bukit Timah

Road was a tidy step from the Cold Storage and with buses either full up or not running, because the drivers were too frightened, it was not easy.

There were, of course, many stories of fifth column activities, arrow signs in the rice fields. In such a mixed community as in Singapore, there must be good and bad, for and against. Some didn't like the British and liked the Japanese but, on the whole, I think the Asiatics bore themselves pretty creditably, mostly staying at their work, some with considerable bravery. Many Europeans left Singapore in those first weeks. We all felt "let them go", those that were in a flap.

I, personally, made no move to go anywhere. I was prepared to stay. I felt sure the Japs would be held somewhere. I just know one thing. Those nervous ones, who left early, were never as incredulous and foolish as I was.

Chapter Twelve – Volcano

Madge Ross arrived in Singapore in January with her three little boys. I had just got myself fixed to go into a boarding house in Cairnhill Road but she persuaded me to share a flat with her. I didn't really want to, I knew that I would be better on my own but, when I saw the flat, I fell.

The block belonged to Guthrie's and the flat she had got belonged to someone high up in Guthrie's. I think that they must have left. Madge didn't like the flat; she really wanted one of the houses. But I thought it was marvellous, a top flat, well furnished in expensive Chinese furniture and red-tiled throughout. And a magnificent view.

I also managed to get an ayah, Essa, old but steady and seemingly not worried by the raids. Madge and I made arrangements to share out the work. She said she would do the cooking and the shopping. This suited her best, she found, as she had her car and she got the two older boys into a school and they had to be taken there each day.

This would have been all right but, unfortunately, Madge never got over the raids as I had. From the first she hated the flat and, after a week, asked the couple living on the ground floor if she could sleep on their dining room floor 'as she was so nervous of the raids and with three children'. They reluctantly agreed and, after that, I had the flat to myself in the evenings. Madge retired at about eight after a nervous supper with the children and me to her mattress on the floor.

She wondered at me, indeed she could not understand how I could be so cool. How I would change into my air-raid suit (one of Ray's khaki overalls and most suitable for the trench) and be prepared for the inevitable raids, sit down and read!

"I can't think how you can!" she exclaimed. "Aren't you nervous by yourself?

"My dear Madge, I like it."

Five minutes later she would ring me up from downstairs to find out how I was. Ray would also ring up and tell me what the war news was and how far 'they' had advanced, say goodnight and "for God's sake, be careful!"

After that I would expect to be in the slit trench any minute. Then, I would get Martin up, collect the coats put in readiness and marshal Madge's amah and Essa, who would not hurry, oh dear, no! Turn off the lights – brownout – and heading down flights of dark stairs, shooing servants in front and with Madge agitating at the bottom of the stairs. It was about 50 yards to the zigzag, covered-in trench, which was the shelter and a very good one it was. It was made in sections. Madge and I would arrange ourselves on the benches and wait – for the crump! crump! crump! That meant the bombs had been unloaded near or far and that the all clear would soon sound.

Most often we would then return to our flats but there might be two more alerts after which the rest of the night would be quiet. But I always slept in my shelter suit so that I should be ready immediately. I got up very early, it was necessary that I did. There was much to be done before the morning raids started. Madge couldn't cope with the cooking so I did it. From six onwards it was a race to be finished before the raids started. I cleaned the living room, my room and the bathroom while Essa saw to Martin. It was lucky that I had her.

Then I laid breakfast for the Ross family and me and Martin, prepared it, peeled potatoes and made two puddings, one for the children's midday meal and one for supper. By the time I had got all the cooking for the day under control, Madge and her three would arrive upstairs. After breakfast, while Madge took Jimmy and Peter to school and did the shopping, I washed up and bathed Martin and have a bath myself if I felt daring and if I thought there was time.

Martin was put down for his rest at about ten thirty, invariably to be disturbed by the raids. I got so fed up with his rests each morning being broken that I told Essa to take him down to the trench and let him sleep there. This proved most successful. Air raids came and air raids went but Martin had his sleep undisturbed. And either I or Essa would stay with him. We would sit on top of the shelter in the shade of a great palm tree. People passing by used to think we were just nervous women, waiting for the air raid!

In between raids in the morning, I tried to get the dinner cooked. It was very irritating as, no sooner had I got the food cooking, I would have to abandon it. But with Martin and Essa already in the shelter, I didn't need to hurry so much as I only had to get myself out.

Gradually the raids steadily got worse and Madge was afraid to take her children to school, much less go to the Cold Storage to do the shopping. I realised we would all starve unless I did that as well. So, having done the housework, the cooking and seen Martin off to sleep with Essa in charge, I went shopping. I went, raid or no raid, sharp on time, in the best way I could, rickshaw, bus, taxi or a lift in some kind person's car. Failing everything, I walked to the Cold Storage, get whatever food was offered, quickly, and be back as soon as possible.

Very naturally, I did not like leaving Martin in air raids. Although Essa was very reliable and never deviated from the instructions I had given her, I couldn't feel at peace leaving him with her. But, what else could I do? Someone had to get food. If I was caught out by an early air raid, I use to take shelter in drains or ditches or took a chance and didn't bother. Much depended on what I saw and heard!

Madge, relieved of the shopping, went to the slit trench each morning and remained there until she was forced out by sheer hunger. I know I was a bit nervous at first but I have never met anyone before or since in such a continual state of panic. She had let it get such a grip on her. She should have left Malaya some weeks be fore.

I remember one night, it was about seven o'clock. Martin had just gone off to sleep and Madge was looking out of the window, saying what a lovely evening. I was about to join her at the window when the siren went. She sprang round, collided with me, nearly knocking me over, and woke Martin, who, frightened by the siren started crying. I lost my temper.

"Really, Madge!" I shouted. "Do control yourself. It's only the siren. Haven't you ever heard it before?"

Oh no – flap! flap!

"Come on! Come on!" she cried. "Quickly, come on, children!"

I let her go on, saw the amahs out, switched the lights off and lifted my sobbing Martin out of his cot and followed on down. I cannot blame her, however, the raids on Singapore were nasty and you knew that, with each one, you were the target. The only relief was when they attacked the Naval base. Mostly, however, the bombs fell around the docks and the airport.

Ardmore Flats were on a hill and., when we emerged from the trench, we could always see where the bombs had fallen by the new fires burning. I dreaded seeing them in the direction of the Airport as it was so near to Ray's camp.

Penang fell. There were terrible tales from Penang, the Runnymede Hotel burned down, looting and worse. One morning, we were all assembled in the trench. The planes were going over. Suddenly there was this hellish scream, a scream that I cannot describe. I cried "Down, down" to Madge and Essa and I went flat on top of Martin. There was a rumbling and an explosion, my ears cracked. After a minute, after finding that we had lived, I got up and peered out cautiously.

Madge was hysterical!

There was a lot of smoke and the smell of gunpowder about. When it cleared, I climbed out. The trench zigzagged to a small dip, which was covered by a thin patch of jungle and the bomb had fallen in this, ten yards from the trench. We were in the section furthest away but I heard cries of agitation coming from the amahs and natives who were in the part nearest to where the bomb fell. None were hurt but they were badly shaken and they must have felt it quite a bit. After that, a number of the amahs refused to go in the trench. It was only a small bomb, fifty pounds I believe. It cleared a neat round in the jungle, fifteen yards across.

This stick of bombs had also got Guthrie's again! After they were bombed in Raffles Square on that first raid, they moved to one of their company houses in Ardmore Park and, blow me, they got a bomb right on it. Mr Horn, the Malacca Guthrie manager, was hurt and also some of the kranies. All the bombs in this raid had fallen on Tanglin.

I went to the Cold Storage later and they had had a hit on the ammonia gas plant. I met Rafferty again, who had come from up-country in much the same condition as Cockerill. He told me that customers had hidden under the counters with their behinds sticking out. He said he longed to go round, giving them a good whack! Then the ammonia started leaking and they cried "Gas! Gas! It's a gas bomb!" And there was quite a small panic.

I rang Ray as soon as I could that morning. I knew how quickly things get round in Singapore and I didn't want him alarmed. I might have spared myself, however, as he wasn't there and I had to leave a message. The Malay, Abu Bakar, to whom I gave it, told him that Ardmore Flats had been bombed so he got compassionate leave and came to see if we were all right. I took him to see the bomb crater but he saw just how close it had fallen.

All through this time, I went each afternoon to see Ray, leaving Martin with Essa. So the next day, I did my usual struggle to the camp, daily getting more difficult with broken mains and burning buildings everywhere. Ray met me in great agitation.
"Where have you been?" he asked.

"Been?" I said, "Nowhere. I went to John Little's this morning, that's all"

"I've been ringing and ringing," he said. "I couldn't make anyone answer at the flat. I tried the Cold Storage, everywhere and I couldn't find you."

"The telephone is broken from the bomb at the flat and, anyway, there's no one there. Madge was probably in the trench but what did you want?"

"I just thought I'd ring up and see if you were all right and then I got worried because I couldn't get you."

We all had to register for Security Cards and while I was in the queue but who should I meet but Mrs Prior, who had been my cabin mate on the 'Glenshiel'. I was very pleased to meet her. I asked her how she came to be in Singapore, a rather stupid question!

"I had to come," she said. "I left everything. The Japanese were in Kuala Lumpur."

"My God, how awful! Was it terrible coming down?"

"It's dangerous because of the machine-gunning. We had always to watch for planes", she explained, "and get out and hide in the ditch, if there was one, or run into the rubber and pray the car would not be damaged."

She told me terrible things of upcountry, Kuala Lumpur was falling. Everybody heading for Singapore. She asked me my news but there wasn't much to tell.

"Do you remember Mrs Yarrow" I asked "saying I would change after I had been here a bit, drinking and so forth?"

"Yes I remember!"

"And you said I wouldn't! Well, I haven't so you were right. I'm so glad to be ale to tell you that."

It was strange to be in Singapore, meeting all the people I knew before. Mary, I saw a little, and her lovely daughters, Nellie and Jean. Mary was very busy getting married. Mrs Parsons and Marian had gone to Australia. I didn't see Fifi at all again but I rang her several times. It was curious going to the Cold Storage again, a very different place now. After we had left, as we had heard, they had had this orgy of sacking what was left of their European staff. Consequently, when every able man was mobilised, they were left at the mercy of an Irish-Australian, who ran it as he pleased. Potts, I heard, was ill somewhere. I had to go down to the Post Office for enquiries about some letters arriving for Mr Bennett and I had a shock when the man in charge said:

"Don't' worry. He'll be here to call for it himself in a few days. Everybody" he continued "will be in Singapore as I see it."

The Japanese got to Tampin. Ray suddenly thought he better get leave and go and collect our things.

"No, no!" I said, remembering what Mrs Prior had told me, "Don't, dearest. It's not worth the risk. You might not get back."

At this point, I sent a cable home to Daddy. 'DON'T WORRY. AM IN SINGAPORE". But it was never received! What their feelings at home must have been, I cannot think. Three days after, Malacca fell. I wondered what happened to the bungalow. I hoped the dresser had put the cats to sleep. I hoped the boy had gone to his jungle.

We heard that Mr Bennett had left with but an hour to spare at was at the Ulu Remis estate. Ray said:

"I have nothing except what I have here."

I said "I have a husband, a baby, two suitcases, a sewing machine, a dressing case, a pram, a cot. Those are my total assets."

Things were getting really grim. We lived chiefly on the flat owner's store of tinned food. The raids were long now, perhaps two or three hours in duration. There were fires that burned for days. Something Daddy had said about a volcano echoed hauntingly in my mind!

I still struggled to the camp at Geylang every afternoon but it was really difficult. Heavier raids than ever in the mornings, the roads congested, flooded with water and choking with smoke from the smouldering houses. It was impossible to get a taxi or rickshaw, bus or tram. People were ever so good over lifts and, whenever possible, a car would stop to offer a lift.

One day after appalling raids, I had just made it to Geylang after a hazardous journey, really hair-raising. Only I never told Ray as he would have had a fit to know his wife had travelled on the bottom step of a tram, sharing it with an ancient Chinese fruit-seller and his basket. Or, as on this occasion, by rickshaw only to be set down in the road and told he could go no further. So there I was, marooned, the road ahead impassable. I re-tracked and an awfully nice European went out of his way to take me to the camp.

On entering the camp gates, Captain Henshaw greeted me.

"Mrs Everard! You aren't still here?"

"Yes. Why? Aren't I supposed to be? I asked, thinking with horror that perhaps some order had been issued that wives were not to visit husbands any more. Just then Ray came.

"Oh Everard, I'm telling your wife she shouldn't be here…"

"What?" said Ray. "Why, sir?"

"Well, you know," he said. "They are all going – or gone".

I smiled. "I'm not flapping off!"

"Well," pulling his moustache down. "Think about it. Things don't look very pleasant to me, and it won't be very pleasant here soon."

"Ray, what do you think we ought to do?"

"I…don't…know", Ray replied slowly. "I'll ask Major Smith, the domestic affairs man and I'll ring you this evening and tell you what he says."

But Henshaw had done the trick. He had woken me from my dream. I was a bit nervous again from that time. At last I saw how desperate things were… We'll hold them at Batu Pahat! My God, they were in Johore, straight on the road to Singapore!

Ray rang me.

"Darling," he said, "under these conditions it would be a wise thing if you put your name down for a boat at the P & O".

"All right, I will".

From that moment, I made preparations. I went to the P & O office. It was a long walk as they had evacuated themselves from Raffles Square to a house in Tanglin for safety. I saw a man Ray knew and had Martin and my name put down for a passage to the UK. He told me to ring him every evening without fail. When I told Madge, she was very worried and could not decide what to do…stay in Singapore?…No, Bill Ross put his foot down. She was left to choose between Australia, South Africa or home. She put her name down for all three.

Every day I rang and every day the same answer. "NO, no news."

I longed to hear there was news, so that I could get Martin away and yet I dreaded it. I made other preparations. I had a T.A.B jab. I got in the two jabs. Martin only had one. I bought all the knitting wool I could find – there wasn't much about and I bought the last tweed suit in John Little's. I didn't bother to try it on. I just went up to the assistant and asked:

"That red suit. How much?"

"Sixty-four dollars, madam".

"Here you are. No, I'll chance it fitting me."

And when I got it back and tried it on, amazingly, it was a perfect fit, perhaps a little long in the skirt.

Martin started cutting his eye-teeth and, as I feared, he was running a temperature. He was now eighteen months old – a large child and a good one.

One day, Ray told me that a convoy was coming in any day and in all probability they would be the boats that would take us off. Also, the Japs were getting unpleasantly nearer. It was not a very nice feeling. I sort of felt a Jap would jump out at me at any minute.

I rang Mary up and told her that I would be going. She said:

"I shall stay, I can't leave Grev. How can I leave Singapore? If the Japs come, we shall shoot ourselves".

"I must go, Mary, because of Martin"

"Yes, you have the child to think of. Of course you must go. Well, goodbye my dear and the best of luck".

(It wasn't until two years later or so when I re-met Mary and heard her terrible story. She had decided to go right at the end. On the 3rd boat out and she had arranged to meet Nellie and Jean on the boat. There was awful confusion and she did not find them that night and the next day at sea she searched for them. They were not on the boat. She heard nothing more of them for years. Then she heard that they would not leave their husbands and had been put on the SS Kuala. This was sunk by the Japanese. Nellie, wife of the No1, Fire Brigade, Singapore, was drowned. Jean, beautiful, young, golden girl she was, had been incredibly brave, going in and out of the water rescuing people, getting them onto the sands of Paluh, a small island off Singapore. Jean had been recaptured and was taken back to Singapore and it was later heard that she was sent to Japan. She was never heard of since.)

But to return… I was all ready, my two suitcases packed and waiting. The tension was terrific and I saw at last the extreme urgency of getting out. On January 29th 1942, I rang Stogden in the morning. I was getting sick of ringing Stogden and always the same answer. Though I dreaded also hearing anything different as it meant parting from Ray, yet I longed to hear something because of Martin. Was ever a woman more torn!

This time, instead of the usual answer, he said:

"Will you ask your husband to ring me this evening?"

Ray was given night leave. At seven, he telephoned Stogden, who told Ray to come over and see him. The siren sounded an alert so Ray left me sitting under the stairs in the hall doorway. Martin had such a temperature I thought I would not risk him in the trench. It was a nasty raid and the building shook and I could see flashes and fires. From Johore, continual flashes….guns!

There were two further raids before Ray returned which was about eleven and the last raid was about to finish.

I was still under the stairs where he had left me.

"I've had a grim time", he said. "Not a taxi…not a car. Walked all through the raids. I sheltered once and when I did get to the end of that God-awful road, Stogden said `It's your wife I want to see and her passport and NOW. QUICK, if she's to get on these boats'. So, quickly, darling, straight away as you are. Madge must come too".

Madge now offered the car and Ray to drive it. So we all got in. All the sleepy Ross children and Martin wrapped in a blanket. There was a congested mass of cars at the bottom of the hill when we arrived at the house. There was a fighting mass of men trying to get their womenfolk into the house. I got in at last, in my turn, leaving Martin with Ray who was talking and listening to a group of men. It was a hot night and the heat was bad in the blacked out overcrowded room. I saw Stogden, seated at a table, surrounded by women.

"Ah, Mrs Everard, here you are at last… Passport in order…good"

All was well and he made out a ticket for me to embark on the "Duchess of Bedford" at twelve the next day.

Madge got into the room and she came up to Stogden. He was horrified.

"Three children and you are in Singapore still! I can't fix you on this boat – go over to that table there".

I'm very fond of Madge but I was glad to see that she wasn't to be on my boat. I had had enough of Madge's nerves. She got put on the "Empress of Japan" (later renamed!). Madge was still undecided where to go.

I rejoined Ray.

"All right?" he asked, anxiously handing over Martin.

"Yes, tomorrow at twelve. `Duchess of Bedford'."

"Thank God for that. I've been through hell out here. Thank God you're on a boat"

I did not say much. I was too upset…too full….too broken….and the whole thing was too big for me. But luckily and fool that I was, I did think that all was well….that Singapore would hold. And that I would be back in a year! I really thought that.

Thank God that I did. Had I thought or had I any vision, I would have had the horror of choosing between husband and child. As it was, I was not bitterly unhappy…only unhappy at leaving Ray. Not crazy with grief as I would have been had I any idea how serious things were and what was going to happen.

Also, Ray did not tell me the Japanese were at the Causeway.

We returned to the flat, Madge weeping to her dining room. She still slept there in spite of the exasperated protests of the owners. I put Martin in his cot for the first time for ages and it was the last time he would ever sleep in it as, we were told, we would not be allowed to take it with me. We ate cold pork pie and went to bed. Ray was very silent and would not talk, saying:

"Let's go to sleep."

I have often thought this over. I believe, now, he was very upset and did not want to talk for fear I would guess how bad everything was and he probably thought, in those circumstances, he would have difficulty getting me to board the boat. We were only allowed to take hand luggage so that meant leaving the cot and the pram behind. So I only had two suitcases in the world so, I decided, whatever was said, my sewing machine was going on board.

Ray and I woke early, both feeling so unhappy. I got all ready in good time before the raids. Ray borrowed a car from one of the Volunteers to take me to the Docks. We got everything downstairs into the hall by nine. And then the raids began and they were very heavy, the guns crashing all around. We kept under shelter till eleven and then there was a lull…and Ray said

"We'll go now".

I said goodbye to Essa, poor thing. I hadn't known her long but she proved herself well, trustworthy and brave. Ray told her he would return and pack up the cot and pram and see her.

Madge had gone off earlier. It took us an hour to get to the docks, which were only about three miles away. I saw thick black smoke in the dock's direction. There were so many detours and traffic jams, owing to the bombing, which with the convoy in the harbour, were all on the docks. We were worried lest we be caught in a raid and too miserable to speak.

Also, it was obvious, that there was a serious fire at the docks and I was sick with fear that it was the boats.

We turned in at the Dock gates. The fire was very close now and black billowing smoke over all. Ray backed the little car by an iron shed. There were fires burning all over the wharf and hoses all over the place and a great fire belching black smoke – but it was on the wharf.

I saw the "Duchess", grey painted. And, carrying Martin, picked my way through the hoses and fires and up the gangway. Ray quickly got my luggage on board, saw my steward and asked him to look after me… What a hope!

He did not stay longer than ten minutes on board. Both of us believe in quick partings. He kissed me twice and also Martin.

"Goodbye dearest, take care of Martin". And he went.

I cried and, crying, looked out of the porthole in the passage and I saw Ray disappearing round a corner of the iron shed. Round a corner!

In my sorrow, I thought of that other time. A brain is an amazing thing. Even so miserable, seeing Ray go, my memory flashed back four years and I saw him again going round the corner of Queens Gate Gardens.

In the afternoon we began moving away. We all crowded on deck, tears running down our faces. There were soldiers cheering and waving as we left. We were going south. I suppose it was the only way, with the Japanese to the north. The little island receded, women were crying, women were trying to comfort each other.

I looked at Singapore with tears streaming down my face. Some woman said to me:

"Terrible to think what is going to happen there…"

We watched till we could no longer pick out landmarks. The "Empress of Japan" was following us with, I presume, Madge on board.

And so we went. And so ended my four years in Malaya, so full, so happy, so abruptly ended.

Interlude – Journey Two

The rest is taken straight from my record, which I wrote up on the last night on board in dock in Liverpool Harbour, so that I should not forget it. We were not allowed to keep a diary on board, for obvious reasons.

March 31st 1942

Well, this voyage is nearly over, safely I hope. I saw England today, Liverpool and barrage balloons. Somebody said to me, "Do you see that buoy? When we round that, you will be safe, from the sea anyway."

What a relief. Sixteen thousand miles of tension, of unceasing vigilance over Martin and two months of carrying, every waking hour, two lifebelts.

We had air raids to Batavia. I saw two bombs fall on the second day out from Singapore. I had just settled myself down on the boat deck with Martin, when the guns fired and there were the bombs whistling down.

Conditions on board were grim. Women with children had the cabins, where possible. Single and childless women were to sleep below where the Indian troops had slept. There had not been any time for cleaning and some women and children were sleeping on deck.

Martin teethed for three weeks and cut his second eye-tooth during the voyage. He, along with the other children, all had gastro enteritis. He was very ill for five days and even brought up water. It took him weeks to recover. He also had impetigo. The filth on board was somewhat shocking. We had to wait on ourselves as far as Durban, which was harrowing as I had to leave Martin all by himself at a dining table and go and fight for food, queuing in the unspeakable kitchen, knowing that, if a submarine popped up at that moment, there would be no hope of getting back to him.

To see Martin, sucking his fingers after crawling around on a deck where, God only knows, what had walked there, has cured me forever of my pretty little frills and fancies on baby hygiene. Anyway, all the children were ill after a week. The food was good but dirty, with cockroaches in things and white maggots with black heads in the bread.

There was no proper hospital on board and one most inadequate ship's doctor, who, to quite him 'was totally unused to women's ailments'. Six babies died; two of enteritis, one of pneumonia, one of septicaemia and one born prematurely. The Purser also died, poor soul, as did an elderly woman of heatstroke. We got quite used to funerals but never used to the pathetic sight of a tiny, white shrouded parcel being commended to Almighty God and the Great Deep. However, Nature counterbalanced, six babies were born on board.

I think that I must have seen all there is to see on a boat. Albatross, whales, sharks, everything.

The way across to Batavia was awful. Batavia (Jakarta, now) looked flat, grey, grim and hot. We did not go ashore and were there for only three days, which was quite long enough. On one of the nights there, we had the worst raids of all, in terms of comfort. All of us were held in the dining room for two hours and really the heat was too much. Many women fainted and babies screamed eternally. I just sat with Martin laying, sweating, on the table in front of me. I now know what the Black Hole of Calcutta was like.

Many troopships, full of cheering men, came in while we were in Batavia harbour. I wonder what happened to them. On our last day, the Empress of Australia arrived with a lot more evacuees. The Empress of Japan had gone on ahead of us two days before from Singapore and so it was all the way. She left soon after we arrived and we left as the Australia arrived. All came through safely, which I think is one of the small great triumphs of the war. Between them, at a very rough reckoning, these three boats must have been carrying at least three thousand women and children.

I did hear a rumour that the Japan sighted a sub. We didn't, all we got were bombs but that was quite enough. We did have the heart-stopping klaxon alert, the signal to marshal to our lifeboat immediately. Oh, what panic every time, collecting one's children. Mostly, they turned out to be whales.

There was one time when the alert went one morning. It was an unknown aircraft but it turned out to be one of ours. It signalled that we were a sitting target for the enemy, with all the white objects on deck. They were the hundreds and hundreds of nappies spread and drying on the decks! After that, we were told they must be dried below decks and, for ever after, the passages were looped with drying nappies.

The ship zigzagged, escorted by the Dutch East Indies Air Force for some of the way to Colombo. The long harbour there was packed with shipping and we anchored nearly at the outer end. Every kind of warship seemed to be there. In town, I changed my Singapore money and spent some on knitting wool and drugs for Martin. He was still very ill, constantly being sick. Colombo had organised an Evacuation Committee, which was most helpful, and a crèche, where I did leave Martin once, hating to do so. But it was so hard, carting him about everywhere. He was just at that stage when he hadn't the confidence to walk alone, so I had to carry him everywhere.

On the boat, I could not leave him alone anywhere for <u>one single minute</u> in case a sub' came along so I did feel that he could be left in the crèche while I did some shopping. We stayed in Colombo for a week and I would like very much to record the kindness of Colombo. This is the sort of thing that occurred.

Martin and I were having a meal in a restaurant that had enormous brass elephants and when I went to pay my bill, I was told, "Madam, the lady over there wishes to pay for your meal." Unknown lady, I have never forgotten you!

I met Madge. She seemed to be having a wonderful time. She told me she had decided to leave the boat at Durban as she was nervous of the Atlantic.

Then we carried on, zigzagging about the Indian Ocean for about ten days. One evening, we heard that Singapore had fallen. There was a hush over the boat that could be felt. I was horrified, too horrified for words. Ray was a prisoner of war.

At last we got to Durban, unhappy, uncomfortable lot of women that we were. Durban was very pleasant. We ate all the nicest things that we could, having been told dreadful tales of starving England by the stewards. I don't know why they did this as there was never anything more untrue.

One hundred and fifty naval men came on board with medical staff. Durban had its horrors for us sure enough. The ship had to be fumigated. It appeared that bugs had been found. I never found any in my cabin, only cockroaches. We were all got off the ship by six in the morning, put on buses and distributed to various hotels. There was a notice on the board that we all had to read. This said that we were all to be back to re-embark in twenty four hours and that we would be fined one hundred pounds if we were later than four o'clock the next day.

Needless to say, I would have given anything to stay in a decent hotel and have a lovely hot bath. We were put in a disgusting room with greasy, torn mats and…bugs and enormous cockroaches that ran along the bedstead. I did not sleep at all that night but Martin did and I kept the horrors off him all night. The sooner I got out of that room the better and at an early breakfast, I met Mrs Ferguson, of Singapore Cold Storage days. She looked rather grim.

"How did you sleep?" I asked.

"Oh, my dear," she said. "Bugs!"

So we worked off our overwrought feelings on the proprietress and decided to get out of there, the twenty four hours being up, and go back to the ship. When we arrived at the dock gates, feeling exhausted and having spent three shillings and nine pence on a taxi, which we could ill afford, we were confronted by a notice on the gangway. Beneath a salubrious picture of a skull and crossbones, were the words:

"SHIP FUMIGATION IN PROGRESS"

A ship guard, as his cap proclaimed him to be, stood on sentry. Well, I was very annoyed and gave vent to a lot of feelings that had been nurturing for some weeks. He listened patiently and then, soothingly, said:

"Come back at two o'clock, it will be all right then, madam. Why don't you go and sit on the beach? Lovely on the beach this morning."

So we took his advice and sat on the beach. Most of the ship's company and passengers were already on the beach. Punctually at two o'clock, we returned but I cannot think why we were so anxious to get back seeing the discomfort of our voyage. The notice was still there and the same guard on duty.

"No, she isn't ready." He said.

I was furious. It did seem to be the last finishing touch to all the trial, irritations and hardships we had to endure and the whole thing seemed totally unnecessary to me. Officialdom! I sat on a soapbox the guard gave me as a peace offering I suppose and I said:

"In about an hour's time, you are going to have nine hundred or so women and babies and children here. You see if I am not right."

And we told him about the threatening notice on the board. He looked very serious and, of course, that's what happened. They began to arrive and soon the quay was packed with tired mothers and children.

A wind rose up, which blew black coal dust at us from an enormous heap nearby. It was hot and we all wanted water to drink. A stevedore kindly got me a cup of tea and Martin obligingly went to sleep on a sack under a boat. I cannot think what those with really young children did. We were all waiting on that wharf until five thirty and what really did annoy us was that the hundred and fifty naval personnel were allowed on board and just had to look on at our discomfort. I learned later that they felt very badly about it. I also learned that the reason why we had to wait was that the crew, the day before, had refused top leave the ship as there was some trouble about shore accommodation and that had made the fumigating late in starting.

Next day, the Duchess sailed for Cape Town with as bad tempered, disgruntled cargo of women as could be found anywhere. However, things did get better. The Navy manned the guns, thereby relieving the crew, and became efficient nursemaids to babies, amused mothers and entertained children and organized a hospital and clinic. In turn, the stewards, who had been doing crew's work, were told to wait on us at table; the cabin stewards then cleaned the cabins, which we had been doing ourselves and so conditions generally improved.

I made a friend of Chief Petty Officer Cook and sometimes he looked after Martin for me. He was in charge of my lifeboat party so Martin could be left safely with him, near the lifeboat, while I went and washed clothes and so on, with the arrangement, if anything happened, I would meet him at the lifeboat with Martin already there. Gradually each man in charge found himself looking after five or six babies!

Cape Town, I thought, was lovely and I wished I had had more money. I did not dare to spend too much, not knowing how or where I would get more. The officials in Cape Town did their best to persuade me to stay in South Africa but I wouldn't consider it. I filled one man with righteous indignation by saying, "No thanks. I'll go to England, I'm tired of colonial muddles", which was really most unfair, rude and ignorant of me. But I do wonder what would have happened to my life if I had decided to stay.

I had heard that Madge did get off at Durban while we were there and then changed her mind and tried to get on the Duchess of Bedford to go to England but they would not let her. Three hundred or so did leave the ship in South Africa and that made for less congestion. The women, who had been sleeping several decks below and on deck even, now had cabins at last.

We stayed five days in Cape Town and then went on to Freetown. No on was allowed off the ship and we only stayed there two days. During that time, the decks, which had been getting cleaner as the crew washed them daily, got filthy again owing to an oiler alongside. The horrible ship spent ages stoking up every five minutes and everything got covered with coal dust. Then we were off again, zigzag, zigzagging without an escort, just relying on speed. Goodness knows where we went, halfway round the Atlantic, it seemed.

And it began to get cold. I kept up my tactics of hardening Martin to it, keeping him on deck all day. He slept in the morning, near our lifeboat, on deck under four blankets. The sea became rough, which I loved. The Duchess rolled everywhere. She was a flat-bottomed boat, designed for the St Lawrence River and was rather high. They called her the 'Drunken Duchess'!

One evening, just before dark, I saw little, red winking lights. It was England or Ireland. I put Martin in the bunk that night, relieved to think that the journey was nearly over. Of Ray, I did not dare to think.

It was some time before we disembarked. There were the same endless queues to be interviewed by Immigration officials. I could understand this at other ports but why at home? We weren't immigrating, we were returning because we had to, to our own country. Inspection of passports, receiving gas masks but none for young children, however.

The Colonial Office, well, they were all very kind but it would not have been fitting if this voyage had not ended in the muddle of all muddles.

All of our heavy luggage had been offloaded the day before and we were told to keep only a little hand luggage for the night but, I think the Captain must have forgotten what he was dealing with, because being females and what with all the paraphernalia that children need, the hand luggage was somewhat alarming when piled up! And this is what caused the muddle. All of the large luggage had been sorted out most carefully, all in correct alphabetical order and then this torrent of 'hand' luggage poured down into the Customs' shed, followed by us all arriving as well. We had to sort it all out so imagine six hundred dispirited and exhausted women, few without children all looking for and only intent on finding their own property.

I found my sewing machine and green suitcase under the letter E section and luckily I got a soldier with an armlet with 'Fatigue' written on it to help me and he found the rattan case.

After an hour and a half, I found my case of foodstuffs and dressing case, all the while carrying Martin around. But it was there and there only that I did better than other women, in losing all my possessions in Malaya. Those who had brought all their stuff, and there were some, I reckoned they would have been lucky to have left that shed in under six hours.

Having gathered my luggage together, I left the soldier on guard over it and joined the queue for the Customs Officer and then one for the railway warrant and, most important, five pounds! After that, I was put in a taxi and sent to the station, where I had an unpleasant ten minutes when my luggage went missing. I found it and it was all put on a truck and I sat Martin on top while I changed my railway warrant for a ticket. Then I got in the train, intending to go to London. But I found it was Easter and so, I got out at Bletchley and stayed over with my aunt and uncle.

As I had been two months at sea, I had no idea where any of my family was and, discovering that it was Easter, my plans were upset. I was afraid that I might not find anyone in London but Aunt Lilla and Uncle George were surely to be found at the Vicarage. So I left the train really on the spur of the moment, got a taxi and, peering through the glass front door, saw the old, family green-leaf plates. Yes, they were there!

The next moment, Aunt Lilla opened the door and was amazed, delighted and thankful to see me, her niece, sitting in tears on the doorstep. I felt weak and dead tired. It seemed so astounding to be back in England.

After Easter, I went on to London; stayed with Daddy, while I sorted out my finances and ration cards. He had given me up for lost and drowned me several times even though I did cable him from Durban.

So what more is there to write? This is the end of the tale of Malaya as I know it. It is four years, this year, 1945, since I saw Ray. Four years, one for each of the happy years in Malaya. Four years, in which I have known utter loneliness, misery and mental worry. I have received four postcards from Ray, for which I thank God. I have waited, seeing no end to this war, through air raids here, Dieppe rehearsals and D Day and its terrific preparations, buzz bombs and Victory in Europe Day, in which I rejoiced with everyone with a hope that I had not had before.

Yesterday, the world was in awe with the news of the atom bomb dropped on Japan. Today, as I finish writing this for you, Martin, to read one day, I hear that Russia has declared war on Japan. So, there is no more to write, only to wait as usual. No, not as usual, but with hope!

(Emsworth, August, 1945)

Chapter Thirteen – The War Years

For the first two years I lived with Ursula in Church Path, Emsworth. She was all alone. Cecil spent his war years mostly in Africa. Life consisted mostly of looking after our children, through endless childish diseases and I going down with severe tonsillitis, endless attacks quite as bad as my 1941 attack. And much the same as one had to fight through them. There was daily shopping and queuing for food to be done. And there were air raids, which prevented one from going to bed when ill. One just had to fight on.

Peter, Ursula, Martin and Barbara, 1943

Quite a bit of time was spent in Ursula's good, deep Anderson shelter, night and day. The back door was never locked and at night our packed suitcases were put by the door so that, having herded sleepy children out of their beds, we could pick them up on our way out. And how good those boys were! Peter, Ursula's eldest, was about three and Martin two. Later, there was David, the result of one of Cecil's period of leave, to be carried out. I think that the children got so used to it, they really walked to the shelter in their sleep, and went straight off in their bunks while Ursula and I listening anxiously.

Sometimes all was quiet and nothing would happen and presently the blessed 'All Clear' would sound. Sometimes, however, we would just have got the children back into the house when the siren would go again. Down we would all go again, this time with searchlights lighting up the sky and the sound of gunfire and knowing we had to be really sharp getting under cover. Then, the sound – 'comer, comer, comer' of the heavily loaded bombers, the guns firing and the crump, crump of bombs falling, close or far off in Portsmouth perhaps.

On one occasion, Martin recalls, part of a plane landed in the Collins' next door garden and we were both excited and horrified as in the ensuing conflagration, its complement of unused shells went off, leaving tracers behind as they exploded and flew over the school wall behind the shelter. A narrow escape but what excitement for the two boys!

As mothers with young children, we could not do much to help the war effort but we knitted and made toys and all sorts of things for numerous Red Cross sales.

I started a little cottage industry – literally.

Country Cottage
from a log of wood

Using pieces of firewood logs, wooden cotton reels and bits of cut up slivers of wood, I glued them together with stinking, brown fish glue, softened in a small cast iron pot, which I still have to this day. I smeared the glue up the sides and when painted, it became ivy. The cotton reels were split in half to make bay windows and I cut up sticks for chimneys, doors, windows and shutters and so on. When painted, they made beautiful doorstops and bookends and raised quite a bit of money right through to 1946 and I still have one of the originals.

The cast iron glue pot

I kept my hand in with some painting, manly water colours of scenes around Emsworth – the mill pond, the harbour and down on the 'Bunny'.

Watercolour scenes around Emsworth, 1944

When the air raids eased off as they did when Hitler decided to concentrate on Russia, Ursula looked after the boys while I took Day turns at the YMCA, cooking and waiting on soldiers, sailors and marines.

Besides Canadians and a Free French camp at the back of Emsworth, there were marines for many months and, one Christmas, Ursula and I put our names down for three marines to have Christmas dinner with us. And how nice they were. They would do anything to repay our hospitality and gave us blankets, which we needed badly. I still have one in use to this day – excellent 'W.D Marines for the use of' blankets. Some of these men are still in Emsworth to this day, having married Emsworth girls. As for the two of us, a friendship with one of them went on for years. I was known as 'Duchess'.

Well, life dragged on for eighteen months and I had had no news of Ray at all and, then, I had a card, months old, just a printed thing but still, it cheered me on a bit.

80336. C.Q.M.S.. EVERARD.

DEAREST BARBARA.
        I AM FIT AND WELL
IN A PRISONER OF WAR CAMP.
I HOPE YOU AND MARTIN
ARE IN GOOD HEALTH.
GIVE MY REGARDS TO ALL AT
HOME. ALL MY LOVE TO YOU
AND MARTIN.
        YOUR DEVOTED HUSBAND
                RAY.

The first card from Ray

I wrote back to him but what I wrote that displeased the censor, I do not know.

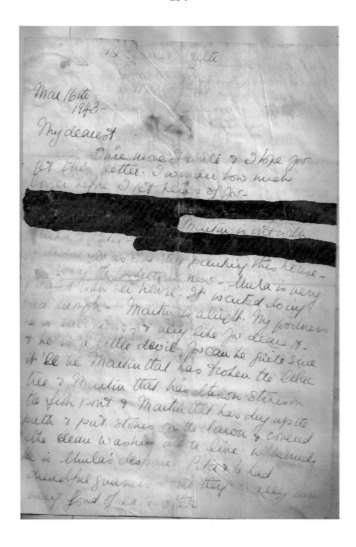

In the whole time that I waited for him, I only received three more cards.

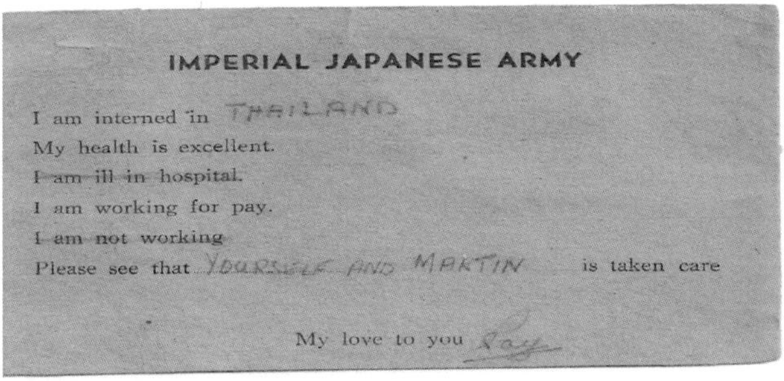

IMPERIAL JAPANESE ARMY

I am interned in *THAILAND*
My health is excellent.
I am ill in hospital.
I am working for pay.
I am not working
Please see that *YOURSELF AND MARTIN* is taken care

My love to you *Ray*

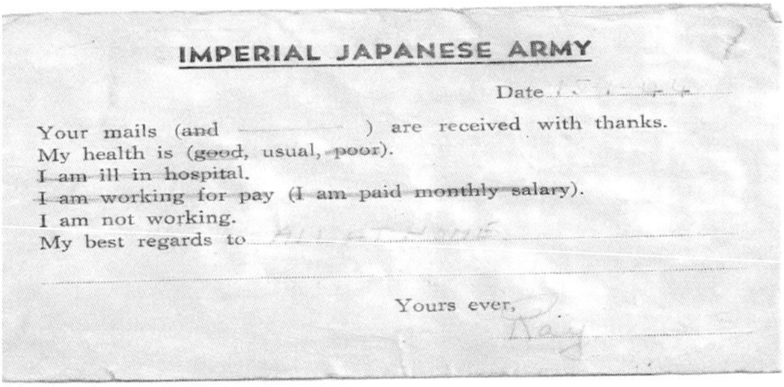

IMPERIAL JAPANESE ARMY

Date _____

Your mails (and _____) are received with thanks.
My health is (good, usual, poor).
I am ill in hospital.
I am working for pay (I am paid monthly salary).
I am not working.
My best regards to _____

Yours ever,
Ray

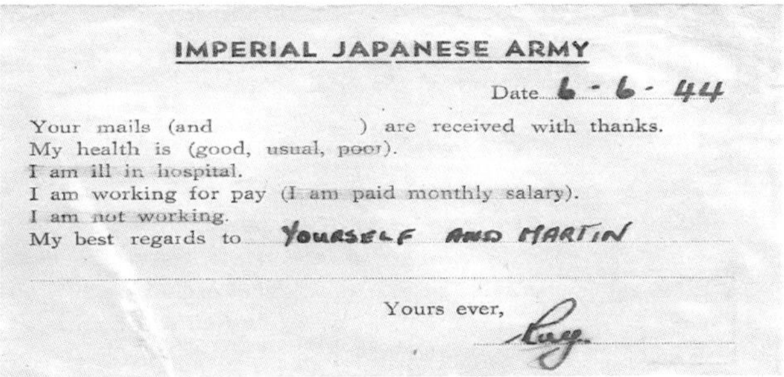

IMPERIAL JAPANESE ARMY

Date **6 - 6 - 44**

Your mails (and _____) are received with thanks.
My health is (good, usual, poor).
I am ill in hospital.
I am working for pay (I am paid monthly salary).
I am not working.
My best regards to *YOURSELF AND MARTIN*

Yours ever,
Ray

I didn't leave Emsworth much as it wasn't fair on Ursula. I saw Daddy once or twice. He was a full time ARP Warden in Notting Hill Gate throughout the blitz. We saw Ruth on occasions. She was having a very bad time with her marriage to Johnny, into which I will not go.

Martin and Barbara, 1943

One day, when Martin and I had been about two years living with Ursula, she dashed in while I was having lunch.

"Barbara, I've just heard that Mrs Patterson has died. Go now and ask Mrs Scaddgell if you can have No 4," she exclaimed.

I went and, although a lot of the people in Church Path though it unfair, she let me have the little house 'because my husband was a prisoner of war'. I had been assiduously collecting house stuff for the last two years and with what Ursula lent me, I was able to furnish very simply the kitchen, living room and one bedroom. It had no bathroom and an outside lavatory. I had an aged hip-bath and I bathed in this every day with a kettle of hot water.

Martin went to school at three and a half years of age! Old Mr and Mrs Ayling were the school caretakers and there was a gap in the wall between their house and the school and, one day, Martin, who used to stand on the top of the air-raid shelter and watch over the wall, was so lonely when Peter went to school that he slipped through and just followed the children back into school after a morning break. When the mistress did the roll call, she realised that there was an extra child there and asked, innocently, whether there was anyone whose name she hadn't called out. Not to be left out, Martin put up his hand! She realised that he would have to be turned out and sent home but I expect that this got to her as, seeing the child's distress, she said, "not now, Martin, but you can come back in the afternoon," as Peter was summoned to take him home. So, I had a bit of time to myself after that.

By annexing a bit of derelict land next door, I acquired the ground where Numbers 1, 2 and 3 Church Path had once been. Their foundations were still there but in the squares between the walls, I grew all the vegetables and soft fruit that I could, strawberries, blackcurrants and raspberries, to supplement our rations. I was quite thin at this time. Most of my rations went to Martin and I never touched sugar, jam or sweets. I think that my chief diet was fried rice and coffee!

No 4 had an upright, brick and block air raid shelter and during the summer months, Martin and I permanently slept in it. Our beds were laid on the bales of straw that I used to protect the strawberries. There was far less worry this way than dragging the child out of the house each time the siren went. Martin had a birthday one year and he became the proud owner of a hammer, a piece of wood and a bag of nails!

Martin with air raid shelter, 1945

Though the great air raids that Ursula had been through were over by the time that I got back to England, we still had some that could be quite nasty and, of course, the doodle bugs, were quite horrible. Lilian, Ray's sister, and her two children, Julia and Marshall, stayed with me for quite a time. They were living in Purley and Frank didn't like her being there so close to London. Lilian used to sing her two children to sleep with a rendition of 'Now the day is over, night is drawing nigh' and, not to be left out, had to do the same for Martin too. Fifi stayed for quite a time to get a rest and I was delighted to have them all.

Hubie, Ray's youngest brother, came and stayed when his ship was in Portsmouth and this enabled me to go off to the cinema as he was able to look after Martin. On the whole, I wasn't too bad a wife in these dreadful years of loneliness and unending worry. No words can describe it, the 'not knowing'. I didn't really go out with men, the three marines used to come and see me but it was all quite harmless.

Then I met an artist and I drifted into a ridiculous affair with him, which shocked Church Path. It was born of sheer loneliness and he was kind but an exasperating sort of individual. He had decorated my hallway with a lovely silvery painting of pansies and, one day, it came over me that I could stick him no more and I told him to clear out and I flung that beautiful painting after him. This is the only time hat I have ever been unfaithful to Ray and it took place after the war in Europe had ended and I had that long wait for the war in the Far East to end.

Martin at the back of No 4 with one of the cats, 1944

Martin and I had two white cats, Bits and Bats, who were both females and who were always having beautiful pastel-coloured kittens. Bits had blue eyes and was stone deaf and Bats had yellow ones and could hear perfectly. One day, I was doing some painting with a pot of red enamel paint, Bats was lying under the table and the pot fell on her. I put her in the sink and wiped her with paraffin first to get the thickest paint off, then I washed her in hot, soapy water. The result was that the thinned paint dyed her beautiful fur a delicate shade of pink. Very beautiful!

She was on the front doorstep one day after that and the Emsworth road sweeper came along. He stared at her.

"Look at that cat!"

"Why, what's the matter with her?" I said, thinking it rather a joke to pretend that she was a normal cat.

"Bless me! Look at her! She's pink!"

"Pink! I can't see any pink!"

"Well, then, I don't know. There must be summat wrong wrong with me eyes," and he shook his head sadly. But I told him the sad story then.

Hubie, being in wireless on his ship, dicked up my radio so that when all the BBC stations had closed down, I could get such places as All India.

I used to listen until late at night as there was always hope of a message as lists of men alive or dead were read out. I had one message via Vatican Radio once and also one from a 'ham' that Ray's name had come over and that he was alive, thank God!

And in August 1945, I was listening, listening and suddenly I heard that it was all over. I could not believe it. I tuned back to the BBC wavelengths from overseas. Yes, they were saying it too!

Martin was asleep in his bed upstairs, safe from all the raids these last few months. All was quiet and still. I went to the front door and then I could hear the ships in Portsmouth Harbour, their sirens going. I went back indoors. Suddenly I felt that I must do something, tell someone or burst. So, I picked up my father's old Sussex sheep bell and tore up and down Church Path, ringing it. They were all jolly cross with me.

"Is that all? We thought it was a fire."

Of course, for them the war had ended months before but, next day, they realised the importance and forgave me. Soon, we had another Street Tea and Bonfire for V. J. Day. Then a very worrying time ensued, a crescendo of worry in which, I think, I was near a nervous breakdown. Many of the wives of P.O.W's had news of their relatives and I had heard nothing at all and I was getting desperate. Then, just when the whole family were beginning to worry as well, this telegram arrived.

"Arrived safely in India. Hope to be home soon. Writing. Ray."

Then at last I had a letter. How wonderful this was. Here it is:

'4th Sept.　　　　　C/O Recovered P.O.W Mail Centre, Bombay, India.

Dearest,

At last I am free and at Rangoon at present. The American Air Force took us out of Thailand.

I find it practically impossible to write anything at the moment as am far too excited with the possibility of seeing you again shortly. The organisation at Rangoon is perfect and the reception given us by the Red Cross was overwhelming. Everybody is doing their utmost to make everything as easy and comfortable as possible.

I have been passed fit by the Medical Officer (Female) here so hope to be on my way very shortly.

Eight years ago was Black Friday, if you remember the day I left 45. Thank God I am fit. There are thousands who unfortunately thanks to the blankety blank Japanese will never return home.

All my love, dearest, to you and a bit for Martin as well.

Your dearest husband,

Ray.'

There! How I treasured it and read and re-read it. And fancy him remembering that date that was the day he left England, all those years ago.

Well, we all waited and made preparations. On November the 5th just as we in Church Path were going to celebrate the first peacetime Guy Fawkes night with fireworks and a huge bonfire, the following telegram arrived, in a 'Priority' marked envelope. 'Service, Liverpool.'

'Arrived safely. See you soon. Ray':

Everybody went dotty with joy and danced and sang all around the bonfire. And then, they all put their flags out and decorated Church Path for he was the C.P.P.O.W!

Next day, Martin met him at Havant station. He was very thin and gaunt and had new, deep lines on his face, which told their story of strain and illness – a quiet, different man yet it was Ray. It must have been a great moment for him to meet his son and that son was a very proud boy, quite overpowered by the occasion, one which he remembers very clearly to this day.

Ray was lucky to have the little house in Church Path to recover in. So many P.O.W's did not, only having a room or, worse, had to live with relatives. As it was he and Martin were able to enjoy and get to know each other and to have a real home life. We consider that this was a great factor in his recovery.

The first few hours were strained and queer. We were two strangers but, in bed, that night the tension snapped. I told him about my affair with the artist and he told me about a nurse in Rangoon, so that was squared up. And we wept and for a man to weep is a terrible experience to see but I personally believe that this is the reason that he has never had the ghastly recurring dreams that so many of these men still have.

Barbara, Ray and Martin by Emsworth Harbour, 1946

We had six months, happy as a whole, which towards the end was somewhat marred by a severe shortage of money. We managed to make Christmas a bit special for Martin. Hubie and Ray constructed and marvellous O gauge railway in one of the bedrooms only for Martin to come out with measles and have to be confined to a darkened room. We spent a lot of time together and Ray had a Jaguar SS and we visited Ruth and her two, Ben and Nicky and went over to Laurel and Johnny Johnson..

Then to my disgust, rage and great unhappiness, Guthries asked him to go out early to get the rubber estates running again. After a frightful flap and a cascade of telegrams – 'passage cancelled', passage not cancelled' and finally 'disregard cancellations' – he finally sailed on the 'Indrapoera' Southampton. Martin and I saw him off, both of us utterly miserable.

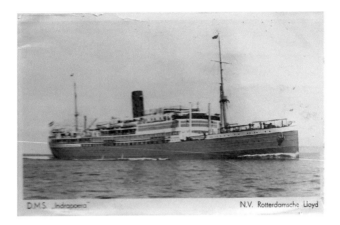

D.M.S Indrapoera

I was so infuriated and grief-stricken at being left behind. The memory of the first parting in 1937 was all too fresh and knowing what a shocking letter writer he was then, I was so afraid the same thing would happen again. Also, it must be remembered, that I had been through a period of great strain and worry and it was hard, after comparatively so short a time, for him to go off again. Anyway, I was most upset. Martin and I returned to the little house in Church Path and sat down and straightaway there started a disgraceful correspondence, of chaotic posts, from a despairing wife; of preparations; moans; much love; and most complicated finances, which I defy anyone to sort out. I can't. It really becomes a sort of diary as I wrote a bit every day.

But what of Ray's traumatic time spent as a P.O.W at the hands of the Japanese for three and a half years. This is his as much as he remembered.

Ray's Story

After I had got Barbara and Martin on to the boat, I went back to the Geylang camp for a while. In early February, 'A' Company, Malacca Volunteer Corp, instead of three platoons of Malays and one of Europeans and HQ staff, consisted of a medley of Europeans from all sorts of units and a few Malays. (All the Malays, except my storeman and a driver disappeared before capitulation). We took up a position in Orchard Road where we were subjected to aerial machine gunning and heavy shelling passing overhead. A mortar bomb did hit our kitchen and put the electricity out of action. By Friday 13th, another Black Friday, the Japs were on the Island and had taken the Thompson Reservoir. I knew that with the main water supply gone, Singapore must fall.

In addition, on the other side of the island, the Japs had pushed their way to the Alexandra Hospital and had entered it and slaughtered a number of patients, including one who was on the operating table. Doctor Donaldson, who was our civilian doctor in private life, not knowing that his wife, a nursing sister, had left Singapore on the morning of the 13th, went in his car to the Hospital and was shot dead on the steps as he got out of his car. So much for the Japs' respect for the Red Cross.

During the evening of this 'Black Friday' the Malay driver was in a garden some two or three houses away from our HQ when he heard a shot fired from a tree the other side of Orchard Road. He fired back and thought that he might have shot a Jap. He was delighted to discover later that he had shot 'a good Jap' – a dead one – caught by his belt to the tree.

On Saturday 14th, we were subjected to further aerial attacks, so our C.O decided to move HQ further away from Orchard Road as planes were machine-gunning the houses and gardens there, presumably spotting for their mortars, which, by then, must have been somewhere near Tanglin. During the night, we moved to a Chinese Towkay's house, which the owner had vacated, leaving two Sikh jaggas in charge. We took over n outhouse, which the Chinese had used for household washing and which now made an ideal kitchen. There were plenty of stores, which the owner had abandoned, cases of tinned meat, beans and other vegetables.

During Sunday 15th, the Capitulation was signed and, on hearing the news, we destroyed all documents and checked all the ammunition in case anyone had lead-nosed or dum-dum bullets, which were against the Geneva Convention. The Pay books and uniforms of the Malay store-man and driver were burned and they changed into civilian clothes and were given ten dollars each and told to find their way back to Malacca, which they did. After the war, I had to testify that they stayed with us to the end so that they could collect all the pay due to them.

When the Sikh jaggas saw us burning the papers, they knew the Japanese had won so they promptly destroyed the glass signs and anything else that would indicate that they had been working for the Chinese. In the evening, orders came through that all military personnel must stay where they were, remove black out curtains, if any, and switch on all lights or light lamps. The electricity was still functioning in this part of Singapore so we switched them all on and, I remember, our Company Commander, with tears running down his cheeks, shaking hands with each one of us that were left. It was impossible at that moment to say anything.

I dragged a mattress out of an air raid shelter and put it on the floor of the living room and tried to sleep. We could not talk. In the morning, I cooked a stew for the twenty or so officers and men, who were by this time gathered at the house and then just mooched around and waited until we were ordered to move to Changi Barracks. We filled our haversacks with all the tinned food we could carry and walked to Changi. By this time, the Japs were arriving by the lorry-load, to me they looked like grinning apes with glasses. We missed the centre of Singapore and so saw few Asiatics; and the shops we passed were al shuttered. It was approximately sixteen miles to Changi, a distance we covered before evening, arriving at the Barracks just before dark.

The OR's (Other Ranks) were allotted space on the first floor of the barrack block, which, I think was designed for forty men in peacetime. There were four rows of ten beds with at least six feet between them, plus the wide verandah each side with the lavatories and washrooms at one end. The Barrack Commander's room was at the other end. I was lucky, being one of the first to arrive as I got a bed and a locker in which to put all the tinned food.

More and more troops arrived so that by morning I had to get out of bed at its foot as, at either side on the floor, were bodies, that three feet of space was occupied by three OR's. The verandahs were also jam packed. I suppose there must have been two hundred troops on each of the two floors.

Other than my army clothes, all I owned was a wallet and a watch that Barbara had given me in 1937.

Subsequently orders were issued that all watches must be handed in as they could be used as a direction finder. I. like a lot of others kept mine hidden until 1944, when the Nips became nasty and threatened that if any more watches were found, all food to the sick would be stopped. Knowing that the little, yellow bastards would, if it was to the detriment of the POW's, keep their word, I decided to hand my watch in. After the war, I collected it from Rangoon, where it had been lodged. Fortunately for me, it was not a well known or popular brand, such as a Rolex. If it had been, I would never have seen it again but it was a stainless steel waterproof watch of Swiss manufacture. A shabby looking old watch with excellent innards as it is still in good order and keeping remarkably good time in 1969, 32 years after it was given to me. (The watch is still going and has been given to my son, Martin).

The first news that Ray had been captured

During this first day of captivity, we were ordered by our own officers to hand in to Central Stores all our tins and other foodstuffs, which we had brought with us. This was done and also, on the orders of the Imperial Japanese Army, all radios, cameras and compasses were to be handed in. All the obvious items were given up but quite a selection of small items were kept and hidden, particularly spare parts for radios and the like. One of the first parties to be called out was to bury the Chinese

Volunteers, who had been machine-gunned on Changi Beach. One man, who dropped as if shot, had been left for dead. He returned with the burial party to the Barracks and remained with us, even going to Siam with one of the working parties. I saw him in Tarsoe in 1944 but I don't remember seeing him again.

It was during these early days that stories of war and surrender circulated, telling of the Ghurkas with Jap ears on strings. When a Jap was killed, they cut off his ear and threaded it in a string so that each soldier could keep an accurate tally of the Japs he had killed.

The British officers of the Ghurka regiments had great difficulty in disarming the Ghurkas on surrender. Their rifles and ammunition were handed over immediately but their kukris were a different matter. It took an awful long time to get the troops to give up this particular piece of equipment, which was not only useful as an everyday knife but which also had uses on religious and tribal ceremonies.

The Indian regiments became the Free Indian Army and joined the Japs and took over guard duties at Changi and elsewhere. Changi itself was divided up into areas with a no-man's land between each, which was patrolled by the Indian sentries. Selarang Barracks was the hospital area and to get there we had to pass through this no-man's land. On passing an Indian sentry, we had to salute him by orders of the I.J.A. However, some of the sentries, providing there were no Nips in sight and on seeing a party of British troops approaching, would have a sudden desire to see what was at the back of his sentry box. So we did not have to salute that particular sentry, such instances being few, though.

Food was in sort supply, right from the start. It was carefully rationed out under the supervision of the Quartermaster. There was not much variety:

Breakfast: A slice of rice bread. Tea – no milk or sugar
Lunch: Rice and a watery vegetable stew.

And that was all.

The usual Barracks' chores had to be done, cleaning and so on, collecting firewood, sick parades, the first of many. Two Volunteers did salt panning, with sea water in trays and leaving it to evaporate in the sun. Without this there would have been no salt with our rice. Gardens were also started, to grow vegetables to help the rice ration.

Dr Chapman was made advisor to the Officer in charge of gardening. On one occasion, he was allowed to go into Singapore to collect some manure. When he got back, he opened the bag and found it was groundnut cake and, knowing what he knew, promptly ate it! The manure then went to the kitchens! When it was given out to us, we didn't eat it for pleasure but medicinally as it tasted horrible. It was peanuts with all the oil taken out, absolutely chockfull of vitamins and had to be eaten raw.

Also, he started to culture Achatina fulica, the giant snail, which can be quite five inches long. They are edible and quite good as a food.

Malaria started to develop and dysentery. Constipation was severe with some men going for weeks and weeks without any bowel action. Ehen at last this did occur, their temperature would rise quite steeply. It was too early for beri-beri (pellagra), which was to be such a menace. But of these Changi days, I remember, chiefly, playing endless bridge, sometimes by moonlight and daily trips down to the beach to bath.
Unfortunately, this was only allowed for the first few weeks as someone swam across the Straits to Johore. Some did try to escape, a very dangerous and risky but brave procedure. What hope was there? A two thousand mile walk to the North and all around enemy held seas, with treacherous natives too terrified of the consequences to help. Mowatt, the District Officer, Alor Gajah, and another did get to the mainland but Malays betrayed them and they were taken to Kuala Lumpur. Others just went. Giles was one. He was detailed off with a party to go somewhere and the last I heard was that he was in Java.

I was in Changi for three months and then fifteen hundred of the reasonably fit men were sent to River Valley Road. This camp had been thoughtfully built by the British to house Japanese POW's! It was built on about five acres, with Singapore River on the west side, running between the camp and the Havelock Road. It consisted of about twelve huts, each one hundred and twenty feet long, made of bamboo and atap. They were open at each end.

To the left of the Gate was the Officers' hut, then the kitchen, and then next, the Volunteers huts, mine being the furthest in one corner. On the right of the Gate was the M.I. Room and then some seven or more huts in which were the British troops and two or three for the Australians. There was a large open square of ground in the middle, the Parade Ground.

The huts accommodated two hundred men in each. They were built in bays, one up, one down with four men to each bay. I was lucky to be in an upper section as the lower bays sloped so low to the ground, the men, if they wanted to stand up, had to use the passage that ran down the middle of the hut. But the upper bays had the slope of the roof in which one could stand upright. The other three men in my bay were McElfish, McKenzie and Hodgeson, all planters from Malacca. We made it as comfortable as we could, with two double bunks on either side.

In the early days at this camp, we were guarded by the crack Black Guards, who were the cream of the Dai Nippon Army, and they treated us like human beings. The villages to the East and West were within bounds so long as everyone was on roll call in the morning and the evening.

So, after a days work, we used to go down to the Chinese coffee shops. This was invaluable for me as I made contacts with the Chinese that I had known from the Cold Storage. I made arrangements with them so that, as we went to the place where we were working, at a pre-arranged spot, knapsacks would be quietly dropped and into which had been put a list of requirements and money.

On our return, at the specified place, the knapsacks would be there, filled with such things as peanut toffee, that famous ointment of the East, Tiger Balm, cigarettes and the like. In the evenings, McElfish and I would go through the huts, I, in front calling out the wares for sale, he following with a large tray full. There were many such knapsacks and sales going on a there were many new arrivals, who did not know how to make contact with the Chinese. One helped immediate neighbours in difficulty but the situation was overwhelming. Hodgeson, for one, had his two bosses stabled in the bay below and one of them disapproved of this trading. This proved rather awkward for him so he was reluctant to help.

These ideals were all very well but how else could one get these things which were so badly needed. And, a very small profit was made. For instance, cigarettes bought at seventeen cents were sold at twenty cents

– and so on. We took the risk of losing every cent we had as the knapsacks could have been confiscated and never seen again. The poor old Chinese could have been shot and we could have been beaten up.

For war work, we were paid twenty-five cents a day by the Japanese and we used this to buy necessities such as eggs, one of which cost a day's pay. Nevertheless, by the time we left River Valley Road, McElfish and I had managed to save fifty dollars.

Then the Black Guards were sent to Java and were replaced by Koreans. Things then did begin to get difficult as the Korean guards got a bit nasty. The first thing they stopped were the trips to the village. This was very annoying as it had been the habit of twelve or so of us to go down to the village early before roll call and get hot rolls for breakfast! The first day that they were on guard, we went to the gate as usual and the guard commander wouldn't let us pass.

"No, no! No, no! Can't go out."

"But we want to get our rolls."

"No, no! No, no!" And then, after persistent requests, he finally said; "How many want?"

"One hundred and fifty."

We gave him the money. He handed his rifle, a .280 with bayonet and all, to Sergeant Major Crabb, who took over guard duty, and the Korean trotted off and got the rolls!

I believe Crabb died in River Valley Road. He was the Representative for Malayan Breweries, selling Tiger beer to the messes in Singapore and to the troops. On an easy day, he would drink about twenty pints and about forty on a tough day, being treated here and there. He was an illustration of the beer drinker being unable to stand up to the changed circumstances while the so-called 'whisky swilling' planter remained fit. I knew of none dying before getting to Siam and certainly not at River Valley Road.

Thursday was the Japanese 'Sunday' so we did no work. Eight of us contributed to a pool of money and bought the ingredients for a curry. Poor old Hodgeson, who had no money, in order that he could enjoy some curry, was prepared to get up early to grate the coconuts and generally prepare it. McElfish and I were going to cook it. So, we drew our normal rations from the cookhouse but made the curry instead of the usual watery stew.

In those days, in 1942, on most Thursdays a show was put on and I remember an exhibition of insects that an R.A.M.C. orderly had collected. It was most impressive with many hundreds of species including Black Widow spiders and others, big and hairy without being poisonous as well as black and brown scorpions.

We had, I believe, our first concert party at River Valley Road. The members of the party had built a stage at the lower end of a long slop, which gave a natural auditorium so that everyone could see the stage. The Jap officers and off duty guards invited themselves and sat themselves where improvised seats had been placed. When the curtain rose and six 'females' came on dancing, the Jap Colonel jumped to his feet.

Everything stopped. Not a sound was to be heard.

He marched up on to the stage and, using the scabbard of his sword, he raised the skirt of each 'female'. Having presumably satisfied himself that they were not what they appeared to be, he returned to his seat and the show continued. At the conclusion, the orchestra struck up the preliminary roll of drums for the National Anthem. The P.O.W's stood to attention.

The Japs looked round and saw everyone standing motionless so they also got to their feet and stood to attention all the way through God Save the King!

The 'females' were six British soldiers, their rank I never knew. Their long flaxen hair was made out of teased manila rope. Their gowns were mosquito nets, taken to pieces and made into clothes without cutting the net so that, if the nets were needed in the hospital, it wouldn't be difficult to sew them up again into their original shape.

River Valley Road was just about the nearest to the Geneva Convention for treatment of prisoners of war ever could be under the Japanese, who have never been able to understand anyone allowing himself to be taken prisoner. Better death than dishonour so to them we were the lowest of the low.

There was water laid on and, I think, electricity. It did become really tricky to get the knapsacks filled and the British Camp Commander said, "Better not risk it." So I sent a note in my knapsack, saying this would be the last time and asking the Chinese to fill them with as much as they possibly could. In the evening, there they were, bulging with stuff. The knapsacks were camouflaged with firewood and any men not carrying one carried more wood and huddled up close as they came through the gate. All the same, how they ever got back into camp without being detected, I do not know.

The British Camp Commandant, Australian and very tall – he was an Olympic hop, step and jump athlete – had to be called out in front of all the camp one day as something had happened to displease the Jap Commandant. He tried to smack the Colonel's face but he missed by five or six inches, not being tall enough to reach. He tried a second time and, again, failed.

The Colonel picked him up and stuck him on a convenient box nearby and stuck his jaw out in front of him. The little Jap was so humiliated and furious at losing 'face' that he jumped off the box, kicked at it wildly and stalked off! The Australians were a tough lot and more than once got the better of the Japs. One time, the Japs were certain the Australians had arms in their huts, which was correct, so they swooped down on the camp and the huts. Ten Japs posted at the doors at each end and the Aussies were ordered to take everything outside.

So the Australians took everything out, trundling backwards and forwards and including the bundles of firewood in which the arms were hidden.

Having cleared their huts, the Japs searched it and then made them put it all back, armoury and all. They then marched over to the gate and, when they were within twenty yards of it, they turned and rushed back to the hut, telling the Aussies to clear it again, with eight men at each door this time. The Aussies picked up their belongings, trundling backwards and forwards, including the firewood in exactly the same way as before. Three times in all this took place before the Japs gave up.

The Australians were very fit and put up a boxing ring and arranged their own bouts. A Korean, who fancied himself as a boxer, demanded to be allowed to fight and an Amateur Lightweight Champion obliged and jumped into the ring and pasted him over. The Korean didn't take too kindly to this treatment and marched the Australian over to Headquarters, where he hoped he would have the Aussie punished. The Colonel stepped in and explained to the Commandant that it was the Korean who wanted to fight, and he succeeded in convincing the Japanese Camp Commandant such that he took them both back to the ring for another go and watched and applauded the obvious victor.

This was typical of a Japanese. Because it was a Korean, it was right that he should take a beating but, if it had been a Japanese, it would have been a different story. Things happened that were not so humourous. Tinnea, or Singapore or athlete's foot as it is known, was becoming widespread. But this was very different to foot rot because it attacked the scrotum and the testicles swelled. Men with it waddled around like ducks.

We were, more or less, work horses, puling barrows backwards and forwards filled with building materials. It was real manual labour, building a go-down by the Way. Over at the side office, a flag would fly. If it was flying, you worked. One chap was going along with his barrow and the flag came down, signalling 'Yasme' meaning rest or tea break. This European, he just sat down on the shafts where he was. This did not suit the Jap in charge, who did not want to sit in the sun for his rest, so he belted the European across his head and across his back. This was all too a frequent occurrence for the slightest thing.

I received no letters in Singapore at all. At River Valley Road, something happened to annoy the Japs and they brought out a laundry basket full of post and made a bonfire out of them. But, at some time in this camp, we had our first postcards given out. The cards were all printed with simple messages such as 'I am ill/well. I am working/not working.' And so on.

At that time, the Gurkhas were in Havelock Road Camp on the other side of the river. They refused to have anything to do with these cards unless they could write what they wanted. A sixteen year old Gurkha was hauled out in front and the Japs put a pencil in between his fingers and crashed down on them, smashing all his fingers. They still would not sign and several more had the same treatment. The Sikhs, who were on guard with the Koreans, would not go anywhere near the Havelock Road Camp!

Towards the end of the time at River Road Valley, parties were beginning to move out to go to Siam. When the camp was about half empty, the Japs suddenly released large quantities of South African Red Cross food and clothing so we were glutted with it. And, when it came time for us to leave, we couldn't take it all with us and it had to be left behind. We were told that whatever we could carry would be taken, provided it could be got to the station. We swopped a packet of cigarettes for some pram wheels and made a trolley, which we piled up with all our paraphernalia like tennis racquets, pillows, blankets, chairs, tables and wood from the bunks. What upset me was having to leave behind a hundredweight of copper wire still buried under the bay of the hut.

We got all this down to the station where a train of goods wagons was awaiting us. Thirty men to each wagon so, apart from our kitbags, everything else was left behind on Singapore station! The amount of stuff taken to that station was remarkable, some chaps even took a piano!

We all piled in. We could just sit down but we had to take turns to lie down. The heat was terrible during the day and very cold at night, consequently everybody wanted to be at the windward end by day and at the sheltered end at night. W, at River Valley Road then, were among the first batches to go up country and were therefore fairly fit men and we more or less weathered this journey. But very few of the poor devils that came after, F Force and H Force, sick men for the most, reached their destination and, if they did, they did not come back.

When the train stopped at a station, there was a rush to get water from the water crane. The journey dragged on endlessly with alternate heat and bitter cold for five and a half days and, at last, we arrived at Bampong, which is where the new railway was going to join up with Bankok. We had been told glowing tales by the Japs of where we were going, of beautiful food and accommodation.

"Oh rice, plentee, plentee!"

So we did not think that conditions would be worse than River Valley Road though we were a little despondent at having to leave our trolley behind. It was the rainy season and Bampong was just a sea of mud. This was only a transit camp, which was just as well as it had tumbledown huts that were so low that when you crept into your bunk space, you touched the roof. The only water for bathing was in a paddy fie ld. The much vaunted food was nowhere. We ate our Red Cross rations. We were there for one night and, next day, after an early meal, we started walking, carrying all we owned.

The way was heavy going through the mud and in the evening we arrived at what appeared to be an aerodrome. I never did know the name of this place. It was great open plain with a few inevitable bamboo and atap huts in one corner. There was a meal of rice cooked for us and afterwards we just crawled into our bunks.

Among the Thai's here, there was a shortage of clothes here, it seemed, and one chap, belonging to the 9th Coastal Defence Royal Artillery, was an ex-gaolbird and a card sharper. Before starting off next day, he sold all his clothes and walked absolutely naked through Siam.

After this night halt at the aerodrome, we hit the jungle. Of course, it was still pouring with rain. A trail had been cut some ten foot wide and was a good none inches deep in mud. I shall never forget the everlasting green of that jungle and the deep green mud and a Jap guard, walking along with a live chicken, plucking its feathers out one by one.

Dr Pavillard must have walked miles and miles extra, going up and down day after day, cheering on the downhearted and helping the sick men to get up and not fall behind. Everybody helped everybody and at times carried other's kitbags. No one gave the naked man anything to carry as it would be certain he would flog it!

Thompson, from the Penang Volunteers, was a dour Scot who had gone through Aberdeen Agricultural College by working with a pick and shovel in his vacations to pay for it, and would just say, "Put one foot in front of the other and say to yourself 'I will not fall."

And so we just plodded...plodded...plodded. I was pretty done in but kept going and did not fall. The pace was slow, it could not be otherwise. The heat in the jungle was not bad being deep shade. This walk in all was about one hundred and fifty miles and must have taken several days. We halted each night at various transit camps where an advance party would have food ready.

My next recollection is arriving at Tarsao. This camp was to become a colossal camp in years to come but when we arrived, it was just a few a\tap huts. All these camps were on or near the River Kwai, the Kwai Nui to give it its full name. The river was our lifeline. It gave us water to drink and, of course, we bathed in it. Tarsao was deep in the jungle, just a clearing, which the very early parties from River Valley Road had been sent up to prepare. Poor devils, no wonder they took the fittest first.

Lice, which were always with us, became so bad that I persuaded a man with a pair of scissors and a razor to take all my hair off as I was beginning to get sores. At Tarsao, we built huts. A lot of the material came up by boat and bamboo was cut from the jungle. There were rations too, rice for us, chickens and pigs for the Jap guards.

After several weeks, a party of Malayan Volunteers and, I think, Royal Artillery and attached Norfolk's were moved to Wan Po Central. Once again it was a clearing in the jungle with one hut. We built, I think it was about eight more and then cleared a road to the line that the railway was to take.

Every morning before light we had breakfast of 'burgee', a sloppy rice dish which was a very poor imitation of porridge. Then it was Roll call and off to the railway to work.

In the hut next to ours were mainly Beds and Herts with a senior N.C.O in charge, who deserves the highest praise as he maintained the morale of not only his own men but all the other's working in the camp. His working party, after Roll call each morning, would leave the parade ground to go to their work, marching as if on a route march and singing all the way to the railway tract and, at the end of the day's work, they would march back again, singing and always led by the N.C.O. On the railway, we were filling, that is, digging earth from some distance and carrying and dumping it at the track site to build an embankment to take the line round the cliff face at Wan Po North.

The allotted task per day was one cubic metre of earth and we were divided into gangs of six. On the completion of your measured task, you could go back to the camp. Not so those under the Beds and Herts N.C.O. Those, who finished their task earlier, either went over and helped others or went and collected firewood to take back to camp.

When all had finished their day's work, they would each pick up a piece of firewood and, with their N.C.O at their head march back to camp, singing loudly.

The 'Nips' tried to stop them on one occasion, I remember, making them march round and round the parade ground, singing, perhaps for two hours before setting off to their allotted task and, when they had finished that, the Japs kept them back on the tract for another three hours. We were back in camp and had had our bath in the river and our meal and were asleep only to be awakened by the gang returning. It was well after midnight and they were still singing!

We cheered them as they entered the camp. They were absolutely deadbeat with hunger and fatigue but they would not let the Japs see it. Next morning, every man who had been out the night before was out on parade and left the camp marching and singing as before!

The embankment had been built to something over twenty-five foot high and, after any unpleasant incident with a Jap guard, this N.C.O would climb up to the top where he could be seen by all of us working in our pits, digging or carrying the rice-sack litters of earth up the embankment. He would then bellow:

"Are we downhearted?"

The chorus from all four hundred of us would be a comparatively tremendous, "No!" And this was usually followed by:

N.C.O: "They're pulling the old pub down."
Chorus: "Boo-oo"
N.C.O: "But they're building a new one."
Chorus: "Hooray"
N.C.O: "Only one bar."
Chorus: "Boo-oo"
N.C.O: "Three mile long."
Chorus: "Hooray"
N.C.O: "With only one barmaid."
Chorus: "Boo-oo"
N.C.O: "To each customer."
Chorus: "Hooray"

And so on.

It was during these days at Wan PO that a 'Nip' guard, who must have known something about Christianity, saw a tattoo of the Crucifixion on the chest of a soldier. The guard was impressed and indicated that the man must be very good. This must have suggested to someone that if they stopped work and stood up with their hands clasped in prayer, they might be able to snatch a few minutes of rest from the continual cries of 'speedo! speedo!'. On this particular occasion, I was the N.C.O in charge of the Malayan Volunteers working party when, to everyone's surprise, a dozen men stopped work at the top of the embankment and put their hands together with heads bowed.

The 'Nip' in charge came running up to me, brandishing his bamboo stick and bellowing at me. I pointed to the tattoo on the soldier's chest and, in English, said they were praying for the death of all Nipponese soldiers. His tone promptly changed and with a muttered 'Soska, soska' he wandered off. We took it in turns after this to have a few minutes break in this way and it lasted for several days but, like all the things we thought of to hold up the work, the 'speedo!' would put an end to it.

On the opposite bank of the river, in the jungle, a saw-mill had been set up to cut the trees into squared baulks of timber to be used on the railway. At first, parties of P.O.W.'s used to cross the river and haul the timber on sledges out of the jungle and then to the river bank. This was very heavy work and eventually the Jap engineers called up a number of elephants with their Siamese mahouts. These magnificent creatures made short work of the haulage and it was all the gang of white coolies could do to keep the elephants supplied with work.

At the end of the day, all would return to the camp side of the river. The elephants would always stop and bathe and play like children, blowing water at each other with their trunks and dowsing the drivers as well. They greatly enjoyed themselves. After bathing, they were taken to a bamboo glade where they were hobbled with chains and left to graze on the leaves of the bamboo. At about one o'clock one morning, we were awakened by the terrific crashing and clanging, interspersed with the jangling of chains. One of the young male elephants had turned rogue, broken his chains and had charged straight through the camp.

Fortunately for us, he missed all the huts that we were sleeping in but went right through the store hut, completely demolishing it, knocked down the cookhouse and a poor, unlucky P.O.W, returning from the latrine, could not get out of the way quickly enough and was caught by the elephant and crushed. Every bone in his body was broken and he was thrown some distance into the jungle. For a long time after that we were vary nervous of the clink of chains during the night.

But the elephants possessed great intelligence. One day, they were hauling logs out of the river. We had put ropes round the logs and the elephants then pulled them up the steep slope of the bank. After several logs had been thus hauled up, one elephant refused to move, the mahout repeatedly goaded him but, for some time, the elephant resisted. Finally, he took one pace forward and the rope snapped. The elephant knew the rope wouldn't hold. The trick one sees in circuses of elephants walking in single file, holding the tail of the one in front, is perfectly natural. They are just following the leader.

The bamboo, which belongs to the grass family, has separate male and female plants and is very distinctive. The female has long thorns, two to three inches in length, very, very sharp and horribly poisonous. A scratch from a bamboo, within forty eight hours, can turn ulcerous. The thorns were so sharp but hollow. By slicing off a piece of the pointed end to expose the hollow tube, after sterilisation, they could be used as needles for hypodermic syringes. We were continually having Typhoid injections and the old metal needles were far blunter.

The male bamboo is smooth without thorns but, like the female, covered in hairs, which would irritate the skin and I believe are used in joke packs. Chopped very finely, the hairs are almost invisible. It was the male bamboo that was used extensively in building huts, tables and chairs. They were used as pipes for water supplies and, when cut at the nodes, they formed useful containers and were used in the hospital wards as urine bottles for those too ill to leave their beds.

Bamboo, four to five inches thick and thirty to forty foot in length, were mainly used in construction work and formed the main supports of all our building, with thinner bamboo used as cross braces and purlins. Female bamboos were burned in the cookhouse. It had to be split before burning or else the moisture in the sealed portions between the nodes would boil, bringing the pressure up inside until the bamboo burst with a tremendous crack. The explosion was known to have extinguished the fire!

During my River Valley Road days, I had, though the help of the Chinese, acquired a small quantity of M & B 693, one of the group of drugs, which, if we could have had larger supplies, would have saved numerous lives. Several Malay Volunteers, who knew the value of the drug, had acquired tablets and when it was known that the incredible Dr Pavillard was seriously ill, asked would anyone donate M & B. Within an hour some 50 tablets were handed in, far more than was required for his recovery, which, as with everything he did, was quickly and quietly cured.

One evening, a patient in his hospital developed appendicitis. He had no operating theatre, no surgical instruments. Fortunately, he did have a cut throat razor, clips, needles and gut. His operating table was made out of six bamboo legs, stuck in the ground for rigidity, bamboo canes lashed to the top of the legs and covered with split bamboo and the whole thing covered with a piece of blanket. Four of us improvised torches from hollowed out bamboo, stuffed with rags and with coconut oil poured in. These gave a bright but smoky light so they could only be used outside the hut. So the operating theatre was out in the open so they could be placed around the table. Fortunately it was the dry season.

The patient was lifted on to the table by an Aussie orderly. I suspect that he had done this before as he had a piece of blanket wrapped round a length of heavy bamboo. When the patient was settled and comparatively relaxed, he hit him hard, right across the forehead. It was a magnificent blow, sufficient to know the patient unconscious and, I am sure, without the patient realising what hit him. Dr Pavillard immediately started work the razor, removed the inflamed part and, just before stitching him up, indicated to the Aussie to give him another blow, which he did. The doctor then finished the stitching and dressed the wound. The patient, still unconscious, was put back in his bed space. When he came to, he complained of a headache, for which he knew of no cause.

When I suggested that to Dr Pavillard that the double shock to the system of being knocked out and then operated on, could have killed him, he replied:

"That, of course, is possible but death would have been painless whereas peritonitis, which is almost certain to have killed him in the end, would have been a very painful death!"

And that was the calm and reasoned thinking that went with all that he did.

Close to the Camp was a Thai house and garden. Four of us took it in turns to sneak out in the early morning and scrounge or buy a hand of bananas to augment our breakfast of two ladles of rice and one teaspoonful of sugar. On our way to the railway tract, we had to pass through a deserted where chillies grew in abundance.. I filled the pockets of my shorts with the little green chillies and chewed them throughout the day. It was being able to eat these sort of things, which, I feel sure, enable me to stave off the awful effect of beri-beri and pellagra, of which so many suffered and died.

The worst that I suffered from these diseases was a mild form of 'rice balls', where the scrotum became inflamed, red and raw, and 'pellagra mouth' when the inside of the mouth became raw, which made it painful to eat even the little we were getting. Some suffered acutely from B group vitamin deficiency and one unfortunate man had his penis elongated in a spiral to a length of about eleven or twelve inches and his testicles swollen to the size of cricket balls. Just to walk a few steps resulted in considerable pain.

Others I have seen with raw and bleeding backs where the skin had just peeled off. Dysentery was common and as we had no microscopes, we could not tell whether it was bacillary or amoebic. The treatment for each was the exact opposite of the other so it was possible that the treatment killed as many as did the disease. The doctors had to take a calculated risk.

More troops arrived at Wan Po Central and parties were sent up to Wan Po North, where the tract was being laid round the face of the cliff. A platform had been cut and tremendous earthworks were required to build the embankment high enough to join up with the platform on the cliff face. I went with a party to Wan Po South, where they were building piers of concrete to take the railway above the level of flood water. At this time, it was dry season so that the river was quite narrow, just a few yards across, and there were a few Thais living in the vicinity, who had planted groundnuts in the now almost dry sides of the river.

During the rainy season, the river would rise and spread to anything up to two hundred yards across. The peanuts, which we later stole, supplemented our rations!

At this camp, the working parties were split into two. One party the hammer and tap men, would drill with cold chisel and sledge hammer, a hole a metre deep in the rock-face and, at the end of the day, dynamite would be put in the holes and fused. When everyone was back in the camp on the other side of the river, the Japs would explode it. The following day, while some were drilling more holes, others would be clearing a rough platform with pick and shovel to take the concrete piers, which the other half of the party was building. Large beams of wood, cut from the jungle, were placed on the concrete piles and boards put across these to form a platform where the concrete was mixed. These platforms, which were not over six feet wide, made it difficult for the 'Nip' guard to pass. For most of the guards, one just stopped working and moved aside so that he could get round the pile of concrete being mixed.

One, who prided himself that he was a bit of an acrobat, would jump round the P.O.W. so that, for a fraction of a second, he was in the air with a fifty or sixty foot drop below. A Dutchman, who had joined us at Wan Po South, said that, if the opportunity occurred, he would kill the 'little bastard'. The opportunity soon came. He jumped as usual and, as he did so the Dutchman moved back, just an inch or so but just sufficient to make him lose his balance and crash down on the rocks below. As the Japanese had seen him fall, the P.O.W's story that he slipped and fell was fortunately accepted so the Dutchman got away with it, for which we were very grateful.

The concrete was a regulation 8 ballast, 4 and 1, but the cement was left out as often as the inattention of the guards would allow. Pieces of wood, bamboo and any old rubbish that could be dropped into the concrete was thrown in to fill the wooden shuttering in which the piles were moulded. One of our N.C.O.'s, although he hated the Japs as much as I did, and still do, made himself agreeable to the Jap N.C.O. in charge of the dynamite and within a week our N.C.O was doing the job of putting the charges in the holes and, of course, when it was possible, he slipped a stick or two into his pocket and brought it back to camp.

After work, at a pre-arranged time, about a dozen swimmers would wander quietly and unobtrusively some distance down river, while at the other end of the camp, when the official explosions started, our N.C.O would detonate a stick of dynamite under the water.

The swimmers would dive in and, as the stunned fish came floating downstream, would gather in as many as they could, flinging them on to the sand, where they were collected by others and whisked off to the cookhouse, once again, to be used to eke out our rations.

The swimmers invariably kept a fish or two for a private fry-up, to be shared with the dynamite stealer. This went on regularly at Wan Po South. I don't know to this day whether or not the Japs knew.

Ray never completed his account as, at this point in his telling, he began to have recurring nightmares and couldn't continue. They were to return later in life when, approaching death from cancer, his memories took over.

At one time, when living in Nutbourne, near Chichester, in West Sussex, he received an invitation to see a special screening of 'The Bridge on the River Kwai',but he and other ex-prisoners refused to go. It was not how it happened and he didn't want to be reminded

He had survived terrible outrages against himself and his fellow prisoners of war and rarely spoke of them. The scars, both physical and mental remained with him until the end.

Below are the correspondence that he was able to send on his release to Barbara and the welcome letter from King George VI.

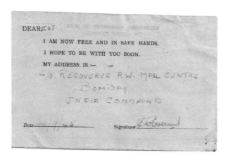

The card from Ray on his release

Telegram confirming Ray's arrival in India

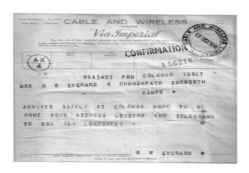

Telegram sent on arrival in Colombo

BUCKINGHAM PALACE

The Queen and I bid you a very warm welcome home.

Through all the great trials and sufferings which you have undergone at the hands of the Japanese, you and your comrades have been constantly in our thoughts. We know from the accounts we have already received how heavy those sufferings have been. We know also that these have been endured by you with the highest courage.

We mourn with you the deaths of so many of your gallant comrades.

With all our hearts, we hope that your return from captivity will bring you and your families a full measure of happiness, which you may long enjoy together.

George R.I.

September 1945.

Welcome Home letter from Buckingham Palace

Book Three: Chapter Fourteen – Return to Malaya

Singapore looked very much the same as it had those many years ago on my first arrival: flat and sun-baked in the mid-morning glare.

Ray was there waiting for us. A very grim reminder was the Japanese P.O.W.s unloading our luggage – Ray's 'grinning apes' in their grey overalls not looking quite so grinning now; little, squat, greasy men. There then began the search for our luggage. I sat Martin on top of a crate under a big letter 'E' and told him not to look at the Japs and, under no circumstances, was he to speak to them. He had my permission to spit at them should they dare approach him.

We did the journey to Malacca by car, very comfortably arriving at Durian Tunggal in the late afternoon. The bungalow looked as usual, but also very different to me as I had never before seen it on its hill, bare and exposed, with all the rubber cut down. It was, however, furnished in a rather higgledy-piggledy sort of way with the flotsam and jetsam of a catastrophe. It was always one of the coolest bungalows in Malacca territory; now it was almost cold.

The few months we were there was great fun, to be all reunited again with Ray, now Acting Manager on his old estate and living in one of the 'plum' bungalows. Transport was rather difficult. At first, Ray only had a motor bike and we had to hire taxis for weekly shopping in Malacca.

Martin's schooling became rather a problem. He was only six so we arranged to send him to the girls' convent in Malacca where he was only one of four boys. Getting him there was difficult. He had to ride on the petrol tank of the bike as we couldn't trust him to ride pillion. Ray would drop him off on his way round to Home Division, the only way to it being via Malacca, and then collect him in the afternoon. To Martin's shame and disgust, he would arrive at either destination with his legs covered in cow dung, splashed up from the front wheel. This was not a very satisfactory arrangement and only the beginning of considerable schooling difficulties.

I went with Ray to Bertam Home Division, when he had a taxi, and walked with him in the rubber while he was inspecting the tapping. When the latex was being weighed, he left me in Mr Bennett's garden, beautiful in its derelict state. The bungalow stood, a ruin, a few windows hanging, no roof, no doors, no stairs, and everything of use had been stripped.

But the garden burgeoned madly; bougainvilleas of several colours clashed happily everywhere, Spathodea, Delonix and Cassia trees, straggling, choked Crotons doing battle with the lallang. The Congea was as magnificent as ever, covering the centre of the 'lawn' in a shimmering mauve haze. The tennis court was barely distinguishable and, the little swimming pool, had I not known its site, I would not have seen it.

Also, I went over to our old bungalow, the old Eight Mile, where we had been so happy. It was just not there. It had been completely removed and even the clearing where the bungalow had been was obliterated, grown over by secondary jungle. Mr Bennett had left Bertam only an hour ahead of the Japanese arrival in Malacca and directly after he left, the Malays went in and took everything. My box, which I had so carefully nailed up for him to take to the bank, never got there.

So, together with the precious Beard christening robe, which had been sent out to me for safekeeping during the war in Europe, my mother's jewellery, my christening mug, given to me by Mr Gorham, and our small valuable wedding presents were all lost. A brooch of Mummy's and a bracelet did surface, found in a kampong house. And these, plus the camphor wood chest, empty, were all we salvaged from the Occupation and have managed to keep all these years.

I think, possibly, that if Ray had been given the management of Bertam, he would probably still be there now. We would have been happy to live at Durian Tunggal as Mr Bennett's and our old bungalow were never rebuilt as there was in the future only to be a Manager of Bertam with no Assistant at all.

And I was happy there, never at my best in the tropical heat and this bungalow, being several degrees cooler, made it easier for me. I enjoyed putting the garden right and looking after all the livestock. Food was still expensive and in short supply and we grew and produced all we could. I experimented with making jam. Pineapple worked well as did guava and lime and pomelo marmalade. Banana was not good!

Furniture could be picked up very cheaply. We got a lovely red and gold lacquer cabinet in two sections at a second-hand furniture dealer for a song, which is still in the family, and several other things plus two useful rush mat carpets, which were already in the bungalow having been just left there by the former Jap occupier of Durian Tunggal bungalow.

Yes, this was a happy time and one wishes it could have lasted, but, eventually, after a few months, Bill and Madge Ross came out and Bill took over management. He had, of course, been Mr Bennett's Senior Assistant before the war so it was only reasonable that he should have Bertam. And we were moved to Asahan.

We were rather dreading this as we had both heard tales of the manager and his wife. I had trouble with them right from the beginning about furniture, something trifling but I forget what. It was impossible to get a servant, and I don't think we even had a kebun, just some estate coolie, detailed off to chop wood for cooking. So I had to do all the bungalow cleaning and cooking. Housework for a European is a hardship but the cooking is really torture. On an open brick fire, using acrid rubber wood, the smoke tried my eyes severely. But I became quite expert even mastering the kerosene tin oven.

You had to get a really hot fire underneath, with glowing bits of charcoaled wood, then, dripping with enough sweat to put it out, pile some of the red hot wood on top to get an even heat all around. I roasted in this and my heady pinnacle of success was a lemon cheese cake with meringue, all correctly browned on top!

As if this wasn't enough, then there was the problem with Martin's schooling, Asahan being thirty-two miles out from Malacca town. So Martin had to go to the Brother's School, boarded out weekly, poor child! And this school, too, was Roman Catholic, so I didn't like that and nor did Ray. And he was the only European. So schooling was a nightmare, it always has been, in Malaya. What upset our plans was the fact that the English schools in the Cameron Highlands had not yet started up, which was where we had intended Martin should go until he was nine and then Rottingdean Prep school for Wellington, but it was not to be.

Ray had to get a car so he found a ramshackle old Morris, which had obviously seen much war service. Ray did not like working under this manager, who shall remain nameless, and it was a bit hard to come down from Acting Manager to be treated like a Junior Assistant, which he certainly wasn't. In fact, we were having to live in the Junior Assistant's bungalow as the Senior Assistant's had been destroyed. It was poor Joe Giles' bungalow before the war, the one where Hetty had not liked to be left. I don't blame her!

But this manager and his wife, certainly, were very autocratic, high-handed and snobbish. It was a very wild estate at the back of beyond with plenty of tiger and elephant in the surrounding jungle but with a magnificent view of Mount Ophir two miles away. Mount Ophir or Bukit Mas in Malay – Gold Mountain – did have a gold mine on it but it wasn't worked as it had been flooded.

There was a beautiful view of the twin jungle-clad summits from the kitchen door. At this time, all I had in the way of paints was an old box of oil paint, which I had picked up in the Emsworth salerooms during the war and it was at Asahan that I started doing a bit of painting again. I made an oil of this view, which I am very fond of, sitting at the door of the kitchen, looking out onto the dry brown lallang and palm trees with the dark green of rubber and blue jungle beyond.

The colours in this paint box lacked cobalt or ultramarine so I was in a spot of trouble with the blue of the sky and the jungle and so looked around me for something to make it up. I hit on Reckitt's washing blue and it served well. It has not lost its colour over the years.

Mount Ophir, seen from Asahan, oil, 1947

Up to now, and during the war, I had done little painting. I was too unhappy. I had only come across this box of oils towards the end of the war, having lost all my pre-war paints to the Japs. I had done an awful lot of making things such as my log cottages, many, many pounds worth, for the Red Cross, which was my only way of helping the war effort. It was difficult for women with little children.

Then we went to Singapore and I found, in an Indian stationer's shop in Raffles Square, a large student's water colour box. What joy! I bought camel hair brushes and poor cartridge paper – anything that was available – and when I got back to Asahan, I started making paintings of the shrubs and plants in the garden. Cestrum nocturnum was one, Ipomea bona nox on a night blue ground, Angelonia, Cannas, Hibiscus, anything that I could lay my hands on.

So I kept busy on Asahan, what with the housework and now the painting and the chickens and the rabbits. These last were a business as rabbits seem incapable of feeding their young on their own and will let them starve. I had to forcibly hold the doe between my knees and fix the blind babies on to her teats. This had to be done until I could wean them and it had to be done several times a day! So I sat on a stool in the kitchen doorway with the view of Mount Ophir for hours. Meat was still very expensive so the rabbits were a necessity.

I didn't go out much on this estate. I did not wish to meet our manager and invite a remark such as I was not needed at the latex collecting. Ray had to get up very early here doing the real old Junior Assistant work like muster every day at six in the morning just before light.

One day, when he was going out before dawn to check on the field work, he came round a corner of the laterite road to be confronted, not by boar or tiger, but by five totally nude Tamil women. They were hopping and dancing around like mad and much put out by the sudden arrival of the Tuan on the scene. Apparently, they had been having a rest on a fallen tree and had inadvertently sat on red Kringa ants and had taken off their garments to shake them out and brush them off their bodies as they bite quite viciously.

I always wanted to walk up Mount Ophir but never did, although we went for a walk by the reservoir on the Muar side. Martin and I were very interested in the orchids growing on the trees. I found Dendrobium teres here and I never found it anywhere else. I collected it and several others and these were the beginnings of my collection of orchids. I planted it in a coconut and it settled down, flowered and I made a painting of it.

We were happily walking along and, then, I noticed the leeches! I had looked up and on the tree leaves above me were these dreadful things, waving about. I shrieked and Ray, who was a bit ahead, came back.

"What on earth is the matter?" he asked.

"Oh, look at these," I said. "Dreadful leeches!"

And then I looked down and they were everywhere on the ground, coming for my bare legs. We rushed on, the joy all gone, and came to a little stream, which had cut itself into a deep ravine. It had a tree trunk placed over it on which to cross. Ray went over and so did Martin. I started and began to sweat in terror. I could not cross over.
"Come on, Mummy, come on! It's easy!" called Martin, irritating boy!

"I can't, I can't cross it. I shall fall."

"No, you won't. Look, it's easy," said he, dancing backwards and forwards across the log. "Look, I'll come and collect you. Take my hand."

I took the boy's hand and got over, but I was a shaking wreck on the other side and soon after this we turned to make the return journey over the log. It is possible that this unfortunate experience, together with the leeches, was the reason why we never went up Mount Ophir and Ray never really encouraged Martin and me to go for walks and, of course, we couldn't go without him.

I had never realised that I had this vertigo. It is a horrible feeling. I cannot cross anything that is narrow and rounded and has nothing to hold on to even if it is only a little stream below. Since this, I have had several such unpleasant moments and always treated with much ridicule by my husband and son – most unkind as it was real agony. Once, I was out on an estate with Ray walking the boundaries along the old Malacca railway tract, which had been removed by the Japs and re-laid in Siam – by Ray, possibly – and we came to a viaduct. This was just too terrible. It had no rails, no sides, only the sleepers on pillars and I had to walk over this and every step I took, I could see the earth thirty feet below.

And later, on another occasion, the thought of which still makes me ill, there was an elephant on the estate, which was being a nuisance. So Ray decided to go after it and he and the estate clerk took various Tamils, Chinese and Malays as beaters, and, of course, fool Mem went too. I love anything like this and would have loved to see a wild elephant. All went well to start with and then we came across quite a large river, I suppose the upper reaches of the Malacca River. Across it had been put a large tree as a bridge.

Of course, everyone tripped across as if it had been Tower Bridge but I held everything up and, in the end, Ray took one hand, the clerk the other and I was edged over but what with the river so far down below me and muddily rushing along, yes, it was a bad experience, the worst of all.

And we never got the damned elephant. All I saw were enormous footprints and we could hear it trampling about. It seems incredible that such a large animal was so difficult to locate with all these people. However, it was just as well as idiotic Ray had only a .280 carbine gun!

We could not stick Asahan, so Ray put in for a transfer and we were moved to Kru Estate, which is fifteen miles out of Malacca and three miles in on a laterite road off the Alor Gajah-Tampin Road. This was slightly better than Asahan. The manager was a Scot and Ray got on fairly well with him.

The Senior Assistant's bungalow at Kru was not very nice. It had no electricity, only hilling oil lamps. It was enormous and its great drawback was a deep landing at the back, running the length of the bungalow. This had no ceiling and was bare to the tiles and the heat of the sun on these made the bungalow unliveable in during the day. We made a sitting area under the bungalow where we did get a faint breeze. I found in most of the old 'aeroplane' shaped bungalows that this is the only habitable spot.

Kru Estate Bungalow, 1947

Air-conditioning was beginning to be considered, but only managers with modern stone-built houses could have it as the old ones were built of slatted wood on high piles. Also it had a very hot, arid garden. Bill and Madge Ross had been here and to follow in her footsteps meant a treeless garden. She always had the trees cut down within a few feet of the bungalow. Sometime, when I was on Kru, we went over to Bertam and I went to look at Mr Bennett's old garden. It was all cut down, even that glorious Congea, which was doing no harm to anything, only beautifying a little bit of this world.

No trees was jolly awkward for me as, by now, I had quite a budding collection of orchids, some of which were wild. People had given me bits of plants, too, and they were all growing happily, excepting Arachnis and some Vandaea, which ask for shaded sun. So, the first thing Ray and I had to do was to construct a pergola near the bungalow. I planted Thunbergia grandiflora, Ipomea bono-nox, Glorosa superba and Cliteria and, within about six weeks, it was well covered. We made it in a lovely circle with a round bed in the middle. It was a real pleasure to walk around it with the orchids hanging in suitable spots in the alcoves.

The pergola

I also had a considerable collection of pot plants, from and enormous specimen of Keng Wah – Epiphyllum hookeri – in an old Shanghai jar to maiden hair ferns, Spathoglottis ground orchids, begonias, blue hydrangeas, dieffenbachia, coleus, croton and, massed around, they looked very well.

Pot gardening in Malaya is very successful as the plants can be placed just where they do best, which is usually in the semi shade of the building especially where you have a garden like this one at Kru; an expanse of open grass, brown, withered stuff with a derelict border far away in the middle, which was composed of a tangled mass of bougainvillea. In one corner, some two hundred feet away was a Spathodea and a young mango tree, either of which would have mad a good host for the orchids but I was not going to trust these precious plants so far away where every wandering cow or goat could eat them.

It had been quite a job to transport us from Asahan. There was one lorry alone for all my plants and the chickens, rabbits and now a goose, a monkey, several cats and a Slow Loris. It seems that at this stage, we rather went in for animals, to amuse Martin, I suppose, but I had all the work of them. The rabbits were perfectly frightful with all the wet nursing to do. The monkey de-fleaed the cats; the goose, Martin's pet, died on its nest, having been poisoned by arsenic from eating treated lallang. And the Slow Loris bit me nearly through the thumb before it succumbed to the same fate, having been given bananas that had been stored in the same arsenic drum. So, except for the cats and the monkey, they gradually went.

The cat being groomed

Martin was still a weekly border at the Brothers school but we were not happy with him being there, it being Roman Catholic and he the only white boy was getting, inevitably, what the Europeans call 'chi-chi'. Nowadays, with all this multi-racial rubbish, it probably does not matter but it did then, and it was not considered suitable for European children to talk Eurasian. To talk in Malay, Tamil or Chinese was fine and, in fact, many children spoke these languages before they spoke English but Pidgin English, no, not ever!

So, we took him away from school and we tried to teach him ourselves in a half-hearted sort of way. But Martin remembers that on the way from the school, I offered him a choice. There had been an outbreak of typhoid or similar disease at the school and there had been the first inklings of the communists starting to cause trouble and, he says, that I offered him the choice – going back to school and risking catching some deadly disease or running the gauntlet of being shot at back on the estate. He chose the latter! Much more exciting!

Edward Fugler, Giar and Martin

I was very busy painting; rather sloppy water colour paintings of al the garden flowers around me. Gradually I was able to get good artist's materials and the work began to improve. We could not afford to buy orchids so I started making a series of paintings of orchids, my wild ones when they flowered, and also any I came on in people's gardens. The Chinese in particular love orchids and have some very fine collections. They loved me to paint their plants and so gradually I had the base of quite an interesting collection of paintings, which were the next best thing to owning the flower.

Barbara with a Dendrobium orchid

One day, we were having tiffin at a young planter's bungalow. He was Nigel Hamilton, Mildred Spong's nephew, whom I had known years ago as a boy of twelve at those Christmases at Chilham Castle. He was rather lonely and new to a Dunlop estate, living all by himself in a bungalow that was even larger than Kru, and he was somewhat overpowered by the great expanses of wooden, cream painted walls.

"Barbara, just look at these walls," he said. "Can't you do something about it? Do me some paintings."

So I went home and painted him some simple Malayan flowers; Allamanda, Hibiscus, Bougainvillea; six in all, and I had them glazed with passé-par-tout and took them over to him. We hung them up and that bit of wall did look a bit better but they looked a bit lost.

"You'll have to do some more," he said.

So, in the end, I painted thirty-six for him and I charged him seven dollars each, which in those days was about sixteen shillings. Nigel was entertaining quite a lot and people saw the paintings and went dotty over them and I suddenly found myself quite busy with orders. So, although I have always painted, this young man did play quite a part in the start of my professional flower painting. The early training in fine detail at Thornton Smith's studio doing the Chinese wallpapers helped. Indeed, I still retained some of this influence, which can be seen in some of these early flower paintings.

It was very good to have a bit extra coming in each month and I could afford to have more servants. I had a young Malay boy and his mother, Kutty. I trained and taught Giar to cook and Kutty looked after the house and was the wash amah. At Kru, I had a very good kebun, provided by the estate, who was the best that I ever had. Karapan really was a gardener and knew what he was doing.

Karapan, the gardener

Most 'gardeners' are just an estate-weeding gang and only fit for wood chopping and wielding a chunkol, but Karapan sterilised earth and grew fine tomatoes in half kerosene tins and even small potatoes. He grew lettuce and many good vegetables and had a knowledge of plants and a love of gardening in the tropics, besides. I learned a lot from him.

He it was who showed me how to purge orchids of unwelcome lodgers. He would go and get some root – derris – and pound this up until it was a thick, milky liquid, add water and put it in a big bucket and then plunge each basket or holed pot of orchids into it. Many a happy hour have I spent watching each pot to see what was evicted. The enormous snails and even the little ones were the chief enemies as they ate the new roots. But four inch-long red centipedes, spiders and brown scorpions took up residence too.

Ray and his piglets

Ray also kept a lot of pigs so we employed a pig boy as well.

These were kept some distance from the bungalow on the other side of the tulip tree. They were fine until a certain thing happened. I have always been fanatical about worms and was always worming everything, animals, servants, child and myself. One day, it was found that Martin and I had tapeworms! So everybody had to be purged and the only person who hadn't been was Ray.

"You should be," I said. "You can't be sure. We've all been done so you must."

"Worms!! Of course I haven't any worms!" he said.

"It wouldn't hurt you to take a dose just to be on the safe side," I insisted.

So, with much indignation, he did and, in due course, out came the most enormous roundworm; a positive <u>snake</u>, which the estate doctor took off in triumph, saying it was the biggest he had ever seen in a human being. It is probably in a jar, preserved to this day! He had caught it from the pigs and after that the pigs were banished. Meat was beginning to get cheaper and the rabbits went too. They were such a bore!

Martin remembers that this was where he smoked his first cigarette – or at least had his first puff. Ray used to smoke fifty Capstan a day and

Martin always had the honour of opening the cylindrical, foiled sealed tins. One day, after Ray took one out while we were watching the pigs, Martin asked if he could have one. Ray said no but I said, "Go on, let him try. He won't like it and maybe he'll learn a lesson."

After one puff, I am pleased to say that I was right!

Martin at Kru

Barbara at play with Martin and Edward

All the estate children were infested with worm, particularly hookworm and Martin was a worry to me. He could not understand why he <u>must</u> wear shoes. He could not understand why all the native children could all go around with none but he, even in the bungalow, must wear them. And, apart from hookworm, which enters through the feet I understood, there was also the risk of Athlete's foot, tinnea.

We used to catch him padding around like Giar and, even, punishing him with a thrashing would not stop him, and I became exasperated with him.

"Very well, Martin, you won't wear shoes. Right! I'll take them away and you can go without them." I said.

And as it happened, it was a Malacca shopping day, in and out of the shops and on the hot pavements, even in the Malacca Club, where everyone laughed at him. When we got home, he asked for his shoes back and I never had any trouble again on that score. Sometimes I have found that, with children and, certainly, Martin, to make the punishment fit the crime, works very well.

Malacca Club Members' wives and children
(Martin, front row centre, Barbara, fourth left on verandah)

I was really very busy with my painting with orders coming in all the time and my painting improving fast. The paintings of the orchids were coming along very quickly and I was continually finding orchids, seeing them on the trees as we used to drive around. Ray still had the aged Morris, which began to be very troublesome. Once going over on the road to the Manager's Home Division and going down a slight incline, we were astonished to see the a back wheel overtake us and rush past!

And a few weeks later on this same road, the engine fell out.

Stuck out in the back of nowhere, in the blazing morning sun, I exploded.

"I will not put up with this car any more! Let us get a new one."

"We will go and look at one tomorrow," said Ray.

So, he got a Standard 12, which was quite a nice car and I did learn to drive a bit in it.

One day, though I was not at the wheel, we were heading into Malacca but were still on the estate road of gravel and earth wheel tracks, when Ray noticed that Martin, sitting in the front passenger seat, hadn't locked the door. This was done by pushing the handle forward but Martin, for some reason, pulled it back towards him. The next thing we knew, he had vanished. The door, hinged at the back, had swung open with the draft and yanked him out of his seat and out of the car. He says that all he remembers was seeing the rear wheel of the car brushing past him as he tumbled head over heels into the dirt. He never heard my shriek from the back seat.

Fortunately, we found no real harm had been done, just a few scratches but a very wounded pride. And from then on, he always road in the back!

Ray's golden goose, which has laid for many years, was just coming in to lay. I was asking and getting twenty-five dollars for the small paintings, and I was also painting and selling large ones showing vases of flowers at a hundred dollars each, making about three hundred dollars a month. I paid for the car and I employed a syce on my wage list now as well as Kutty.

At about this time, the manager went on leave and his place was taken by the Malacca Rubber Plantation 'senior' Senior Assistant, who could not understand how we afforded our ménage on Ray's salary. He was certain we had put all the servants on the estate roll, disguised as weeders and such and he spent hours and hours checking to find the evidence. Of course, he never did as they were my servants but we never bothered to tell him. It was rather unkind of us in a way as it was quite unknown for any estate wife to make money. But one would have thought he would have noticed my paintings all over Malacca.

It was very nice to have a new car but she didn't remain new for very long. The 'grey pig', as she became known, literally shook to bits on the estate roads.

Standard 12 'The Grey Pig'

Chapter Fifteen – The Emergency

Then, suddenly, as a bolt from the blue, we woke one day and found we had the Malayan Emergency upon us. I understand now that the original plan had been that all the Europeans, tin miners and planters, living in isolated places, would be attacked simultaneously. Luckily, this plan had misfired and some poor devil had been attacked two weeks ahead of time. For about three weeks, it was very unpleasant and nervy on Kru.

We were isolated and, at this time, unprotected on journeys into Malacca and particularly coming back over the three miles of our lane. From now on, every journey that I went was an ordeal, expecting to be ambushed at any minute, the first sign of which was usually a fallen tree put across the road and then shots from the bank verge.

So many were shot and killed that way. Payday was particularly dangerous for Europeans coming home with many thousands of dollars to pay the estate workers their wages. The bandits, at first, relied on this method for their funds but later, when planters and miners were better protected by police, they took to extorting money from wealthy Chinese.

Planters were being attacked all around us but it wasn't so bad in the Malacca Territory as it didn't have the great tracts of jungle like Johore or further upcountry. Anywhere bordering on deep jungle was not good.

Before all this happened, I had been getting on quite well with my driving and was even driving in Malacca Town. I still could not reverse and I had done little night driving, except on the estate roads with Ray when pig hunting. But, with the Emergency, I gave it up as I felt uncertain of what I would do if bandits jumped out at me and, really, I never cared for it. I got a bit fed up too as Ray promptly went to sleep when I drove. Also, I found it difficult to look for orchids when driving!

All unnecessary journeys had to come to an end. Dinner and Mah Jongg parties and so on were forfeit and, if possible, we only went into Malacca on Pay Day and Ray's Masonic nights. Much against my wishes, he had become a Mason. For some reason that I cannot fathom, I did not like this at all. I did not like him having secrets from me and promptly read his little, blue book right through and ridiculed it. And yet it is a worthy sect, doing much good. I think that I was just plain jealous and also a little apprehensive at the cost as some men let it get out of all proportion, joining Lodges right and left, and all the trappings can be very expensive. I remembered Auntie Lilla telling me about Uncle George, who was Worshipful Diddledumps of this and that!

So for Masonic night, we used to put up at the Rest House, which was quite near to the Lodge and we wives, around ten o'clock, would hear a tune, which I would swear was:

> *"Twinkle, twinkle, little star,*
> *How I wonder what you are…"*

The vision of these, mostly, middle-aged men, clad in dear, little housemaid blue aprons, decorated with chains, made most of us die with laughter. Once, I said to Bill Ross, a propos of some remark that he had made, "Yes, that's all jolly fine, Bill. You may be all Brothers but we are not necessarily all sisters!"

And, long afterwards, when he was Worshipful Master of Malacca Lodge, he quoted this, amid shrieks of laughter, in his speech on Ladies Night. I don't know whether it was known that I was the awful woman who had said it! And, far off though the time might be, the thought of Ladies Night worried me because as sure as night follows day, Ray, in his turn would become Worshipful Master. It was their main, great ambition, going step by step to this goal by uncomfortable ceremonial ritual. They always held this Ladies Night, which was very nice really except that the Worshipful Mistress (my description!) had to make a speech. Now, I have always been a shy and nervous speaker and this really would have been the end. I think that, if I had the choice, I would rather cross fifty rivers with trees across them than go through that ordeal!

And it was a good thing that I was selling paintings so well because staying at the Rest House was expensive.

Martin's schooling suffered from the Emergency. The Brothers' school anyway was not suitable and our plan to send him to the Cameron Highlands' school was right out. The school never really got going there and we decided against it anyway because of the dangers of getting him there. So Martin had come back to the estate.

Then, at last, on the estate, we were armed. Ray was issued with a Belgian shotgun and I had a pistol, which I was taught to fire and kept loaded beside my paint-box all day. Very nice! God knows what would have happened if I had had to use it! We were given Malay police and two police sergeants.

The garden, way out on its perimeter, had to be strongly wired in, and at night the hissing oil lamps in their post-mounted kerosene cans were put up at intervals to light up the rubber beyond. The police patrolled along this, watch by watch.

Under the bungalow, the corners were sandbagged, which interfered with my plants and my light for painting. One was a sitting duck from anywhere in the rubber, which was all around us, and all privacy was gone as there was always a Malay policeman on guard, usually standing and watching the artwork with interest! They were a damn nuisance and it was questionable whether one didn't stand as much in danger from them and their weapons as from the bandits.

One thing, however, is quite certain. Had there been an attack, no lot of men would have fought more bravely than these little brown men, because the Malay, basically indolent and lazy, when roused is a ferocious fighter and never more so if confronted by Chinese, whom they dislike intensely in the form of bandits. I was never allowed to go out of the garden and Ray, who of course had to inspect the estate, was fully armed with a sergeant with a Sten gun and flanked by two police with rifles wherever he went.

Of course, there were unfortunate circumstances. One was caught on guard at night asleep. Another let his gun off by accident and the shot went right through Martin's bedroom floor! As for the tell-tale patches of dark green on the lallang lawn, the Mem was not amused! When seeing it, I would say in my kampong Malay, "Appa orang adda kinshing sini?" (Who has made water here?) "Te tow, te tow, Mem. Blum siah…." (Don't know, not I)

And I would tell the sergeant off, threatening dire repercussions if I found my garden thus deface again.

On another occasion, Martin reminds me, because we had decided that it was too dangerous to take him with us at night when we visited friends for dinner, we left him behind with a Sikh guard. Normally we would take him with us, putting him to bed in a bedroom while we were entertained and, still asleep, lift him out and put him back in the car and drive home. He would wake up back in his own bed totally unaware of the move. However, the Sikh guard sat under Martin's bedroom with a shotgun across his knees and we had total trust in him. Like the Malays, he would have defended his charge to the death. Only later did we discover that this same guard had become the leader of a local bandit cell!

Soon we were allocated two European Police Sergeants – ex-Palestine Police – billeted with us, and all this indiscipline stopped and we became like a military garrison.

I

Two Palestine Police join Barbara, Ray and Martin,
seen here with the syce and gardener

The Palestine Police with their platoon of Malay guards

The police were drilled well and everything became very orderly. Trenches were dug near the wire and the sandbags were mostly removed from the bungalow as the police guarded and patrolled from the trenches. Their bedroom had a cupboard that was filled with arms and ammunition. Martin adored them both and proudly wore service badges that they sewed onto his shirt, and Ray carved a wooden gun for him. He used to march around guarding me while I painted.

Now, armed, we did go out a bit. Always taking the police with us, we went to the Ross's for tiffin and to play Mah Jongg until we had to leave in time to get home before dark, and on Sundays we resumed going to the Malacca Swimming Club at Tanjong Bruas. People congregated there all day at weekends. It had a lovely cool breeze off the sea. It was simply a round atap-roofed shelter, open on all sides with tables and chairs underneath, beside a swimming pool, which was always full of clear sea water as it was changed daily by the tides.

Here, Martin learned to swim.

Martin and Ray at Malacca Swimming Club

This was rather an event, as children were not allowed in the pool by themselves until they could swim the length unaided. Every so often, some child would feel able to do this and the whole pool would be cleared and everyone would watch, cheering and applauding the small child puffing and blowing its way across, to be awarded with a small badge, proudly to be sewn on to their swimming shorts.

Martin, 1950, still wearing his
Malacca Club swimming badge

At first I used to gaily take my latest paintings in for people to see, never thinking, until some person began to make pointed remarks that I was using the Club to sell my paintings. As I was most sensitive on the subject of selling paintings, I didn't like this to be thought of in this way, and so people, who wanted to see them, then had to come out to Kru or we had to take them to them. We would lay out twenty-four or so 'samples' all over the floor. It was amusing for us to watch people deciding which they would have. Each would make a decision, singling out which ones they particularly liked and would mark those they wanted. Then I went home and painted copies! Over and over again, I did this. My paintings of the Tulip tree – Spathodea campanulata – of which I still have the original, have been painted by me no less than twenty-eight times! On average I had orders for up to six or twelve paintings and it was not only Malacca but all over the place. And it was not only Europeans, wealthy Chinese loved them.

On occasions, the Rosses would come over to us. If Kru had been an awful bungalow before, it was even worse now; no wireless, no music except for a wind-up gramophone and a carefully selected collection of 78 rpm records. I didn't want Martin to hear the cheap jazz music first so I carefully chose Beethoven symphonies, Swan Lake, opera, Moonlight Sonata, Edward German's Merrie England, and many other songs and carols. We also found some Malayan songs such as Terang Bulan and Selamat Tidor, a lullaby.

Martin, who had a glorious boy's voice, true as a bell and right on the note, chirruped and sang them all and it was a joy to hear him. Each night, he had a repertoire of songs, some of which Ray had sung to him, with which he sang himself to sleep. Imagine, perhaps we would be playing Mah Jongg with the Rosses and Martin would be in his bed in the next room, singing away. We would have to stop our play and listen to this perfect singing, it was so lovely. Pure music, classical tunes sung note for note. And it would end sleepily with a 'God Save the King'!

Madge Ross said on more than one occasion, "I feel His Majesty (*George VI*) would have been most gratified to know that in the midst of this Emergency one small boy on a rubber plantation in the back of beyond is winding up his day with the National Anthem."

Martin's ability to imitate the Malayan pigeons resulted in them answering him and, as for Kutty, she would get so cross with him as he could imitate Giar calling her 'Mat! Mat!' And she would come running along, leaving whatever she was doing, only to find it was only Martin. He spoke kampong Malay perfectly. He was and still is a good parrot!
It was a bit of a shame, life on the estate what with the police and the bandits, though we, thank God, had nothing happen on Kru itself. Needless to say, it was all around us and we never knew whether we wouldn't be next. Many a visit to neighbours, albeit many miles away, would be interrupted by a force of soldiers suddenly appearing out of

the surrounding rubber or jungle and taking up positions all around us while we might be having tea on the lawn.

There were some gruesome tales, such as the couple on an estate upcountry, who, on waking up when it was still dark, got up and put on the lights and - bang! bang! bang! bang! They were all shot dead in a wooden bungalow. They had no protection; the only safe place to be was to get to the bathroom and crouch down as there, there were concrete walls. One learned to put on the light and wait. The big bandit hideouts were upcountry and anywhere bordering deep jungle. Malacca, on the whole, was peaceful other than an odd horrid incident. Around Mount Ophir, which bordered on Johore, it was very jungley.

Pay Day grabs still happened. For planters, Pay Day was always a worry, carrying home some fourteen thousand dollars or more. In the first few months, one used secrecy and stayed overnight in town and we divided up the money, putting some in the boot and so on. I used to tuck a few thousand dollars in my bra. Of course, later, when we had the police around, it became a military operation with the car bursting with police and bristling with guns. Ray drove with a loaded revolver in the glove box; a guard with a sten gun took the front passenger seat; two guards sat in the rear seat, rifles poking out of the open windows while I sat between them with Martin squashed between my knees.

Later on, we realised why Kru was left alone. In the area, where the elephant chase had taken place, was a swamp in which Chinese squatters lived. And there was a bandit camp right behind the coolie lines, and we never knew and there we were with all those police. The bandits daren't reveal their presence for fear of being disturbed.

One time, for some reason, we had to go to Malacca in the evening and we had to leave Martin. Why, for the life of me, I cannot remember! So we left him with Noorasami, the estate official pig-shooter, sitting on guard beneath his bedroom with his shotgun across his knees. Well, of course, Martin was quite safe as the Asiatics adore children, and Martin was no exception. Noorasami would probably have laid down his life to protect the child. Only later, did we discover that he was one of the bandits.

This was the thing; one just didn't know who, where – some all the time, others just helping or forced to help. Others, part-time bandits and even estate workers. It was a time of great uncertainty. We had horrible journeys in the car, always with police around us. On parts of the road where the bank was at a level with the car, we would make Martin lie down on the floor of the car. He had his instructions. In the event of us being fired on, he was to get down onto the floor at our feet. How he would have managed, heaven knows but that was how we travelled around. He was very brave, stoically saying little, but it must have been very alarming for him. He was only seven or eight.

Fifi came to stay with us. She stayed for around two months and Edward and Martin played around together happily. Martin had waited for several months for his major Christmas present, which arrived in much excitement shipped out from Harrods, perfect for rushing around the bungalow between the pillars, and much in keeping with the military activity, which surrounded us at the time.

Martin and Edward Fugler
and the Harrods Christmas present

I don't know why they were with us for so long, but I went down with a very bad go of tonsillitis, not as bad as the last one in Malaya in 1941 during the bombing of Singapore, but as bad as any I had had in England. Anyway, I had to go into Malacca Hospital and have millions of grams of penicillin pumped into my bottom. When I came out, Martin went down with measles and he was rather ill with it and shortly after he had to go into Malacca Hospital, as he came out with boils and he had to have the same treatment. But he refused to have the indignity of having his injections in his bottom, insisting on the nurses to give them every three hours in alternative thighs!

Martin recovering from measles

I think that several years of lack of a proper diet with such things as powdered milk, KLIM, had not given him a chance to build up strength and resistance. It was pretty grim in the bungalow, night after night with only oil lamps to see by, so woeful to read by and always flickering with mosquitoes, cicadas and other insects.

All of a sudden, I had the bright idea of making a doll's house and so we set to. Ray did the carpentry, making it out of a rubber chest, cutting out the windows and door openings, and putting hinges on the front and back. It was to be Georgian in style and it had to be quite planned out. It had a long room as a drawing room, a hall, stairs, dining room and kitchen; upstairs, a long bedroom, bathroom above the kitchen, a nursery and a big landing. It was great fun. We built it up from the ground floor. The first job was to score the parquet flooring with pencil and then painting it seven or eight times so that the floors were made with the best polish. Then followed the making of the fireplaces and the painting of the walls.

It opened front and back and had two dormer windows, and was very balanced with a white balcony above the pillared front door, which was recessed and flanked by square bay windows. The whole thing was gay, with painted bricks and white stone and gradually it grew. Then came the fun of fitting out the kitchen and making the bathroom equipment, right down to the toilet roll holder and roll! Furniture was made for all the rooms and I painted miniatures for the walls and curtains, and we made tiny chandeliers and carpets. The police were absolutely fascinated with the 'kitchy rumah' – little home – which was the most English-looking of houses. We were most happy making this doll's house.

Then there came the time that Managers were due to go on leave, and we were moved from Kru and on to Ulu Sawah. But I was glad to get away from Kru. The heat of the bungalow affected me, and Martin was looking peaky so it probably wore him down too.

Ulu Sawah was quite a different place, being more a modern house with Terrazzo floors downstairs and in the bedrooms upstairs. It was on a slight hill and there was a rubber replant going on, so there was a breeze and it was many degrees cooler than Kru had been. It had electric light and fans and a nice garden with lime trees.

It had only recently been rebuilt on the site of an old bungalow, and the broken up floors of the old one had been broken up further to be used for the paths and had only been roughly laid so that they were home to the many scorpions. Martin and I enjoyed ourselves going round on weekly scorpion hunts. Some were the big blue and black chaps and some the more dangerous brown ones. It was a good idea to leave shoes downstairs at night as scorpions are very partial to getting in shoes.

Anyway, this estate was a lovely change and was closer to Port Dickson than the Malacca and there was a lovely bit of beach not too far way called Masjid Tanah – Magic Earth

.

At Masjid Tanah

Deserted beach and a low tide at Masjid Tanah

We used to go there on Sundays to picnic and bathe. It was completely deserted, with big volcanic rocks jutting from the sea.

Ray, Barbara and Martin, showing an early interest in yachting

There were supposed to be crocodiles here but we never saw any. Vandaea orchids hung in festoons from the trees and I collected shells and lovely seeds. I wish now that I had made a collection of seeds but then there are so many things I could have done in Malaya. Never mind the 'Happy Years' – 'Call them the Wasted Years' could have been better. We used to come to Masjid Tanah without the police. I think that it must have been safer on the estate as there was not much jungle to protect the bandits.

We even went there once at night. Ray and I bathed and I was frightened by the black water. I was always nervous of bathing in Malaya. I never really swam, never went more than knee deep. I always feared sharks and with good reason as they were always around. What a difference to the days when I used to swim between the two piers at Brighton!

Chapter Sixteen – Fraser's Hill

In 1951, after we had been at Ulu Sawah for about eighteen months, Ray got a carbuncle on the back of his leg just below the buttock. This became enormous and he had to have penicillin treatment and was in Seramban hospital for a bit. One journey there gave him so much pain that he couldn't do the drive and I had to and this was the last time. I had decided to give up driving because of the Emergency, which was still very much in evidence. I could not visualize what I would do if we were attacked while I was at the wheel.

Ray's carbuncle had four funnels and was really shocking. There was talk of him and us going home for advanced leave but that proved difficult as there was no passage available at that moment. So Guthries sent us on local leave for two weeks, paying for Ray and me while we paid for Martin. We went to the Rest House at Fraser's Hill. I had often heard of this cooling-off spot but had never been there. At any other time, we would have enjoyed the journey but, as it was, it was most unpleasant as we had to run the gauntlet at the terrible Gap, where Sir Henry Gurney, the British High Commissioner had been murdered. I didn't like the journey anyway as it was mountainous with nothing at the edge of the road except air and jungle way, way down and this upset my vertigo, of course.

However, on the way, I saw large specimens of Nepenthes (Pitcher plants) and also Audina barbusfolia in large clumps and many tree ferns. However, it was lovely at the Rest House when we eventually got there and we found Sergeant Blair was also on leave. It was beautifully cool, surrounded by jungley mountains. They grow vegetables here. Quite a lot of the expensive English vegetables come from the Cameron Highlands and Frazer's Hill such as cauliflowers and cabbage, as well as many English summer flowers. There were dahlias and roses but what fascinated me was the jungle all around.

Here it was safe to walk around the Hill and we found a lot of orchids and, if they were flowering, I collected and painted them. In fact, I did quite a lot of painting on that holiday as there was nothing else to do other than golf, which we do not play, and walking, which is what we did. Along the little tracks and paths, there were leeches so we picked up a few of them and, of course, I had some horrid moments crossing ravines and streams, with just a tree trunk on which to cross and, as

ever, Martin, maddeningly, dancing back and forth as is his wont!
"Come on, Mummy, it's easy! Look!" and off he would go again.

Fraser's Hill, 1949

I had no means of knowing the names of the orchid plants that I
collected. At that time, there were no reference books on orchids in
Malaya and I could only get Burkill, which is hopeless as it is only an
enormous dictionary and orchids are the most useless plants ever. Few
were listed and if they were, such as vanilla, which is the only orchid
with a vestige of food value, incidentally, it would be the one or two
that can be rubbed on your stomach. A fat lot of good that is when one
is trying to identify one! The Malays have no use for orchids at all and
consider them useless, just 'bungas' and weeds. I used to send plants to
Mr Holtum, later Professor R.E.Holtum, at Singapore Botanic Gardens,
who would name them for me. I suppose I must have sent him a good
thirty from Fraser's Hill.

Bulbophyllum ericsonae was one, which had a labellum that closed
with a snap, and I remember an Anochistiles, which was a nice, little

ground growing orchid and is in Burkill, called 'daron loh' writing flower on account of the curious markings on the leaves. It also made me itch as these leaves are very irritant. Dendrobium roseatum was another, trailing up a tree like a creeper. None were very large and spectacular as, on the whole, the wild Malayan orchids are rather small and insignificant. I also painted a fine, scarlet passion flower.

Martin enjoyed himself and distinguished himself on the first morning to other people staying there. An important high-up in Guthries was staying there and probably would not have spoken to us at all had he not been wakened by a flute like rendering of 'Swan Lake' on the clear air - 'Deda, da, dedaa; deda da, dedaa' – and went to the window to look out and saw a small golden, red-haired boy, singing his heart out. Martin, of course, who else? He turned to his wife and said, "At least they have good music on the estate." We had a drink with them later and I showed them my paintings.

We did go on one very long walk with Sergeant Blair for a few miles and not realizing quite how far. Of course, it was only really safe near the Hill. We met no one, of course, but I suddenly saw the path was going to go round a horrid bit of cliff, falling away around the corner and I became very nervous. So we turned for home and went back rather more hurriedly as neither Ray nor Sergeant Blair was armed. Fortunately, nothing happened.

We enjoyed this holiday very much and felt all the better for it. The rest House had roaring fires at night on our private sitting room. It was much needed as were woollen jumpers. It was wonderful for me to breathe cold air again, never at my best in the heat. On the return journey, we stopped at *Teh* and saw Fifi and Fugie. I seem to remember we stayed one night with them. We went to the Batu Caves as I wanted to show them to Martin. Some of them were rather 'bandity' but the main one, which had steps up to it, was safe enough. The enormous, deep caverns in the limestone with vast roofs went deep into the hill and I think had not been properly explored. They were full of Flying Foxes and were very awe inspiring and majestic.

Then we returned to Ulu Sawah and Ray had got his carbuncle under control. It was clear that he would get another one. The trouble with the Tropics is that, once you get ill, everything is far more accentuated and, with his P.O.W. days not all that far behind, Guthries could not take risks with him. So they decided to send us home to England on leave as soon as a passage became available. Then there was a cancellation on a Danish boat, SS Selandia and so we had to pack up all our possessions and store them in the rubber store on the estate. I believe the manager had my orchids to look after. By this time, through my sales of paintings, we had quite a lot of nice things such as the Chinese lacquer cabinets. I had a nice little Siamese cat called Wendy and she had to be boarded out in Malacca.

It is quite a business, going on leave. Normally one starts preparing for it months ahead but, with a suddenly advance leave, we had to pack up and get ourselves ready in two or three weeks. We sailed on the 'SS Selandia' from Port Swettenham. She had only some seventy passengers on board. The people, who had cancelled, were 'high-ups No. One' in Guthries so we had a gorgeous double cabin with private bathroom. What luxury after my two previous horror voyages!

SS Selandia

The food was marvellous, especially the smorgasbord. We seemed to find ourselves very tired and for some days, just sat and looked at the sea. Martin found a new world, full of excitement and delights, as one was allowed full run of the ship with the exception of the crew's quarters and the engine room. There were some twelve other children and we rarely saw him all day, what with the pool and the games. He had by now learned that there were things that we insisted on being obeyed or we generally felt we could trust him to be sensible and we had no trouble.

The ship called first at Penang, just up the coast. I hadn't been to Penang since 1938. I didn't remember what it had been like anyway.

The Runnymede had been completely gutted by the Japs but we took a trip on the Mountain Railway to the top of Penang Hill. I didn't like the 'nothingness' below me on the way and look resolutely up. I noticed several ground orchids, a yellow Spathoglotis, which I painted back on board. I also saw a Calanthe but I couldn't reach it as I was in the carriage going down the mountain!

This being a cargo boat, it stopped at some unusual places. Madras was next, where Ray was most interested to see the Tamil living conditions and found them much worse than in Malaya. After docking in Columbo, then still in Ceylon, where we went up to the Temple of the Tooth on Mount Kandy, before heading across the Indian Ocean towards Aden and Port Sudan. This was the longest leg and one where Martin tried our patience a bit. In a storm, he was not to be found and we feared for him. A search proved fruitless until someone spotted him standing on a bollard on the walkway below the bridge, bracing himself against the rise and fall of the bow as the ship crashed into each monumental wave sending cascades of water over him and me, as I grabbed him and brought him back to safety.

On another occasion, free to go anywhere from stem to stern, all that could be seen of him was this small bottom framed in one of the hawser holes in the bows. With his arms to hold him back, he was leaning right out over the water to watch the bow cutting through the water and the flying fish and dolphins rising way down below. I nearly had a heart attack but couldn't call him just in case he let go! One of the crew went and carefully prised him away!

Port Sudan was fun. It was nice to hear the Sudanese singing rhythmically as they worked. The sea was so clear you could see the whole underwater outline of the ship and, looking deep into it, see the most fascinatingly coloured fish. Turquoise, ultramarine, reds and coral – I could have stayed there a long time except it was very hot. After the Red Sea, the Suez Canal and Port Said where we didn't dock, we crossed the Mediterranean and through the Straits of Messina towards Genoa and Europe.

Going through the Straits was exciting with the mountain scenery on either side and the endless mountains and rivers draining down into the sea. Mt Etna was not erupting but Stromboli had been recently. Covered in yellow flowers, it had a deep brown gash down one side with rocks and lava still being thrown up and flowing down, hissing into the sea, with steam and smoke escaping from the crater. As the first boat in the vicinity, we sailed round the whole island, surveying and re-charting the sea bed.

Martin may have missed out on his education a bit while on the rubber estates but he certainly learned much during that voyage. He took a deep interest in the maps of the world so that he could relate to where he was and so learned geography.

In fact it was poured into him – India, Ceylon, Aden, the Sudan, Egypt, Genoa, Marseilles and Gibraltar – what a voyage for a receptive boy. The daily run was fascinating, using the compass and seeing the navigation, all there for him to watch as we were allowed into the bridge and the Captain and the officers bent over backwards to answer all the questions fired at them.

We arrived back in London, in Tilbury docks on my birthday, July 27th, 1949. Saying goodbye to the other passengers and watching the one shipboard romance that had kept us all fascinated during the voyage come to an end – or did it, we never knew, as the young boy disembarked while his love stayed on board to finish the voyage in Denmark! – was sad.

We took some rooms in Mitcham and took Martin to see as many things as we could. He had his first experience in so many years of fresh milk on his cereals and always had to have the top of the milk. London double-decker buses were a new experience and we went to see South Pacific and Call Me Madam and the Café de Paris and the Trocadero. But London was suffering from a bit of a heat wave and even Ray found it too hot. So, we left and went down to Emsworth, where we boarded in Victoria Road. I did a bit of painting but all of a sudden, things started to happen.

I took my orchid paintings, numbering about a hundred and fifty, quite a few of them wild species that I had collected myself and a few hybrids to the Herbarium at Kew and showed them to Victor. S. Summerhayes, who was the curator. While we were talking, another older man, who had been walking around outside, put his head round the door and said:

"I heard such exciting names being spoken, I couldn't resist finding out what it was all about."

Summerhayes said. "Come and meet Mrs. Everard." And he introduced us to David Sanders of the Royal Orchid Nursery at St Albans – that most famous of orchid nurseries that had been started by his grandfather in the 1880's. "Look at these paintings".

David looked and was most interested and on learning that we were going back to Malaya was still more interested. He invited us to come up to the Nursery, which we did later. At this time, I also became a Fellow of the Royal Horticultural Society with David Sanders sponsoring me. Nowadays, this procedure is no longer needed as anyone can become a Fellow on payment of a subscription.

I promised him I would send him orchid seeds whenever I have pods. But here was a lost opportunity. I would have had a wonderful time collecting plants and such like for Kew but, of course, even going back to Malaya with the Emergency, there was no way I could go anywhere collecting.

It was a nice, uneventful leave, in which Ray rested and got quite well. I saw all the relations, of course. Daddy, now a very old man, was still living in the Norland Square flat, not working obviously and, I think, leading rather a lovely life with Tommy working somewhere in London and more or less keeping him.

But the whole leave was tinged by one sadness. We had to arrange schooling for Martin and it was arranged that he should go to Rottingdean Preparatory School at the start of the next term, the winter term. Ruth was going to have him during school holidays as both her boys, Ben and Nicholas, were there and that seemed very suitable. There were so many family connections too. Steyning Beard had sold the land to the school many years ago. It was a lovely big piece at the back and to the north of Rottingdean. Uncle Ernest and Aunt Elizabeth were living at The Elms, Rudyard Kipling's old home. It belonged to Sir Roderick Jones, who, when he heard that Ernest Beard wanted a home in Rottingdean, immediately put it at his disposal, as he said:

"It is not right that a Beard cannot find a home in Rottingdean." How nice of him!

The Elms, Rottingdean

We outfitted Martin at great expense at Billings and Edmunds at a cost of £80. It seemed as I remember that he needed four of everything, indoor and outdoor shoes, so many pairs of socks, rugby boots and, of course, the wooden tuck-box. That item is the only one that has survived all these years. (*currently in the garden shed in London - Martin!)* And it worked out that we would see him settled at Rottingdean before we left.

It was good of Ruth to have him in the holidays. She was having a very tough time bringing up her two boys, having gone through a very unfair divorce from Johnny and he remarried. She was, however, being very successful in Fleet Street and making good money but this meant leaving the boys in the holidays in the care of her housekeeper, Hilda. Martin, of course, is a most reticent boy and it is only over the course of the years that I have realised the boy did not have a happy time. He was the 'odd man out'. The two cousins were not exactly unkind to him but he did not get on with Hilda and I can see now that Martin must have been quite lonely. Having said that, neither Ben nor Nicholas has ever admitted to liking Hilda either!

We were able to go to Rottingdean for one or two weekends to take Martin out. As well as taking in the delights of the Palace Pier, the Aquarium and crumpets and walnut cake at Fuller's Restaurant, we went to Telscombe of course. It looked much the same except for some unpleasant new houses at the bottom of the Tye and one overlooking Telscombe itself. The building in Saltdean was very threatening. Mr

Gorham had died some years ago and typically, when his will was read, he had left Telscombe, well, all that he owned anyway to Brighton Corporation. What a thing to do! It was a most remarkable will and gained considerable publicity. '…that Telscombe may be preserved with its rural characteristics….' And lots of bequests and conditions, no new buildings, no alterations and so on. Quite a will!

Some years ago, Ernest Thornton-Smith had bought The Manor. The house seemingly looked the same. We never went in the house, indeed I have never been in since the family left, but, looking over the wall, at Gregory's Cottage, disturbing things had happened to the old farmyard where the cowsheds had been. It was all flagged and with a view through to the barn and chickens walking about. The house pond had been renovated and was now a rock pool with rockery stone and an alien swan – a live one – on it!

The Windlass's also had come and Oak Cottage had wrought iron gates – yes, there were changes. The Winlaws had long gone and a Rector, called Haines, was the incumbent now, Miss Kirkby was still there, living in one of the hated council houses above The Manor, a blot on Telscombe to this day! I went to see her. She was very old but glad to see me. She was surrounded with all the photos of past glories of Telscombe and had the wonderful signed Stables visitors' books around her. She was full of memories of the old days.

At last the day came when we had to take Martin out and say goodbye to him for three years. Martin, being Martin, did not show his sorrow, just kissed us goodbye and turned back into school. This is the curse of those that work in the Far East, sooner or later the family must break up. The children must return back to England either for schooling or health and either the wife leaves the husband to be with the children or the children are left behind while the parents must head back.

With us, Martin would be at school most of the time and, as we thought, with only the holidays to be arranged for. It was obviously best for me to be out east with Ray. I certainly couldn't trust him to be faithful on his own. And so, we set off sadly on the P & O ship 'Corfu'. I cannot remember anything really outstanding about the voyage except our get up for the Fancy Dress dance.

I hit on the idea of dressing up as Tamils, Ray a tapper and I his wife. We managed to get brown grease paint in Aden and I slicked my hair back and put a lipstick caste mark on my forehead. I stuck a press stud on my nostril and wore a red and white sari and went barefoot. I caused quite a sensation and quite a lot of old men wanted to dance with me, which must have been quite unpleasant as I was sweating through all the grease paint. I was told I was 'more Tamil than Tamil' and the Lascars came up from below decks to have a look.

Well, I giggled away quite happily through it and followed Ray around, who with is hair on end and dirty vest and pants, was chewing betel nut and going up to all the Tuan Besars and saluting them in Tamil and begging for money –

'Caas ille, caas ille!'

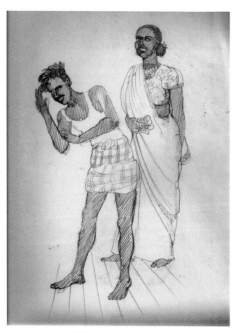

Ray and Barbara win First Prize
Fancy Dress, P & O Corfu, 1949

Oh it was great fun, and we won First Prize! No one had really noticed me up to this time as I was very busy embroidering the carpets for my doll's house and next morning, people couldn't believe this sedate female with hair plaited really was the old Tamil woman of the night before.

The ship was very comfortable and although I liked the Selandia very much, I still think that I prefer the P & O boats best. We were not really terribly happy, feeling the break with Martin, and I was worried whether he would be all right, uncertain also whether I had done the right thing, leaving him wife or mother, mother or wife.

Chapter Seventeen – Back with Rubber

This time we were going to a quite new estate. Ray was to be the Senior Assistant on Temiang Seramban Estate under Huby Wally, a rather elderly man on the verge of retirement. The estate lay all around Seramban town, the manager's division being on one side and our division quite near to the town itself.

We collected our possessions from Ulu Sawah. I was upset to find that a rat had made a nest in my lovely cut-work Chinese dinner mats and to hear from the woman in Malacca that Wendy had died mysteriously.

The bungalow at Temiang was small, with electric light and a fan, thank heavens. It was perched halfway up a hill with aged mango trees close to the house and, when I got the orchids settled in, they liked this very much. There was nothing much of a garden and Ray and I began to make it quite nice.

We were still very much in a bandit area. All around Seramban, it was very bad. At the bottom of the hill, the road ran through a small group of atap houses and passed ponds with lotus growing in them and beyond this, it was very dangerous. I was surrounded by Malay police all day and, although I missed Martin, I was occupied enough busy with my paintings for Robinsons in Kuala Lumpur, who were selling them well. And so, my collection of paintings was growing rapidly. I painted several new ones on Temiang – Hibiscus mutabilis, Spider Lily and many orchids.

Hibiscus mutabilis

And while there, I had my first exhibition. This was at the Singapore Orchid Show and was the first to be held after the war at the Happy World Dance Hall.

Singapore Orchid Show, 1950

We had a carpenter in Seramban make several large wooden stands and had them sent down to Singapore in advance. We followed on by car loaded with all the pictures, some just behind glass with passé-par-tout and quite a lot of the large framed ones. I had been given a lovely site on the dais and they looked very well, surrounded by hundreds and thousands of sweet smelling orchids. The scent of massed orchids is something one never experiences in England.

The paintings caused much interest and I even painted several more during the two days of the show. These included Dendrobium Gatton Sunray and Jeremiah Coleman's cross, with its butter coloured flowers measuring four inches across.

Barbara painting   *Dendrobium Gatton Sunray*
Dendrobium Gatton Sunra
y

Then there were the five hybrid Vandas, including Nam Kee, Josephine van Brero, Teres gigantea and Andersonii, both with lovely pearl white petals.

Vanda Nam Kee   *Vanda Josephine van Brero*

Dendrobium undulatum was planted in a huge pot two and a half feet wide and consisted of many pseudobulbs at least five foot in length and many, many scapes of flowers. I also painted its offspring Constance, which was even bigger.

Doing this painting was quite hard work as I usually had an audience of Chinese breathing heavily down my back and murmuring in Chinese and then exclaiming, in their guttural, staccato voices, admiring remarks (one hopes!). And all the while I was painting, Ray would be talking about the paintings and selling them and, when the show closed at about eleven on the last evening, we found that we had sold about a thousand dollars worth. This was incredible. I looked at Ray and suddenly felt very tired and hungry.

"Why, we're rich! Let's go and celebrate. Where can we go at eleven o'clock to eat?"

"The airport is always open," said Ray. "Let's go there".

So, we did and had Prawn Cocktails, Oysters flown in that day, Fillet Steak, Strawberries and Cream and lots of champagne.

That was my first exhibition and what great fun it was. And there were good results. I met all the orchid people in Singapore – John Laycock, Mr Holtum and the manager of the *(Fern?)* nursery, Nam Kee. After that and from now on, Robinsons of Kuala Lumpur had paintings displayed on their staircase and they sold well there and I received nice cheques from them from time to time.

Orchids in a crystal bowl, found in a loft in 2010, now framed in a Private Collection possibly painted in England after 1952

I had the time in Malaya to do their large paintings that take four or more days to do. I painted bowls of flowers with incredible flower arrangements of lush orchids. They were wonderful. I wonder where they all are now.

So, from now on, I was really quite busy. Back on the estate, with the bombing and strafing still going on around me in the neighbouring jungle, I painted on. The other interesting outcome was meeting the little Chinese manager of a Nursery. He was badly in need of someone to send him plants and cuttings of specie orchids but being Chinese he was too frightened to come on to the mainland so we said we would send them to him. Of course, I knew places where the Scorpion orchid grew and several of the more showy ones. He particularly wanted Arundina bambusfolia. I also knew of a tree that was covered with Renanthera elongate so, together with the plants from our collection, we sent him a nice collection.

We had an arrangement whereby we sent him a list of the orchids that we wanted in exchange. We wanted Vanda Coerulea, Phalanopsis grandiflora and several more. They would arrive in due course and very soon we had a collection of some four hundred plants.

All four Phalanopsis plants flowered and looked lovely, hanging from the mango trees, all white and ghostly. For some reason, little owls used to sit on them. Vanda Coerulea flowered and I made a good painting and also crossed the lowest flower with Maggie Ooi and a great big pod formed, which I subsequently sent home to David Sanders. He grew several plants on the arrangement that I was to have half of them. But the subsequent demise of the Royal Orchid Nursery and auction sale that followed meant that these plants were sold and I don't know what happened to them.

Anyway, this was all great fun and Ray and I went off hunting. It was a bit dangerous at times. Going into such danger spots as the Jelebu Pass, Ray had devised an ingenious tool to get the plants down from the trees. It was rather reminiscent of a sweep's gear with a series of rods that screwed into each other with a claw-like rake at the end.

Coelogyne mayeriana

We collected Coelogyne mayeriana from Jelebu and when I came home, I was horrified what we had risked, but we had seen no one, no Chinese at all except for an old woodman on one occasion, who cut us a lovely rattan cane. I think that, possibly, the Chinese thought we were harmlessly mad. There were in fact a few who could go around unmolested. One was a European man, who managed a Chinese temple.

He lived near us somewhere and was generally thought to be slightly dotty by all. He used to come and go wherever he liked, wandering about in the jungle and through the villages. But he wasn't all that mad as it transpired that he used to input valuable information to the police and because he was so supposedly mad, no one suspected him. Of course, he may have also given valuable information to the bandits!

Estate doctors could go anywhere. Somehow, along the grapevine maybe, their cars were known and they were never attacked. Dr Chapman, the soils chemist, was another. He was orchid mad too and had a few nice ones. He was a most eccentric individual and when I first met him, he was engaged in an experiment to grow lettuces without earth. He had been a P.O.W with Ray. He did not care in the slightest how he ate his food. He used to put it all on one plate, potatoes, meat, pudding and all!

He came orchid hunting with us sometimes. It could be quite an operation some times, getting orchids down. Grammatophyllum speciosum, the Tiger orchid, has always been my bane. I had tried many times to collect a plant of this splendid orchid, the biggest in Malaya. Indeed, while we were on Kru, I committed quite a crime. We had located a nice plant about half way up a tree and Ray, nothing loath, had taken a couple of estate workers over and we cut down a tree and leant it against the other so that they could shin up it. In order to do this, we had to rearrange the trees and had laid it across the road. So, along comes a most staid old planter and his wife and they nearly die of fright because they thought it was a hold-up! There was some talk about naughty Mrs Everard but nothing happened. I have learned better ways since then but what one does in one's ignorance…..

I had located a nice specimen of Grammatophyllum, growing quite low on a stump in scrub. Dr. Chapman was most excited so armed with parangs and saws, we went to get it. All went well and just as we were about to get it dislodged, round the corner came a police jeep, bristling with policemen and guns. Out jumped a police sergeant.

"What are you doing here," he demanded.

"Only collecting a plant."

We indicated the nearly severed half a hundredweight of Grammatophyllum.

"You can't stay here. There's been a police raid and there are bandits all over here. We've got a dead one in the Jeep."

We looked across at the Jeep and there were two feet sticking out! I was all for clearing out as quickly as possible and leaving the orchid, but not Ray and Dr. Chapman. Bandits or no, they got the plant and we brought it home and carefully divided it and planted it. The sadness is that it never flowered so I have no painting of it.

On the whole, there were some nice orchids growing around Seramban. I found Phalanopsis cornu-cervi in flower and growing just outside the Residency gates and also an Aerides Luisa in a hedge. Also, there was a lot of the lovely Aerides odoratum growing on a tree, which men were actually cutting down.

Arides odoratum

So I collected them all up and kept a plant for myself and sent the rest to Singapore. I had another exhibition, in Seremban, which was quite good but not on the level of the Singapore show. If I hadn't been so busy, I suppose I'd have been lonely. Ray was away a good bit, all day on other divisions so I had long hours of painting with only the Malay police to talk to. So my kampong Malay got quite good. . While guarding the bungalow, they would watch what I was painting and show great interest.

The mango trees flowered and I made a big painting of a branch. While I was doing this, the most appalling bombing with swooping planes overhead was going on quite close to the lanes and then there was a huge explosion in the lanes. Really, we were living quite close to a most troublesome spot although we never saw anything. We had one or two scares. One evening, the sergeant came in.

"Tuan, there is something in the rubber." he warned.

We all went to look. Sure enough, in the terraces of the trees, there is something white, large and moving around furtively. Ray gets a gun and he and the police go off to investigate. It was only a cow!

We got few real letters from Martin, just the school letter, written under duress. He was too young to articulate on paper so we assumed.

Chapter Eighteen – The End of an Era

Looking back, I suppose my marriage was an ordinary affair. I was still very much in love with Ray, more so than he ever was with me. I don't think that it was ever a great success, sexually. With Ray, all was over and done with before I'd even started. In all my married sexual life, I only achieved two climaxes and then there was only the brief time before Martin's conception when there wasn't birth control. Before the war, as Ray would do nothing about it, I had been using a douche and this is guaranteed to kill any romance. To have to go and prepare oneself with some jelly stuff and then, after it's all over, drag oneself to the bathroom to douche. Only to return and find your husband fast asleep is not very conducive.

On the last leave, I had myself fitted with a coil, I think it's called. This was at least a bit better as I would fit it in any time it suited and then take it out and douche the next morning.

But now, though sexually the same, Ray seemed to be changing. We had the normal rows and arguments that all people have but now he seemed moody and morose and no longer <u>talking</u> to me. He became impatient and sulked and more and more I felt alone. There were dreadful silences and, as far as I can see, all over nothing. I could not see what I had done. Up to now, he had been loving enough, indulgent, always trying to make me happy.

Now, of course, in the course of years, I know what it was but a woman does not realize it when it first happens. It was another woman, harmless enough I think but just enough to upset his conscience. There was another worrying thing, which even I could not help but notice. There was disturbing news in the Straits Times about Korea and the impending war there. I became quite worried whether we should be swamped again and the same 1942 horror overtake us again. My terror this time was that we would be trapped out in Malaya in a war and Martin would be in England.

Well, things went on with Ray acting in a way that I couldn't understand and I worried about Martin. News had filtered through that he wasn't all that happy in the holidays when left to Ruth's housekeeper. I suppose the other boys left him out. He had, however, a wonderful holiday in Cornwall with Laurie Pascal, now married, which somehow brightened his bleak, lonely little life. Laurie was a brilliant photographer and either felt sorry for Martin or considered her a surrogate mother. Many were the photographs taken at their house in their Duke's Head Yard house on Highgate Hill.

The school fees were going up and up too but, luckily, the paintings were still selling well and, although we had to live carefully, we could still manage it. Then, I went and caught malaria. This, I didn't understand as I had been taking my mepacine pretty regularly. Suddenly I got a temperature and felt jolly ill. Dr. Brown came and said I had malaria and would have to go to hospital. So, into Seramban hospital I went and it was jolly unpleasant. They gave me quinine, which is terrible and I couldn't take it. My head was agony and on and off, up and down with this high temperature; the chill and surges of this rising temperature; then the terrible sweat on and on for days. How Ray ever lived through thirty seven bouts on that railway during the last year, I can't think. Luckily it was Subtertian malaria not Benign Tertian malaria. Apparently, there are these two kinds, the latter recurs all through life and this must have been what Daddy got when he went to South America as a young man because he was always going down with malarial chills. Ray also was lucky as he ended his bouts with a subtertian, which cancelled out all the other so there is no re-occurrence. Nor has here been and nor have I ever had one. But it was terrible and I felt so ill. In fact, I suppose this was the most serious illness I have ever had. I was severely told off for not taking my mepacine but I <u>had</u> been taking it.

At first, blame was put on the orchid hunting but then they found that mosquitoes in the stagnant water of the slow flowing ditch just below the bungalow and the oil man purged it. Gradually, I got better but I was in hospital for some time. Then, one day, Ray, on one of his visits, told me he had been at Huby Walters bungalow and one of Guthries' office wallahs, with whom Ray did not get on very well, had been talking about moves.

"He says we may go back to Kru," Ray said, heavily.

This was too much. What with my weakness, worry about Martin and the war, I broke down and implored him not to allow us to go back to Kru.

"I just couldn't. I couldn't stand it, not Kru, that terrible bungalow."

"Well, there's no one to take over Acting Manager," said Ray.

"I don't care. I can't go back to Kru," I said. "For God's sake, let's leave. I just can't stand any more. Let's chuck it and go home."

"All right," replied Ray. I'll see what I can do."

I cried and cried and probably was ill again. Ray saw Guthries and they were so helpful. He was down to go to Kru but, very worried and frightened, he sent in his notice. We were dreadfully worried whether we'd done the right thing. He stood to lose quite $1000 in commission. We would have to pay our own fare and have no job to go to. To this day, I don't know whether we did right. It was one of those steps one takes that alters life. Had we stayed, Ray could have taken over Kru and go on for years as Acting Manager. Undoubtedly, I should have had to go home to sort Martin out. Ray would then have got deeper in with this woman (whom I know nothing about) but as it was, after many nasty remarks – 'rats leaving the sinking ship' – Guthries accepted Ray's notice and we started packing up. We arranged to sail on the P & O ship Carthage.

Now, this voyage was a bit different. There was no leaving things behind in some rubber store but packing up a home into packing cases – and what a pack it was! The Chinese lacquer cabinets had to have enormous chests specially made. All my beautiful, green vine leaf patterned china had to be carefully packed. Fancy me taking that beautiful china out to Malaya! I had about twelve fruit plates and two beautiful round, fruit dishes on a plinth, given to me by Aunt Lilla and which had been in Uncle George's Welsh family for years. Of course, I had thought that Malaya was to be our home for years and that we would get a management posting soon. Then, at least, when one gets an estate to manage, a planter can settle down and make a home. But we seem to have hit this Senior Assistant/Acting Manager stint. With so many managers going home for their first leave, it fell to Ray's lot to have to take over, 'Acting', which meant that I could never make a home. It was very unsettling and now to have Kru thrust on me, it was too much. What with the Emergency going on a strongly as ever and as worse, the threat now of the Korean War and Martin not happy in England.

And so we packed some eighteen cases, great chests, not the little tea chests. We packed them all ourselves even the beautiful acid-drop demijohns, which I had found in a heap of four hundred green ones in the Ulu Sawah rubber store and which I used as lamp bases; the doll's house, naturally; the camphor wood chest and the rice table with its four little tables and all the paintings had to come back from Robinsons to be crated. Indeed, it was very, very tiring with so much to be disposed of; two refrigerators and all the orchids. A Chinese collector took many of the hybrids; Dr Chapman had some of my great treasures – the Phalanopsis and Vanda Coerulea went to him. The orchid disposal was the real wrench for me leaving Malaya. I loved Malaya itself, the land and I've always said 'it would be a lovely place if it wasn't for the people in it'.

Ray, of course, didn't like this leaving at all. He loved the life, the ease of it, but the Emergency and the strain of always having police with him together with the disappointment of further Acting as manager rather than management made him fed up with it. As I have said, whether we made a mistake, we will never know. If we had stayed, we would have been dead. I think our marriage would have suffered as I would have had to go home because of Martin and I know that Ray would have got embroiled with other women.

Many planters, like the Ross's, still living on Durian Tungaal but with two of the boys at school in Australia and only the youngest, David, living on the estate, had decided to chuck it all in. This was the case particularly for the poor devils on outlying estates, whose only way out now was by helicopter, who daily endured the bombing and strafing, surrounded by bandits. So many were killed on their final day, shot to death in their cars running the gauntlet as they tried to leave. And now we had to do it. All went well as we went at breakneck speed, with me expecting the worst at every turn in the road, when Ray ran low on petrol. So, we had to stop to fill up with petrol, thus giving plenty of time for every bandit to finish us off.

Nothing happened, fortunately, and we rushed on and at last, once more, we came to that blessed Causeway, which so many years before, I had been so glad to cross. I bought a few things as mementoes – two carved Bali heads, a mandarin coat and some carved chechas. We went to the Cold Storage and found out that Holt had left and was running a rival, called Fitzpatrick's Cold Storage at the bottom of Orchard Road. Originally, Fitzpatrick had joined the Singapore Cold Storage around 1941 and they paid dearly for that orgy of sacking as they found they were severely depleted of European staff when the war ended and they re-opened the store. So many of the old Europeans had died in Changi or were too old or ill to come back out to Singapore again.

They found that they were more or less left with Fitzpatrick, an Irish-Australian, who proceeded to more or less run the Cold Storage as he pleased together with Holt. Then, something happened and the two of them decided to open a rival and they were doing this very successfully. We went and saw the owner of the Nursery and he gave me an enormous bunch of orchids, which, me being me, I proceeded to paint on board and painted until we got to Aden.

We had our last curry, our last Mee Hoom Prawn Fritters and, with very mixed feelings went on board.

This was a very different return journey, not just a joyful departure, but a journey paid for by us and no job at the end of it. Ray started worrying and he was really impossible and, of course, he upset me, naturally. He cast his worries on everybody around so that the whole voyage we just sat in two deck chairs and worried. At last, he said he would get off the boat and fly the rest of the way home and look for a job. The idea was that he would have one by the time I arrived. I thought that this was most unnecessary and a waste of seventy three pounds but he insisted and so off he went and I was left all alone. I had an attack of some gastric thing, caught in the Red Sea, where it was so hot in the day and cold at night.

It was a miserable way to finish the journey on my own like that but Ray and Martin met me, which was lovely and made up for all the misery. And Ray was on the verge of getting a job.

Barbara Everard

This is the end of what Barbara wrote but of course the story does not end there. Between 1952 and 1990, she made a name for herself as one of the world's great botanical artists, the story of which may be told at a later date.

Those interested in further reading might like to go on the internet to the website, www.barbara-everard.com. There a virtual gallery has been created to show some of her work from the years in Malaya and during this rest of her artistic career.

Martin Everard, 2011